HOLDING AND INTERPRETATION

HOLDING AND INTERPRETATION

FRAGMENT OF AN ANALYSIS

by

D. W. WINNICOTT

The definitive text, with an Introduction by
M. MASUD R. KHAN

GROVE PRESS
New York

First published in 1986 by The Hogarth Press Ltd, London

Published by Grove Press, Inc.
920 Broadway
New York, N.Y. 10010

Library of Congress Cataloging-in-Publication Data

Winnicott, D. W. (Donald Woods), 1896-1971.
Holding and interpretation.

Reprint. Originally published: London: Hogarth Press, 1986.
Includes index.
1. Psychoses—Case studies. 2. Depression, Mental—Case
studies. I. Title.
RC512.W55 1987   616.89'09   86-31871
ISBN 0-394-55563-5

Manufactured in the United States of America
First Edition 1987

10   9   8   7   6   5   4   3   2   1

CONTENTS

INTRODUCTION
by
M. Masud R. Khan

SOME six months before Dr Winnicott's death in January 1971, a group of young Anglican priests invited him to come to talk to them. He accepted, and in a casual exchange of conversation they told him that what they needed guidance about was how to differentiate between a person who seeks their help because he is sick and needs psychiatric treatment, and one who is capable of helping himself through talking with them. Telling this story to me, Winnicott said that he had been taken aback by the awesome simplicity of their question. He had paused a long while, thought and then replied:

> 'If a person comes and talks to you and, listening to him, you feel he is *boring* you, then he is sick, and needs psychiatric treatment. But if he sustains your interest, no matter how grave his distress or conflict, then you can help him alright.'

I was deeply impressed by the wisdom of Winnicott's reply, and since then, whenever I see a person in consultation, this statement of his is never out of my mind.

Re-reading Winnicott's 'Fragment of an Analysis' has brought that question into an even sharper focus for me. We have two accounts of this patient from Winnicott, one which he recorded in his paper 'Withdrawal and Regression' (Winnicott 1954a, reproduced in the Appendix to this volume), and the other presented in 'Fragment of an Analysis', of which this is the definitive text.[1] It is instructive to compare these accounts in their style, character and content.

For my argument it is important to distinguish between *boring* and *boredom*. *The Oxford English Dictionary* defines the verbal substantive *boring* as 'the practice of annoying and wearying others', and the noun *boredom* as 'the state of being bored; tedium, ennui'. It is my hypothesis here that *boring* has the quality of the 'anti-social tendency' (Winnicott 1956) and implies a demand and a hopefulness, whereas *boredom* is an organised and defensive mood and a psychic structure. Similarly feeling bored is a normal state and

---

[1] An earlier version was published in Giovacchini (1972).

different from boring. When I re-searched into Winnicott's writings for the antecedents of his idea that boring is a symptom of psychiatric sickness, I found that one can trace it, though in indirect and obverse ways, from his earliest writings.

Winnicott (1936) himself has told us that 'careful history-taking has had a profound effect on my outlook. . . .' To witness his way of observing infants and children is often very revealing towards a true understanding of his later sophisticated psychoanalytical hypotheses. The cases presented in his first book, *Clinical Notes on Disorders of Childhood* (1931), already establish his distinctive style and sensibility as a clinician. He always observes the infant and a child as a *whole* person in his *given* caretaking environment. Two chapters from that first book have been republished in his collection of papers, *Through Paediatrics to Psycho-Analysis* (1975).

What stands out from his case-material in those chapters is how Winnicott singles out restlessness and fidgetiness in children for special observation. The fidgety child cannot process and master psychically, *through playing*, his excitement and anxiety. He turns them into behavioural 'nuisances', e.g. tics, fidgetiness, disorders of appetite, constipation etc, as appeal to the environment. This phase of Winnicott's clinical experience finds its first theoretical statement in his paper 'The Manic Defence' (1935). My purpose here will be to find out what are the psychodynamics of that psychic state which compel a person to be boring.

It is not an accident that, moving from his clinical data from paediatric work with children to analysis of adults, Winnicott should write his first serious analytic paper on manic defence, which is an intra-psychic way of dealing with anxieties that have their behavioural counterparts, fidgetiness and restlessness, which he had observed in children. Winnicott (1935) postulates that he has come 'to compare external reality not so much with fantasy as with an inner reality'. This seemingly casual statement carries a vital shift in Winnicott's approach to psychic experience. Later he was to see in compulsive fantasying a negation of psychic reality: 'fantasying remains an isolated phenomenon absorbing energy but not contributing – in to dreaming or to living' (Winnicott 1971). Winnicott sees in manic defence an attempt to deny inner reality, a flight to external reality and an attempt to maintain 'suspended animation'. He gives four clinical samples to make his point (Winnicott 1935). The first is of Billy, aged five. He had been referred for restlessness and inability to enjoy what he had acquired. In analysis, Billy's games were not *playing* but wild attacks. As the child's persecutory anxiety lessens, he begins to be able to use material for playing and expressing concern for the characters of his fantasy. The second, David (aged eight), an asocial child, came to analysis for being turned out of school on account of 'sex and lavatory obsession'. In an early session the child had remarked: 'I hope I am not tiring you', and Winnicott adds that 'the aim to tire me out soon asserted itself'. But alongside there was in this child the need to save the analyst from exhaustion, and he provided Winnicott with compulsory rest periods. What became clear was 'that it was he who was becoming exhausted'. One can see how clearly tiring and boring are related together, as techniques of coping with inner stress. The boring patient is trying to maintain omnipotent control over his inner reality by obsessional over-control of language and material. His narrative is a petrified space where nothing can happen.

Winnicott's next case of Charlotte (aged 30), who was clinically a depressive with suicidal fears, gives account of how the patient reported a stock dream: 'she comes to a railway where there is a train, *but the train never starts*'. After she had settled into her analysis she had a dream where the *train started*. Winnicott interprets: 'In simple language, trains which start to move are liable to accidents.' The need in manic defence is to freeze all possibility of anything happening. This is why I am extending Winnicott's concept to postulate that the patient who compels boring narrative on us is not letting language and metaphor elaborate or change his experience. He creates a space of discourse where both he and the analyst are paralysed by the technique of the narrative as well as its monotonous and repetitive contents.

The fourth case is of an obsessional patient, Mathilda (aged 39). When, in a session (from which Winnicott reports), she had brought a Polyfoto of herself (48 images) for him to look at, Winnicott had discovered in it the patient's wish for 'a denial of her deadness by looking and seeing', and how the patient had *'felt it more real for me to see her photo* (a 48th of her) than for me to see her herself. The analytic situation (which she has spent four years proclaiming to be the reality for her) now seemed to her for the first time to be unreal, or at least a narcissistic relationship, a relationship to the analyst that is valuable to her chiefly for her own relief, a taking without giving, a relationship with her own internal objects. She remembered that a day or two before she had suddenly thought, "how awful to be really oneself, how terribly lonely".'

In these clinical vignettes we already have the essentials of Winnicott's approach to the patient. Here we can already see him questioning the *authenticity* for the patient of what he or she produces or presents in the analytic situation and relationship. From this I would conclude that that which is boring is inherently inauthentic, both for the patient and the analyst. And yet we have to learn to tolerate this counterfeit discourse in order to help the patient. Freud (1895), in the very first case where he totally abandoned hypnotic techniques and worked exclusively with free-association method, had encountered this 'boring factor', and remarked:

'The story which Fräulein Elisabeth told of her illness was a *wearisome* one. . . .' (my italics).

In the context the next important paper by Winnicott is 'Reparation in Respect of Mother's Organized Defence against Depression' (1948a). Here Winnicott introduced his concept of 'a false reparation', which derives from 'the patient's identification with the mother and the dominating factor is not the patient's own guilt but the mother's organized defence against depression and unconscious guilt.' Winnicott's work here was an attempt to find some answer to a climate of acrid debate in the British Psycho-Analytical Society during the previous decade between Melanie Klein and her followers who placed total emphasis on unconscious fantasies and others (chiefly Edward Glover) who considered some of the fantasies attributed to the patient as the subjective creations of the analysts themselves. Winnicott tried to show how much the mother's mood can impinge upon a young child's growing psychic reality and dislocate it from finding its own character.

We shall see how later Winnicott was to extend this hypothesis into his concepts of the true and false self organization of personality. A more dramatic clinical example of the intrusive effect of mother on a child Winnicott gives in his paper: 'Mother's Madness appearing in the Clinical Material as an Ego-alien Factor' (1972).

Already in his paper 'Primitive Emotional Development' (1945) Winnicott had given a succinct account of how he saw the infant–mother relationship:

> 'In terms of baby and mother's breast (I am not claiming that the breast is essential as a vehicle of mother-love) the baby has instinctual urges and predatory ideas. The mother has a breast and the power to produce milk, and the idea that she would like to be attacked by a hungry baby. These two phenomena do not come into relation with each other till the mother and child *live an experience together*. The mother being mature and physically able has to be the one with tolerance and understanding, so that it is she who produces a situation that may with luck result in the first tie the infant makes with an external object, an object that is external to the self from the infant's point of view.
>
> 'I think of the process as if two lines came from opposite directions, liable to come near each other. If they overlap there is a moment of *illusion* – a bit of experience which the infant can take as *either* his hallucination *or* a thing belonging to external reality.'

In this paper we have in rudimentary form all of Winnicott's later concepts, e.g. holding, transitional object and dependence. It was on the

primary model of mother–infant relationship that Winnicott was to elaborate the nature and character of transference and the role of the analytic
setting. He was to emphasise one process, 'that of the individual's contact
with shared reality, and the development of this from the start of the infant's
life.' (Winnicott 1948.) Winnicott sees a hazard for the analyst in such an
undertaking: '. . . many treatments of schizoid types of adolescent fail
because they are planned on a basis that ignores the child's ability to "think
up" – in a way, to *create* – an analyst, a role into which the real analyst can
try to fit himself' (Winnicott 1948).

In his paper 'Birth Memories, Birth Trauma, and Anxiety' (1949)
Winnicott states that 'there is evidence that the personal birth experience is
significant, and is held as memory material' but he insists that *'there is no such
thing as treatment by the analysis of the birth trauma alone'*. He recounts certain
episodes from the analysis of a female patient Miss H. (aged 50), and
concludes: 'In the very close and detailed observation of one case I have
been able to satisfy myself that the *patient was able to bring to the analytic hour,
under certain very specialized conditions, a regression of part of the self to an
intra-uterine state.'* What is even more significant is Winnicott's statement: 'It
seems to me that *it is in relation to the border-line of intolerable reaction phases that
the intellect begins to work as something distinct from the psyche.*' It was this
differentiation of precocious intellectual functioning in reaction to impinge-
ments that was to lead Winnicott to see in fantasying a pathological mental
functioning that is a negation of psychic reality, and of which a certain type
of compulsive free-association is the symptom in analytic process. Some
vicissitudes of this type of developmental distortion of mental function
Winnicott discusses in his paper 'Mind and its Relation to the Psyche-
Soma' (1949a). The need in some patients 'to be relieved of the *mind activity*'
in order to refind their psycho-somatic wholeness of being is seen in their
demand for ECT.

In his paper 'Anxiety Associated with Insecurity' (1952) Winnicott spells
out three main types of anxiety resulting from failure in technique of
infant-care:

> 'unintegration, becoming a feeling of disintegration; lack of rela-
> tionship of psyche to soma, becoming a sense of depersonalization;
> also the feeling that the centre of gravity of consciousness transfers
> from the kernel to the shell, from the individual to the care, the
> technique.'

This memorization of the technique that fails I consider to constitute the
essence of the technique of the patient who is boring. Such patients twist
and abuse the analytic process we offer them to impose upon it an arid
technique of relating (through discourse in the adult situation) of which

they have been the victim in childhood. Behind it, as Winnicott (1952) points out, there is an ungraspable fear of madness in them:

> 'There is a state of affairs in which the fear is of a madness, that is to say a fear of a *lack of anxiety at regression* to an unintegrated state, to absence of a sense of living in the body, etc. The fear is that there will be no anxiety, that is to say, that there will be a regression, from which there may be no return.'

The tyrannical repetitiveness of the boring patient's narrative congeals this latent 'madness' into an interminable verbiage.

The clinical means for dealing with such highly organized *mental habits* Winnicott discusses in his paper 'Metapsychological and Clinical Aspects of Regression within the Psycho-Analytical Set-up' (1954c). Essential for Winnicott is the issue of classification and choice of case. He distinguishes three types of cases. First are those who can operate as whole persons and whose difficulties are in terms of interpersonal relations. The second are those in whom wholeness of personality is precariously held. Here analytic work relates to the developmental stage of concern (cf Winnicott 1963). The *survival* of *the analyst* Winnicott considers the dynamic factor in the treatment of these patients (cf Winnicott 1963). The third are those whose analysis must deal with the very beginnings of personality formation as a differentiating entity in itself. Here the emphasis is on management, and the clinical handling of regression to dependence in the analytic situation.

For Winnicott 'the word regression simply means the reverse of progress' and *'there cannot be a simple reversal of progress'*. There has to be an ego organization which *enables* regression to occur. Hence the capacity to regress is the result of favourable environmental care in infancy and childhood. It is this positive aspect of infant-care in these patients that, according to Winnicott, engenders in them *a belief* in the possibility of the correction of the original failure, through specialized (clinical) environmental provision, towards new forward emotional development.

In the care and treatment of these patients the emphasis shifts to the *quality* of the analytic situation. One passage from Winnicott states (1954c) it lucidly:

> 'It is proper to speak of the patient's *wishes,* the wish (for instance) to be quiet. With the regressed patient the word wish is incorrect; instead we use the word *need*. If a regressed patient *needs* quiet, then without it nothing can be done at all. If the need is not met the result is not anger, only a reproduction of the environmental failure situation which stopped the processes of self growth. The individual's capacity

to "wish" has become interfered with, and we witness the reappearance of the original cause of a sense of futility.

The regressed patient is near to a reliving of dream and memory situations; an acting out of a dream may be the way the patient discovers what is urgent, and talking about what was acted out follows the action but cannot precede it.'

The understanding and *management* of regressive states, explicit or cloaked, were the primary concern of Winnicott's clinical work. Freud and other analysts had established the ubiquitous presence of regression in all psychiatric illnesses and in the transference relationship. Their emphasis had been largely on regression to more primitive stages of libido development, with corresponding fantasies and wishes. Winnicott added to this the emphasis on the element of *need* in regressive phenomena and states.

That said, let us return to the present clinical material. I am deeply indebted and grateful to Mrs Clare Winnicott for making available to me the total notes that Winnicott kept on this case.

As Winnicott indicates in his brief introductory remarks to the material presented here, this patient had been in analysis with him earlier, during the war. In fact there are three separate sets of extensive notes from three stages of the two analyses of this patient with Winnicott.

From the beginning of the analysis Winnicott had decided to take notes. The first set of notes belong to the first analysis and are titled 'Fragment from an analysis'. Winnicott had written it up in a draft form but never published it. What he says there is so revealing that I shall quote his introduction to those notes directly from the typescript:

'In this paper I wish to make use of some rather unusual clinical material.

'It is difficult to report analytical material. First, there is the immensity of the task of remembering an hour's work and then of writing it down. Second, there is the quantity of material and the difficulty there must be in choosing from it. Third, there is the special difficulty analysts seem to find in recording what they themselves said.

Here, however, all these three difficulties are to some extent overcome. My patient spoke slowly and deliberately, and what he said could be easily recorded; I chose a special moment to make records, one which I knew would be decisive for the analysis; and I actually wrote down what I said whether I was pleased or ashamed of it.

In the analysis of a young man of 19 a stage was reached which was obviously likely to prove critical. After a long and steady pull the patient and I were reaching the top of a hill and seeing more and more, partly because, as we reached the top, the work itself became less arduous. We were to cash in on a year's analysis and, in order to learn as much as possible from what was happening, I took down several hours almost verbatim. I think I can say in this case the patient did not know that I was adopting this unusual procedure. Of course I would not have done it if it would have really mattered a great deal had the patient discovered it.

Without describing the whole case, I would say that in this analysis the striking feature was the ease with which the patient was in touch with his feelings towards the objects of his inner world and the ease with which he told me about these as long as he felt that I was in this inner world with him. Going with this, as might be expected, was a stubborn resistance in the form of a dissociation in the patient's personality, so that he in analysis had very little relation to himself in the external world. The fragment of analysis which I wish to report marks the period of the breakdown of this resistance.

This analysis was a straightforward one. It had that momentum of its own which is so nice for both analyst and patient. In spite of big interruptions because of the fact that the patient's university was evacuated from London, the patient had acted as if he knew he needed help, believed that he could get help. Moreover, he did not behave as if he felt – as some patients do – that the analysis would be snatched away at any moment if he did not hurry.

I might describe how his analysis started because it throws light on the character of the transference. One day the patient's mother rang me up and said that she was in analysis with So-and-so and she had a son aged 19 who wished for analysis for himself. Would I see him? I replied Yes, send him at 5 o'clock tomorrow. At 5 o'clock the next day the boy came into my room, lay down on the couch and started analysis exactly as he would do a year or two later. In other words, analysis for him meant something which he already believed in. As he left the room he went up to my bookcase and saw two books which he said were in the bookshelves at his home. In this and in every way he showed that he placed in my chair someone who already belonged to his inner world, and it is roughly speaking true to say that I remained an object of his inner world until the moment which I am about to describe in the first of the analytic hours which I took down verbatim.

In other words, up to this point, which was roughly speaking a year, interrupted by evacuation during terms, the patient's relation to me was an extremely artificial one unless one understands just what was happening. The material was rich and the work done considerable, but it was impossible to reach, for instance, the dynamics of the Oedipus situation. The period of transition was in fact heralded by the patient's first recognition of the reality of jealousy in the external world in the form of a casual statement that he had read something about a thing called the Oedipus complex and didn't hold with it. During this first half of analysis I made no attempt to force the situation because I knew, from the type of the transference, that it would be absolutely futile to do so, and also because the analysis was steadily progressing so that one could expect eventually the development which would throw light on what might be called a resistance or a negative therapeutic reaction.

Going ahead of the clinical material, in order to give the reader something to catch on to, I would say that the vital change in the analysis came with the analysis of the patient's fear of completing analysis. There is a number of ways in which anxiety is produced by the idea of completion of a job, and with this patient the accent was on one way, namely the disappearance of the hallucinated breast or subjective good external object at the moment of gratification and cessation of desire.

For him this was worse than aggression towards the love object – it annihilated it.

Up to this point in the analysis I had been an internalized person, and analysis had gone along swimmingly in its own way and within its own limitations. After it, however, the analysis and the patient's life changed. In analysis he became able to relate me to external phenomena, and to lose his serious dissociation, so that he now brought external matters into the associations. At home he started a new relation to his mother, one based on observation of her real self; and the patient changed from a self-satisfied, self-centred, lazy young man who dressed in abnormal garments and affected a beard, into a man who wanted a job and who eventually took and is holding a responsible war job in a factory. Moreover, the Oedipus situation, which had previously been unreal to him, and which had not been able to be brought into the analysis, now became real to him in the classical manner.'

The clinical notes that follow give a verbatim account from five sessions towards the very end of that analysis, which had lasted roughly two years. It had ended because the patient had become able to take a war job in an engineering firm. Two themes preoccupy the patient: fear of ending analysis and it becoming a 'complete' experience; and the confusion of this with the patient's dread of 'the violently hostile content of satisfaction at the end of the meal, which means annihilation of desire and annihilation of subjective breast followed by hostility to persisting objective breast' (Winnicott's interpretation to the patient in one of the sessions). The acute fear of satisfaction from a good, or rather ideal, feed features persistently in the material of the five sessions. One interpretation of Winnicott to the patient in this context is worth quoting here:

> 'Satisfaction means something more important to you than the blotting out of the breast. It means the loss of desire for it, and at that moment you do not know whether you will ever recover that desire; and in so far as the breast is a subjective phenomenon this means that you have no knowledge that the breast will come again. You are at the mercy of your instincts and your capacity for instinctual gratification, unless you recognize someone with breasts as objective phenomenon and dependence.'

The first analysis had lasted nearly two years, with long holiday breaks. The patient, who had been considered suffering from a schizophrenic-type illness, had made good recovery.

Some eight years later Winnicott wrote spontaneously to the patient's mother:

> 'You may be surprised to get a letter from me, but I would very much like a note from you about B.
>
> I know that on the whole it is not a very good idea to get into touch with past patients, and for that reason I am writing to you and not to B himself. Nevertheless one's work becomes much more interesting if one can follow up cases, and as I remember B's analysis very clearly I have often intended to ask you to let me know about him.
>
> I hope you are well and that he is well.'

The mother wrote back eagerly, and Winnicott asked her to see him. I quote his account of the interview with the mother:

> 'Mrs X came to see me at my request, although she was pleased to do this and to give me a report on the family. It was interesting to note that a great change had come over her description of B's home life. In the intervening years Mrs X has herself had a long analysis and she now describes herself as having been very ill.
>
> In the first interview with me she had said that if any child had ever had a perfect childhood it was B. It was in her own analysis that she discovered that her perfection as a mother had a symptomatic quality. She simply had to be perfect, and this allowed for no flexibility and

was derived from very great anxiety in herself. This unexpected bit of news completely confirms the main conclusion drawn from the analysis of B, since what we unexpectedly found there was that in reliving the very early breast-feeding experience he felt completely annihilated at the end of a feed and for this reason he had been unable to let himself go in any feeding experience. The subsequent development of this boy may be said to have been satisfactory. I would say that the only non-satisfactory feature from my point of view is that he is a communist, but of course, it is not necessary that membership of this party should be a symptom of illness. In my opinion this is one relic of his need to defend himself against his mother, who in spite of herself rather obviously dislikes these political views of her son.

The main feature of the recovery of this man is that he acknowledges nothing at all from his analysis. I always recognised it to be extremely important that no claim for recognition or gratitude whatever should be made. A perfect analysis would be just as difficult for him as a perfect management of infancy and would annihilate him. His only possible way is for him to have changed as a result of it, and I now regret having once allowed myself to stop him in the street to ask him how he was, although this apparently did no harm.

His return to analysis will almost certainly come through the fact that he has now become a medical student, and it is quite likely that he will come round eventually to wanting to be an analyst. He would probably be the last person to know this, and it is a point to remember that in his own analysis which must precede his becoming an analyst he will have to arrive at some consciousness of the way in which he was helped in his own analysis. If he is not to be an analyst there is no reason at all why he should ever know.

After the end of the analysis he changed and, after changing from an introverted man with indeterminate sex and a big liability to be turned over into homosexuality by a seduction, he suddenly went into an engineering works where he was soon managing other men. He was able to change his job when he found that he had to, but he always knew that engineering was not his interest, it being simply the kind of life he had to lead because of the war. He was not really well enough to join the army, and in any case one would think that his roots in Great Britain are not deep enough for him to want to die for the country. At the end of the war he was able to reconsider his position and he decided to be a doctor. He is now married and will soon have a child. An important part of his management came through the mother's recovery in her own analysis so that she was able to turn him out of her own house. In other words, the analysis in this man did not go far enough to enable him to get away from his mother with her as well as she was at the time when he was under treatment. The benefit of the double analysis is clear. His younger sister is fairly straightforward, married, with a family, but his older sister is a schizophrenic having analysis and at present being cared for in a hospital. B had retained his very great interest in music and he seems to have found a wife who can understand him and can take the place of his mother without being like the mother. In other words, it seems as if he has not had to find another ill mother, although to some extent he has found someone rather like his mother is now she has recovered through having had a long analysis.'

Nothing seems to happen for another four years, though from some notes it appears that Winnicott kept in touch with the mother spasmodically during this period. The next we hear of this patient is when he goes voluntarily to a hospital specialising in treatment of neuroses and is an in-patient there. The psychiatrist in charge of him had got in touch with Winnicott and informed him that the patient, after qualifying in medicine, had a break-down and was admitted to that hospital. The patient himself was resistant to returning to Winnicott for further analysis. A note scribbled in pencil around this time by Winnicott states: 'I heard that the patient was in a certain hospital and I got in touch with the doctors there, knowing that the time must have come for the continuation of the analysis. I had kept in touch with the mother. The patient had no capacity to come and look for me.' From the existing correspondence it seems that around this time the mother also rang Winnicott and came to see him. Two days after this consultation, the mother wrote to Winnicott: 'I have just spoken to B and gave him your address and phone number – I do hope he comes to see you and is able to start analysis soon.' The reason the mother had to give her son Winnicott's address was that since the first analysis Winnicott had moved to a new address. The patient started the analysis a week later, while still an in-patient at the hospital. So the second analysis starts some thirteen years after the end of the first. A note in pencil by Winnicott about the beginning of the new analysis is very telling:

'When the analysis restarted it was hardly true to say that he came to see me. Rather it seemed that an observer of life came and talked with me in a rather well arranged rhetoric. We sometimes talked of the patient. Gradually I would say we have become two nursery maids talking about a boy (the patient), and in time the nursery maid brought the boy – even the baby – to see me. I got a few glimpses of a real child.'

At first the patient came five times a week but some four months after starting analysis he was able to leave the hospital and take up a medical appointment, which necessitated his coming three times only. This analysis lasted just over two years.

There are two sets of notes from this second analysis. The first set consists of notes Winnicott wrote retrospectively about the on-going analysis, and they cover, by and large, the first sixteen months of the analysis. From the end of this phase of analysis Winnicott abstracted five episodes which he has reported in his paper 'Withdrawal and Regression' (1954a). Then there is a gap of three months, and after that Winnicott keeps a verbatim record of the sessions of the last six months of analysis, which are published here.

To end the account of Winnicott's dealings with this patient it only remains to be stated that Winnicott again wrote to the patient, from his own initiative, some fourteen years after the termination of his second analysis. I quote the letter:

> 'You may be surprised to hear from me: indeed you may have forgotten me. But the fact is that I would very much like to hear a word from you about yourself, your work, your family. I'm at the age at which one looks back and wonders.
> I send you my very good wishes.'

The patient answered promptly with a very long letter, giving news of himself and his family, and telling Winnicott of the sad death of his mother after a distressing and long illness. He had fared well in his own work and life. Winnicott replied to him:

> 'I was so very pleased to get your reply to my letter. Thank you for the trouble you took going over things. I am sorry your mother had an uncomfortable end. She was indeed a personality.
> I am impressed by the way you have used your life instead of perpetual psychotherapy. Perhaps that's what life *is*. (I might write to you again one day.)'

In his Preface to the Second Edition of *The Gay Science* in 1886, Nietzsche wrote:

> 'This book may need more than one preface, and in the end there will still remain room for doubt whether anyone who had never lived through similar experiences could be brought closer to the *experience* of this book by means of prefaces.'

I feel a similar sentiment faced with the task of introducing Winnicott's extraordinary verbatim record of the last six months of the long-stretched analysis of his patient. The virtue of Winnicott's clinical narrative rests in the fact that its drift is as undecided as its psychodynamics are open-ended. Even though in his brief introductory remarks Winnicott frames his account in the context of the Depressive Position, the actual events of the 'subtle interplay' (p. 173 below) between him and the patient are untrammelled by any intrusive theoretical presuppositions. This should not be mistaken for naïveté on Winnicott's part. He was a clinician endowed with a complex sensibility, and over the years he had actualized in himself a mercurial intellectuality that informed all his clinical work. However, he had also cultivated in himself the generous discipline of letting the patient's psychic reality find its mood and character in the analytic space. Therefore each of us, who reads his narrative, will turn it into a discourse according to the needs and bias of his own sensibility.

I shall discuss it under three headings:

(a)   the patient's way of relating to himself;
(b)   the patient's use of Winnicott;
(c)   Winnicott's style of presenting and dosing himself to this patient.

Winnicott was an indefatigable note-taker of his clinical encounters. Where he found the energy and the time is a mystery. All the same, he did not take such extensive notes on all his patients. Something about the *manner* in which this patient presented himself and took hold of the clinical space struck Winnicott from the very beginning. In his first draft notes from the start of the analysis, quoted above, one hears Winnicott tell that he was impressed by 'the ease with which the patient was in touch with his feelings towards the objects of his inner world', and that the patient had little difficulty in verbalizing these thoughts, even though ponderously. When the patient starts his second analysis, Winnicott notes: 'Rather it seemed that an observer of life came and talked with me. . . . We sometimes talked of the patient.' This curious and calculated stance of the patient persists right through to the end. One could argue that for this patient nothing existed but his *thoughts*, and that his basic attitude was: I refuse, therefore *I am*. It is this *refusal* and these thoughts that are the contents of the perpetual chatter that goes on in his head, and which Winnicott (1971) was to call *fantasying*. It is this mentation that isolates his subjective self from others, and even from his own reflective self-awareness. Towards the outside world he is merely reactive. Towards his true self, if one may use that phrase, he has only a protective attitude. He can never reach it and live from it. Hence his complaints of lack of spontaneity and initiative. What established this irrevocable dissociation in him Winnicott attributes to the 'ideal' feeding experiences in infancy that robbed the patient of all initiative from need and desire. Instinctual urgency of hunger or lust push one towards the object.

That is the one risk he cannot take. Hence he lived in the *oubliette* of that objectless space, which constitutes *le terrain interne*, of his mentation and self-observation. In it every experience is represented by thoughts, but no experience or person is internalized. The patient himself remarks: 'chatter is talking to no person' (p. 143 below).

From the very beginning Winnicott was aware that the whole manner of talking and relating in this patient inherently carried a negative therapeutic reaction. The patient gives his own diagnosis: 'I never became human. I have missed it' (p. 96) and 'To sum up, my own problem is how to find a struggle that never was' (p. 165). Winnicott was not daunted by this. Nor did he set out to cure it. He allowed for its functioning as the necessary condition for this patient to *exist* in life. Because this patient rarely does more than exist. Furthermore, once Winnicott realised that the withdrawn affable mentation of this patient was not hostile in intent towards him, the analyst, he was challenged by the *paradox* of this patient's total acceptance of the clinical situation and space, with a parallel refusal of inter-personal relating and to initiate any play from spontaneous impulse. I advisedly use the word paradox. To have seen it in conflictual terms of ambivalence would have been a false over-simplification. It is through sustaining this paradox for some thirteen years of relating to this patient (one must not forget that for Winnicott this analysis lasted thirteen years and after; Winnicott had kept the patient alive in his memory all that time) that Winnicott was able to witness how this patient relates to himself and what is the character of that self-relating. It was *boring-ness*, not boredom! Boredom is a static, inert psychic mood. Boring-ness is an active existential stance, maintained through incessant mentation. Hence the eerie and mellow fatigue that we find in this patient, and which so readily enables him to shift levels of consciousness at any threat or prospect of true encounter with Winnicott, and drift into sleep.

This 'couch-sleep' provided this patient the truest experiences of himself, and this couch-sleep is a secret space to which even his dreams yield no clues. What monumental capacity Winnicott had to contain unknowing. He lets it all happen. The patient frets: 'The thing is to wake up. . . . I would like to wake up, that is, get up, go away' (p. 168). But that he'll never achieve. He shall stay in the *oubliette* of his mentation. Hence he can have no aims. Where there is no route, there is no aim. When the patient raised 'the vague problem of aim' (p. 169), Winnicott promptly reminds him that he couldn't even come to Winnicott for his second analysis, and adds: 'I had more or less to go and look for you' (p. 170). At best this patient could only reach a point where he can be the isolated surround of his True Self, but cannot risk to live from it. Hence he bores himself with his techniques of self-care and self-cure all life long.

When Winnicott had decided to frame this material in terms of the Depressive Position, he had good reasons to do so. The Depressive Position connotes an intra-psychic state, entailing specific affective capacities and other ego-functions. It is not an accident, perhaps, that soon after writing the first account of this patient's analysis in his paper 'Withdrawal and Regression' (1954a), the next paper by Winnicott should be 'The Depressive Postition in Normal Emotional Development' (1954b). For Winnicott the Depressive Position constitutes an *achievement* in emotional development. The crucial passages in Winnicott's argument are:

> 'The child (or adult) who has reached that capacity for interpersonal relationships which characterizes the toddler stage in health, and for whom ordinary analysis of the infinite variations of triangular human relationships is feasible, has passed *through and beyond* the depressive position. On the other hand, the child (or adult) who is chiefly concerned with the innate problems of personality integration and with the initiation of a relationship with environment is not yet at the depressive position in personal development.
>
> In terms of environment; the toddler is in a family situation, working out an instinctual life in interpersonal relationships, and the baby is being held by a mother who adapts to ego needs; in between the two is the infant or small child arriving at the depressive position, being held by the mother, but more than that, being held over a phase of living. It will be noted that *a time factor* has entered, and the mother *holds a situation* so that the infant has the chance to work through the consequences of instinctual experiences; as we shall see, the working through is quite comparable to the digestive process, and is comparably complex.
>
> The mother holds the situation, and does so over and over again, and at a critical period in the baby's life. The consequence is that something can be done about something. The mother's technique enables the infant's co-existing love and hate to be come sorted out and interrelated and gradually brought under control from within in a way that is healthy.'

The essential concepts for the understanding of this patient's use of Winnicott are in the phrases 'the mother *holds a situation*' and 'the mother's technique'. If one examines carefully this patient's transference relationship, one feature stands out remarkably: the diligence with which he observes Winnicott's technique of analysing and takes it into his language immediately. All the way he refuses and negates the objective object Winnicott, in order to isolate Winnicott's technique of analysing and make it his own. What he leaves to Winnicott is the holding of the clinical situation and space. Furthermore, language provides this patient with all the barriers he needs to keep Winnicott distanced. Whenever the clinical process edges him towards mutuality, he falls asleep. His verbal 'demands' for physical contact are merely another ruse of his mind precociously to usurp an emergent need and/or wish in order to hand it over to language, where they then stay petrified and inert. Winnicott reassures him on this count: 'I would say that a correct interpretation that is well-timed is a physical contact of a kind' (p. 160). Winnicott senses all the way how precarious is the inner protective shield of this patient. Any accidental influx of actualized excitement in a physical mutuality of tenderness or concern could easily have played havoc with the perpetual gamesmanship of this man's mental apparatus. So Winnicott stays in the area of deliberate language as the exclusive mode of usage by this patient. Hence the patient never reaches his capacity for playing. It remains a nostalgic possibility in his thoughts. Winnicott is profoundly aware of the constrictions this patient has to live with. He tells the patient that he is 'cluttered up with reparation capacity' (p. 29), and this carries an ominous threat for this patient because 'satisfaction annihilates the object for him' (p. 30). Given these limits, the patient could *use* Winnicott in a very specialized and distant way only. His basic use of Winnicott is to find a personalized space where he can spread out his thoughts and what he has *observed* of his experiences, and tentatively allow for interaction between them. But even here *sleep* is both his refuge and his only experience of dependence. Winnicott interprets after one of his *sleeps*: 'You had a need then to be held with someone else in charge while you slept' (p. 162). The persistent use that this patient makes of Winnicott is that of a certain reticence in Winnicott. The patient knows Winnicott knows more of him that he ever interprets. This is one shared secret between them. The other is Winnicott's note-taking.

Now I come to the last issue I wish to discuss: Winnicott's presentation and dosage of himself to this patient. In his paper, 'Delinquency as a Sign of Hope' (1973), discussing the anti-social tendency in a child who may steal a fountain pen from some shop Winnicott postulates:

> '. . . it is not the object that was being sought, and in any case *the child is looking for the capacity to find, not for an object*' (author's italics).

I believe Winnicott sensed from the very beginning that this patient was searching to *find a capacity* in himself and not a relationship with an object. And this decided Winnicott to set a specific tenor to his relationship with this patient. Like the patient, he too became partially an *observer* of the clinical process. In him it took the form of taking notes. In another paper, 'The Mother–Infant Experience of Mutuality' (1970), discussing *the experi-*

ence of mutuality Winnicott states: 'This mutuality belongs to the mother's capacity to adapt to the baby's needs', and he elaborates it in terms of the clinical process as follows:

> 'Analysts with a rigid analytic morality that does not allow touch miss a great deal of that which is now being described. One thing they never know, for instance, is that the analyst makes a little twitch whenever he or she goes to sleep for a moment or even wanders over in the mind (as may well happen) to some fantasy of his or her own. This twitch is the equivalent of a failure to hold in terms of mother and baby. The mind has dropped the patient.'

I believe that one other function the note-taking served for Winnicott was to keep him awake and aware during the patient's long pauses or lapses into sleep, and even during the assault of the patient's organized dense rhetoric in the sessions, which foreclosed mutuality by its very method. The printed narrative lends a somewhat false momentum to the verbal exchange between the patient and his analyst. The calculated idiom with which this patient manufactured his narrative was inordinately boring and the patient is aware of it. Somewhere, quite unconsciously, Winnicott drew upon his vast experience of doodling with children in consultation and used the space of the paper to doodle notes. His way of scribbling notes during the session comes much nearer to doodling than writing. He scrawled all over the paper, in all directions and sometimes upside down. Thus he himself stayed alive in somatic attention and his mind never 'dropped' the patient. Such patients provoke a very uncanny sort of hate-response in the counter-transference which compels the analyst to intrude with interpretations to ease the tension generated or to lapse into a silence that is more inert and boring than the patient's narrative.

Winnicott also creates a secret space in the area of note-taking that matches the patient's secret space in couch-sleep. Thus both are safe with each other, and survive each other. Each is aware of the other's secret and *lives* with it, without questioning it.

The lessons for all clinicians who read this clinical narrative are many indeed. Perhaps the most important one is that one must not try to cure a patient beyond his need and his psychic resources to sustain and live from that cure.

M.M.R.K.

Fragment of an Analysis

THIS fragment of an analysis is given as an illustration of the depressive position as it can appear in the course of an analysis.

The patient is a man of thirty, married, and with two children. He had a period of analysis with me during the war, and this had to be broken off because of war conditions as soon as he became clinically well enough to work. In this first phase he came in a state of depression with a strong homosexual colouring, but without manifest homosexuality. He was in a bemused state and rather unreal. He developed little insight although he improved clinically so that he could do war work. His very good brain enabled him to juggle with concepts and to philosophize, and in serious conversation he was generally thought of as an interesting man with ideas.

He qualified in his father's profession, but this did not satisfy him and he soon became a medical student, probably (unconsciously) retaining thereby his use of myself as a father-figure displacing his real father, who had died.

He married, and in doing so offered a girl who needed it a chance for therapy through dependence. He hoped (unconsciously) that in his marriage he was laying down a basis for a therapy through dependence for himself, but (as so often happens) when he in turn claimed special tolerance from his wife he failed to get it. She fortunately refused to be his therapist, and it was partly his recognition of this fact that led him to a new phase of illness. He broke down at work (as a doctor in a hospital) and was admitted into an institution himself because of unreality feelings, and a general inability to cope with work and with life.

He was not aware at that time that he was seeking out his former analyst, and was quite incapable of asking even for analysis, although as it turned out later this is what he was precisely doing and nothing else would have been of value.

After about a month of the new analysis he was able to resume work as a hospital officer.

He was by this time a schizoid case. His sister had had a schizophrenic illness treated (with considerable success) by psychoanalysis. He came to analysis saying that he could not talk freely, that he had no small talk or imaginative or play capacity, and that he could not make a spontaneous gesture or get excited.

At first it can be said that he came to analysis and talked. His speech was deliberate and rhetorical. Gradually it became clear that he was listening to conversations that were going on within, and reporting any parts of these conversations that he thought might interest me. In time it could be said that he brought himself to analysis and talked about himself, as a mother or father might bring a child to me and talk about him. In these early phases (lasting six months) I had no chance of direct conversation with the child (himself).[1]

The evolution of the analysis at this stage is described elsewhere.[2]

By a very special route the analysis changed in quality, so that I became able to deal directly with the child, which was the patient.

There was a rather definite end to this phase, and the patient himself said that he *now came himself* for treatment, and for the first time *felt hopeful*. He was more than ever conscious of being unexcitable and lacking in spontaneity. He could scarcely blame his wife for finding him a dull companion, unalive except in serious discussion on a topic set by someone else. Actual potency was not disturbed, but he could not make love, and he could not get generally excited about sex. He had one child, and has since had a second.

In this new phase the material gradually led up to a transference neurosis of classical type. There came a short phase leading obviously to excitement, oral in quality. This excitement was not experienced, but it led to the work described in detail in the case notes that follow. The case notes refer to the work done between the excitement that arrived in the transference but which was not felt, and the *experience* of the excitement.

The first sign of the new development was reported as a feeling, quite new, of love for his daughter. This he felt on the way home from a cinema where he had actually cried. He had cried tears twice in that week, and this seemed to him to be a good omen, as he had been unable either to cry or to laugh, just as he had been unable to love.

By force of circumstances this man could attend only three times a week, but I have allowed this, since the analysis has obviously gone with a swing and has even been a rapid one.

---

[1] Cf 'Clinical Varieties of Transference' (Winnicott 1955) and 'Ego Distortion in Terms of True and False Self' (Winnicott 1960).
[2] In 'Withdrawal and Regression' (Winnicott 1954a), reproduced in the Appendix to this volume.

Thursday, 27 January

Patient The patient said that he had nothing much to report except that he had had a cough. Probably this was an ordinary cold. It did occur to him, however, to think in terms of TB, and he had been going over in his mind the use he could make of it if it should turn out that he should have to go to a hospital. He could say to his wife: 'Now here I am . . .'

Analyst Various interpretations were possible here and I chose the following: I said that what was ignored was the relationship of this illness to the analysis. I was thinking in terms of the break it would make in the treatment. I said that I was not at all sure that this rather superficial working out of the consequences was the most important part of the anxiety. At the same time I dealt with the reality aspect and said that I was going to leave it to him. He was conscious of the fact that he wanted me to deal with this as material for analysis and he did not want me to take part in actual diagnosing.

Patient After my interpretation he said that in fact the idea came at him not as TB, but as cancer of the lung.

Analyst I now had more powerful material to work with and I made the interpretation that he was telling me about suicide. It was as if there was what I called a five percent suicide. I said: 'I think you have not really had to deal with a suicidal urge in your life, have you?'

Patient He said this was only partially true. He had threatened suicide with his wife but he had not meant it. This was not important. On the other hand he had at times felt that suicide was part of the make-up; in any case he said there was the fact of his sister's two suicide attempts; they were partial suicides and not designed to succeed. Nevertheless, they showed him how real suicide could be, even when not an urge involving the whole personality.

He now linked this up with the barrier that he felt he had to get through to get further.

Analyst I reminded him (and he had forgotten) that he felt that there was a person preventing him from getting through the barrier.

Patient He said he felt the barrier as a wall that he must break down or hit himself against; and he had the sensation of having to be carried bodily over the difficult patch.

Analyst I said that we therefore had evidence that between him and health was suicide and that I must know about this as I must see that he did not die.

Patient He had the idea of various forms of starting life again with things different. *Pause.* He spoke about his lateness which had become a feature recently. This was due to the fact that something new had happened; he could have come, setting aside all his work and hanging around for a quarter of an hour so as to be on time. Instead of that his work had become more important and he now finished things off before coming; with luck he might have been on time. He put it that the analysis had now become less important than his work in some sense.

Analyst I made an interpretation here, gathering together the material of the past and pointing out that I could see this more easily than he could: first he could only contribute into himself, then he could contribute into the analysis; and now he could contribute to the analysis in his work. I joined this up with the guilt which underlies the whole of this phase including the suicide. I reminded him that the thing that the analysis was leading up to was excitement with instinct including eating. The guilt about the ruthless destruction here was too great except insofar as constructive urges and capacities reveal themselves.[1]

Pause.

Patient The effect of these interpretations was revealed in the next remark when he said in a much more easy way: 'I now think of the illness in amusing terms; it might be measles, a childhood thing.'

Analyst I pointed out that a change had come over him since I had taken away the suicide communication which was hidden in the fantasies about the illness.

Patient Following this he said that for the first time he felt if opportunity occurred he could use an affair and balance this with his wife's infidelity.

Analyst I pointed out that this indicated a lessening of the dependence elements of his relationship to his wife, these having been gathered into the analysis.

The week following 27 January

The report of the next three sessions is condensed into the following statement.

Patient The patient reported that before the last session he had in fact slept with the girl friend. This was after a party. All feeling was damped down. He said that it might have happened at any time apart from analysis. He felt no love (potency was not disturbed).

The whole of this session was toneless and unconsciously designed to make the analyst feel that nothing important was happening.

---

[1] Cf 'The Development of the Capacity for Concern' (Winnicott 1963).

Patient Following this he reported that he had expected a great result. He had expected me to know without being told that he had had an experience with excitement in it.

The information came indirectly at first.

Analyst I pointed out to him that he had so damped down the report of what had happened that I had been unable to make use of it. I was now able to interpret the transference significance of the incident and at first I said that the girl represented himself so that in the affair he as a female had had intercourse with me as a male.

Patient He half accepted this interpretation but he was disappointed because there was no natural evolution belonging to the interpretation.

Analyst The following day he was depressed and I made a new interpretation, stating that my previous one had obviously been wrong. I said that the girl was the analyst (in the transference neurosis).

Patient There followed an immediate release of feeling. The interpretation led to the theme not of erotic experience but of dependence.

The analysis now came out of the difficult phase which had lasted throughout the week, and a powerful relationship to me developed which frightened the patient.

Patient His question was: 'Can you stand it?' He spoke about his father in particular among the people from whom he had sought the right to be dependent. His father could take it up to a certain stage, but then always he would hand him over to his mother. His mother was of no use, having already failed (i.e. in the patient's infancy).

Analyst I made another interpretation, which I had to withdraw because I could tell from the effect that it was wrong. I reminded him of the female version of himself that hovered around his male self throughout his childhood, and I equated my new position in the transference neurosis with this female shadow self. After withdrawing this I saw the correct interpretation. I said that now at last his thumb had come to mean something again. He had been a persistent thumb-sucker till eleven, and it would seem likely now that he gave it up because he had no one for it to stand for.[1]

This interpretation of the thumb was clearly correct, and incidentally it produced an alteration in his very stereotyped hand-movements. For the first time in the whole of his analysis, without being aware of doing so, he put his left thumb up into the air and brought it towards his mouth.

---

[1] See 'Transitional Objects and Transitional Phenomena' (Winnicott 1951).

Tuesday, 8 February

The doorbell being out of order, he was kept waiting three minutes on the doorstep.

Patient He reported having a formula for starting, and compared it with history-taking. Patients assume that you know more than you do.

Analyst 'I have to bear in mind that you may have been upset by the waiting.' (Very unusual in the case of this patient.)

Patient He went on with the description of how one gets stuck in history-taking between going into great detail or simply satisfying the patient, presumably pretending that one knows as much as one is expected to know. Somewhere in the middle of this he had a withdrawal.[1] Recovering from the momentary withdrawal, he managed to report the fantasy belonging to the withdrawal, in which he was very annoyed with a surgeon who stopped midway in an operation. It was not so much that the surgeon was angry with the patient as that the patient was just out of luck; he was being operated on when the surgeon went on strike.

Analyst I linked this with the reaction to the weekend following my accept- ance of the dependence role. I brought in the bell failure, but this was relatively unimportant; whereas the long breaks linked up directly with his statement at the end of the previous hour that I might not be able to stand his need for an extreme dependence, such as his living with me.

  The effect of this interpretation was very marked; the analysis came alive and remained alive throughout the hour.

Patient The patient spoke of his negativity, how it bores him and makes him depressed. It leaves him high and dry. When he gets sleepy he gets annoyed with himself. This negativity is a challenge. Sometimes speech is not worth the effort. He feels literally dried up. Sleep means lack of emotion. Nothing presents itself. He then described the contrast between his wife's attitude and his own. His wife feels things and cannot stand his own intellectual approach to everything and his absence of feelings. He began to discuss the word love, not its sexual aspect.

  He then spoke about Jones' article in *The Observer*,[2] mentioning especially the child with the button and the way Jones linked this up with cannibalism.

  I made no interpretation, knowing that he was coming the next day, and that the theme would reappear.

[1] Cf 'Withdrawal and Regression' in the Appendix to this volume.
[2] 'The Dawn of Conscience' in *The Observer* of 6 February 1955.

Wednesday, 9 February

The patient came excited.

Patient 'I feel better.' (Elation.) He reported having laughed with people. There was something new about all this. It was natural.

Analyst I found that he could not remember what happened last time and I gave a summary. In giving this I was unable to remember the content of the withdrawal fantasy and said so. It always helps this man if I am able to remind him of the material of the last hour.)

Patient He said that this liberation brought about by his feeling better made him independent of his wife. He now had a bargaining weapon with her which he could use, although he felt no vindictiveness against her. He did not need to beg for sympathy any longer. It used to be nothing but himself, hopeless.

Analyst I said that it seemed to have strengthened his whole personality, his getting a little bit nearer to cannibalism and to instincts.

Patient He said that to make matters better he had had a discussion with a surgeon, very friendly, very satisfactory in result.

Analyst Here I remembered his withdrawal fantasy and reminded him of it.

Patient He continued that the surgeon had argued against the idea of an operation in regard to a certain treatment of a patient. The surgeon understood, but in a sense he had downed tools.

Pause.

Analyst I interpreted that excitement was present but well under control because it brings its own anxieties.

Patient He reported other minor incidents. 'I can afford to be excited. A year ago the same things happened but as I could not afford to be excited they passed over me. I allowed an intellectual appreciation only. I could not afford to do without my depression. In fact I could not understand how anyone could get excited, and I had no conception of feeling competent. Now, because of the progress that seems to be maintained here in this treatment, I can let things go.' *Pause.* 'I do not want to talk about excitement.'

Analyst 'The point of excitement is being excited.'

Patient 'There is a risk involved. You look silly. People might laugh if you prattle.' (This word belongs in the analysis to a phase of his early childhood in which it was said that he prattled before he became sullen and withdrawn.) 'And then you are left holding the baby.' (Meaning excitement.)

Pause.

Analyst I made an interpretation joining together the prattling and the holding of the baby.[1]

Patient 'People despise adult prattling. I have always beeen serious-minded. Now I feel that I could prattle naturally outside the analysis. In the analysis I can only be serious even now or I can be excited about something. There is something different about excitement in its own right. The danger is that if you are excited you lose it. You have it taken away or undermined.'

Analyst 'If you show excitement it gets bagged.' (I might have interpreted the castration anxiety here but refrained.)

Patient 'Yes. You are light-hearted and then you become heavy if the excitement is claimed and considered to be attached to something. It is important to be fancy free, but this can only happen in the absence of a love relationship. I was thinking of this last night. The relationship to the girl is a fancy free affair. The relationship to my wife cannot be so.'

Analyst I reminded him that he was also talking about masturbation, and he developed the theme as he already was on the point of doing so.

Patient 'The advantage is that there is no risk taken; no social complications.' He was struck by the unexpected fact that when he was married the need continued, even though this jeopardized his potency.

At this point there were bell noises; a man was mending the bell. This caused an interruption, and the patient was surprised to find that he minded.

'It is usually the other way. You seem to be overworried when there are interruptions and I cannot see that they matter. Just now, however, with such intimate matters under discussion, I see for the first time the truth of what you have said about the setting of analysis and its importance.'

Analyst I linked this up with the theme of dependence.

Thursday, 10 February

Patient He continued to report excitement, although this was at a low level compared with the elation.

Analyst 'It appears that you have lived most of your life at a level below par in regard to excitement, and now when you come even to ordinary excitability you feel conscious of it.'

Patient 'Yes, I find I am able to be gay and lighthearted with less effort. I

---

[1] For the concept of 'holding' see 'The Theory of the Parent–Infant Relationship' (Winnicott 1960a).

used to be able at times but it was always an act. Something happened today which made me realize, however, that caution is needed. There are still unanswered questions to do with work and family. I feel apprehensiveness and guilt at feeling well, and of course at having a secret affair. It would be dangerous to get too excited, that is to say, at the expense of the future. I cannot afford to ignore what remains to be done. But there is a difference. I can now look forward to a future. In the past it seemed that I had difficulties in the present with no solution, as well as no prosect for the future. There was no hope of living an ordinary life ever. My depression was something to do with looking for dependence. I could say that in the dependence and therefore in the depression I was claiming my birthright.'

Analyst 'The hopelessness about the future and the present therefore turns out to be a hopelessness in the past which you did not know about. What you are looking for is your capacity to love, and, without our knowing all the details, we can say that some failure in your early life made you doubt your capacity to love.'

Patient After agreeing with all this, he said: 'There is the task still to be done.'

Analyst I made a rather wide interpretation linking up the reality that belonged to his discovering his love of his daughter and reminding him that this followed tears at the cinema.

Patient 'I have always had an intellectual idea of pleasure associated with pain. Similarly I associate love with sadness. I told somebody this once. It was at a Youth Club talk on sex. I said that there was an association between love and sadness, and I was forcibly rebuked and called sadistic.'

Analyst I remarked that nevertheless he knew that he was right and that the speaker was wrong.

Patient 'Perhaps she (the speaker) knew but she found it inconvenient to agree with this point in the setting.'

Analyst 'There is no need for me to try to answer this because the answer is evolving in your analysis.'

Patient 'I was not being sadistic, and this comment was therefore not true.'

Analyst Here I started making a rather more comprehensive interpretation, bringing in the word cannibalism which came from Ernest Jones' article in *The Observer*.[1]

Patient He filled out my remark by saying that he had always recognized that biting was important in love-making.

Analyst In the comprehensive interpretation I spoke of this infancy situa-

---

[1] See p. 24.

tion which he had missed in some way and which he was needing me
to provide in the analysis, speaking of the holding of a situation in
time, so that the dependence phenomena could be tested in relation to
the instinctual moments and ideas. I happened to say in illustration
that an infant might have three nurses in the course of a day in an
institution, thus presenting a difficulty in regard to reparation.[2]

Patient He picked up the idea of my interpretation quickly and said: 'In my
case there seemed to be four, because of my four lives – hospital,
home, analysis, and the girl. Everything depends on my being able to
describe in the analysis what happens in the other phases.' He then
said: 'But adversely what is happening is that this split in the total
situation is giving me more to talk about. In any one of the four places
I have a lot to say, whereas usually I feel exhausted if I say anything
and have nothing more to say.'

Analyst I spoke first about his need to feel that he was contributing in this
analysis and that if he has nothing to say he has often felt awkward
and deficient. I said: 'We are also talking about one of the origins of
conversation in which each individual is integrating all the material of
the split-off experiences by talking in one situation about another,
there being in health a basic unified pattern.'

Previously all he had been able to find were various examples of the
original pattern which he was all the time seeking. Now in the analysis
he had found the pattern and could benefit from being able to split it
up.

Pause.

Patient 'There is a danger of going too far. One could get confused.'

Analyst At first I thought that he meant that my interpretation had been too
complex. He was referring, however, to the innumerable odd things
that he could bring into the analysis, and I was reminded of his having
been noted for prattling until a certain age in early childhood when he
changed over into being unable to talk except seriously.

Patient He now told me about the fear of a hopeless jumble of bits and
pieces, something that he called being too widely split. He chose to
speak about the ward round that he does on Thursdays with Dr X,
especially as this always affects the Thursday evening session. I had
never been told this fact before. Dr X's round is never simple. It is
always a series of challenges. He is full of ideas and demands. At
present there is a new development in that the patient has innumerable ideas of his own and he now stands up to his chief, and they both
enjoy the contact. There was also the matter of a rather difficult

[2] Cf 'The Development of the Capacity for Concern' (Winnicott 1963).

surgeon. He had written a history of a patient, and had received an amusing letter back thanking him for his very detailed and comprehensive report. This letter was praise, and it came just when the patient was in a mood to receive praise, perhaps for the first time for many years. He certainly welcomed it. Just now there seemed to be too much of everything. He became worried always when there were innumerable bits, and for this reason had developed a technique of generalizing and thereby simplifying issues.

Analyst The alternative to an ordering of the material was getting lost in innumerable fragments. It would seem that the patient here was describing his growing ability to tolerate disintegration or unintegration.

Patient He said that these ideas felt like too many children.

Analyst My job as analyst was to help deal with these children and to sort them out and get some sort of order into the management of them. I pointed out that he was cluttered up with reparation capacity when he had not yet found the sadism that would indicate the use of the reparation phenomenon. The excitement in relation to me had only been indicated and had not appeared.

Patient He then described the analytic situation as a difficult one for the excited patient. Analysts are well protected. They avoid violation by special mechanisms for protection. This was especially evident at the Institution, where patients and doctors do not meet except professionally, and appointments are arranged indirectly. The doctors also are having analysis. It is only possible to hurt them by actual physical violence. Once some men tried to break through and succeeded in annoying some of the doctors by deliberate rudeness and were rebuked. An analyst ought not to act that way. Or why do they? 'There are two ideas,' he added here. 'One, I am annoyed that the analysts were not immune to verbal trauma. At the same time I am annoyed at their invulnerability. You can only annoy an analyst by not turning up, but that's foolish.'

Analyst I said that he had omitted talking about not turning up (I ought to have said playing at, but I left this out). It was as if he had told me a dream in which he had not turned up, and we could now look into the meaning of this dream. We could see that it contains sadism for him at the moment and that the sadism leads us to cannibalism.

As an additional interpretation I said that, in joining together all the different phases of his life, there was one which was the surgeon's praise. I had been likened to the surgeon in the material of the previous hour, and it was important to him that I should be able to see that I have praised him through the surgeon.

Patient His response to this was that he thought that I ought to be able to show excitement along with his excitement. Why could I not be proud of his achievement?

Analyst I replied to this that I was indeed excited, although perhaps not as excited as he would be since I was also not so much in despair during his despair periods. I was in a position to see the thing as a whole.

Patient He continued on the theme of the analyst's ability to be excited at progress in patients and I said:

Analyst 'You can take it from me that I do this kind of work because I think it is the most exciting thing a doctor can do, and it is certainly better from my point of view when patients are doing well than when they are not.'

Monday, 14 February

Patient He reported that the phase of excitement had subsided. The novelty of it was lost. There were three factors. One of these was that he was tired; another was that the excitement could not solve all his problems. (I noted the end of a phase of elation.) While he was excited he had expected that his difficulties with his wife, etc., would automatically solve themselves, but he realized now that they were as before.

Analyst I brought in the end of the last hour when he hoped that I would be excited too. I pointed out that we were dealing with elation and that it was important to him that I had not shared his elation although I had shared his excitement.

why?

Patient He said that the change had persisted to some extent; for instance, he noticed a lessened need for putting on an act – living in itself had become less of a heavy burden and deliberate activity. His talking, although still difficult, was now not a permanent problem; it often seemed unimportant that he was not talking like others. *Pause.* He said that the end of excitement brought anxiety because during the excited time he had plenty to say in the analysis. Now he had nothing again.

Analyst 'Really you are letting me know that you have nothing whatever to say.'

Patient 'That took the lid off. It showed that all I had been saying was of no value whatever. I feel exposed.' *Pause.* He reported definitely not wanting to speak.

Analyst Here I made a comprehensive interpretation, bringing in a previous one in which I linked up the present analysis with the first phase which was completed in the war without his having achieved much insight. I said that satisfaction annihilates the object for him. He had obtained some satisfaction last week and now I, as the object, had become annihilated.

Patient 'That makes me think, because I was concerned that the girl friend was no more of interest to me.'

He then made a review of his relationship to his wife in the light of this interpretation of mine. He observed how satisfactions had to some extent always led to anxiety associated with annihilation of the object.

Analyst I made an interpretation concerning the continuation of my interest in the period in which I seemed to be annihilated.

Patient He reported that intellectually he could understand my interest continuing and the continuation of the object, but there had been an effort required to get to the feeling of the reality of these things.

Analyst I drew attention to his use of frustration which keeps satisfaction incomplete and preserves the object from annihilation. → *how* ?

Pause.

Patient 'I now feel we have got down to important things. Looking back I am able to recognize the reality of this problem.

'I wonder if this sort of reaction is unusual or uncommon or whether I am like other people.'

Analyst I discussed with him the two aspects of this question; firstly, he was talking about a universal phenomenon, and secondly, he was dealing with something which is more important to him than to some people.

Patient 'How does this affect the baby having a breast feed?' (Here he was getting very closely back to the essential features of the first analysis.)

Analyst I now gave him a longer and more detailed description of the two possible reactions, the schizoid and the depressive (without using those terms). I spoke in terms of the buttons of the coat pulled at by the child, which was associated in the patient's mind with the word cannibalism. I said that for him when he had got the button the important thing was that he was satisfied, and therefore the button became unimportant (decathected). 'There is another possible reaction, which I mention because it is there in your analysis but you are not yet able to see it. This would be concerned about the coat that was now devoid of a button, and also concerned about the fate of the button.'

Patient He obviously understood what I was saying. *Pause.* He said that he had been thinking a great deal over the weekend about which of two extremes to follow in his career. On the one hand there is the intellect and the highbrow line of development, with pleasures despised. Alternatively there is pleasure, which he could make the most important pursuit. In practice the first meant following the advice of his chief, writing up case histories and starting off on a career in medicine based on intellectual attitude. His chief's whole life is in medicine and on an intellectual plane. He was tempted to follow this spartan regime but, he said, this would leave himself out of the picture, and the alternative would also be unsatisfactory as he would go out purely for pleasure. He could drift into some line between the two extremes, but drifting would not be satisfactory either.

Analyst I related this to the material at hand. I said that, if his analysis got no further than it had got at present, he was left with exactly the problem that he had described which belongs to the first of the two reactions (the schizoid). I said that it would be possible to talk about the future, and to say that his analysis already did show that he was on the brink of the alternative line of development with concern about the object. Should his analysis cover this issue, then a new solution would automatically appear to the main problem of the management of his career.

Patient He said that he wondered how there could be hope of getting at something here in the analysis which had never been before. 'Is it possible to get at something in one's nature that does not yet exist? How can one achieve concern when it has never been there before? Can something be created out of nothing? Alternatively, is there something buried which can be discovered?'

Analyst I said that to some extent we might find that he had achieved concern and had lost this capacity through hopelessness in some infantile situation. Nevertheless, it would not seem impossible to make a step in analysis that had never been made before. These things depended not only on himself but also on his analyst.

Patient 'Well, of course the baby has to get at these things for the first time with the mother.'

Analyst 'In the last few minutes we have been talking intellectually and talking about your analysis, and this is rather different from doing analysis.'

Patient 'I do feel, however, that it is of positive value to talk about things intellectually.'

Analyst (I could not help comparing this state of affairs with that which obtained at the end of the first analysis, when very big changes had occurred in the man's personality and external relationships, but insight was not a feature.)

Tuesday, 15 February

Patient 'I was thinking about the end of yesterday. You said we were talking around the subject. For some reason or other this made me laugh. It was really a very marked reaction. I could not help feeling that it was very funny. It was as if we had said, "We are only pretending to be serious." We were playing round in a lighthearted way. There was a break in our serious attention to matters, and I laughed and felt very excited.'

Analyst 'Your word "playing" reminds me that I might have brought in this word "play" in connection with the ideas around your phrase "fancy free" in the previous session. At the end of last hour you and I were playing together, talking round the subject, and you enjoyed it, and felt the contrast with the usual hard work.'

Patient 'That reminds me of something from Molière. Someone told a man that he had been speaking prose all his life. He was amazed. He had been unaware of this fact and it excited him.'

Analyst 'I think there is a feeling that we were caught playing together.'

Patient 'The same thing in medicine generally. I can see now how important it is when something lighthearted turns up in the middle of a serious subject. It can be bad taste, but occasionally it is very helpful in the middle of a serious medical discussion to have a little game, a wisecrack of a play on words. I spoke about the two extremes: should I undertake very serious work like a hermit or an ascetic, or should I go out for pleasure and avoid everything serious? There seems now the possibility of a blend, which is different from seeking a midway path. The blend includes both extremes at the same time.'

Analyst 'This is the same subject as that of the thumb and your interest in it and your having me for it to stand for.'

Pause.

Patient 'A new subject cropped up today. It had to do with the girl friend. I saw her just now. My attitude to her is changing. Originally I was only attracted intellectually. Firstly there was a demonstration of bravado in relation to my wife, and secondly there was a physical excitement, but this made me worried because I knew that boredom and exhaustion were bound to appear. Today there was a change. I actually experienced warmth of feeling and an interest in what she was doing and saying. I wonder if I might be starting to be in love. This would be absolutely new. I cannot judge. It never happened before. I don't want to pin a label onto it. There is a sharp contrast between my ease with this girl today and my general difficulty which continues with my wife. It is the same with work. There seems to have

arrived a bridge. In relation to the girl, when there is a hiatus, she
continues with ideas from her end which my wife can no longer
manage. Probably she used to, but she has given up hope. A striking
example would be that I phoned this girl for half an hour. This is
absolutely new. I have never phoned anyone for more than three
minutes, as there was never anything to say except business arrangements. At home there is a great easing of tension, because it no longer
matters about my wife and her boy friend.'

Analyst I asked about his wife and about how much she knows.

Patient 'Probably she knows pretty well, but I prefer to make a mystery of it.
It would be too cold-blooded to open up a frank discussion on the
subject. Whoever starts the subject is in a weak position.'

(Incidentally the patient is showing that he knows that this episode
with the girl is part of the analysis and not an attempt to break up the
marriage. He is always hoping that he can get well and that the
marriage will mend.)

Analyst I attempted to show that the various separated episodes in his life
all came together in the transference.

Patient He went on to speak about the way his wife expects him to be
dominant, while she likes to be in the dependent position. With the
girl, neither is dominant. It occurred to him to say that this relationship with the girl is like that of a brother and sister, whereas with
his wife the relationship is of father and daughter. Occasionally he
had this relationship with his younger sister, but they have drifted
apart. The advantage with the girl is that, while providing a relationship of this kind, there is an absence of incest taboo. They can help
each other. This provides an exciting novelty, discovering the possibilities. *Pause.* He reported that he was stuck.

Analyst I continued with the theme of the bringing together of all the
attitudes in relation to the analyst and the experiencing of conflicts
which are avoided through the acting out in compartments. In
speaking of this I referred to masturbation.

Patient 'I was thinking that you were sure to say that this relationship to
this girl is something to do with masturbation, partly because masturbation has become very much less compulsive since the relationship started. I thought: "He will say you are only acting out a
fantasy."'

Analyst I pointed out that the introduction of the word 'only' was important, a word that I had not used.

Patient 'Yes, you would pour cold water on it.'

Analyst I dealt with the reality of the masturbation fantasies which formerly
we could not find, but which he has discovered in relation to the girl

and particularly in the interplay which has turned up and which follows developments in his relation to myself.

Friday, 18 February

Patient 'The first thing that occurs to me to say is that it was three days ago when I came last. It seems a much longer time. There was a part of a dream which I had in the morning which I remembered. When I woke I was still in it, and then, as I gradually woke further, I just remembered it, by which time I became worried because I felt I ought to be horrified, whereas it seemed quite natural. The dream was that I had seduced my daughter. For a time I lost the memory of this dream and then it came back.'

Analyst I pointed out that this dream followed on his having felt love for her after crying. I asked what he meant by seduced.

Patient 'Probably I simply mean that I had intercourse with her. I remember now that recently, when she was on my lap, I had some sexual excitement, something needing suppression. This occurred last week during a period of excitement and during the time when I was having occasional intercourse with the girl friend. It was all part of this same thing, and in this period I was not masturbating. I did not want to. Also I was able to suppress it by conscious effort, in preparation for potency.'

All this reminded the patient of the problem belonging to several years ago, at home, with his wife. He reported for the first time difficulties in getting excited and premature ejaculation. At that time he would masturbate to relieve tension in order to get better control.

Analyst I reminded him that he had likened his relationship to his wife to a father–daughter relationship, and that the dream therefore indicated something happening in his relation to his wife.

Patient 'That links up with what I was going to say. I have been depressed because I have been seeing the girl friend since the dream and I have been getting fond of her, but I now have found that she has become cold.'

An earlier partner had turned up, so my patient was being pushed out. She herself had been seduced by her father at sixteen and therefore she hated him. There is the point that society does not frown on such a seduction as much as it does on incest between son and mother. In anthropology a father–daughter relationship may develop, but not that of mother and son.

He said that in several relationships girls tend to lean on him because he is sympathetic, and the relationship tends to end in a father–daughter way. He feels this as a defect of his personality. He is not able to be aggressive.

Analyst 'What you are leading up to is that you have not been able to get to your hate of the man in the triangular relationship.'

Patient 'This only comes afterwards. It is not spontaneous. It is an academic point.'

Now there had been an advance and there was danger of it all getting out of hand. How would it all end? He knew the rival with the girl friend.

Analyst Here I made a sweeping integration of the four elements which only joined together in the transference: dependence, instinctual gratification, incestuous dream, the marriage relationship.

Patient After this he said that he just remembered that many years ago he dreamed of intercourse with a woman, and it now seemed that she could have been his mother. There was certainly some element of his mother in the woman of the dream. All this came on top of the practical dilemma in regard to the girl. There are unsatisfactory alternatives:

  1. compete with the man
  2. retreat
  3. terminate the relationship.

He recognized all three as unsatisfactory and was angry. Such ends would only be convenient. Also he had been thinking on the way to analysis today, 'A life without sex must be unsatisfactory, even although worries could be avoided in that way. If there were no expectations it would not be a life.' He said that, from early on, somehow or other he had acquired the idea that intercourse is desirable; something he knew he would want even if he did not need it.

Analyst I pointed out the absence of the father in the dreams.

Patient It was here that he told me more of the rival with the girl friend, also a married man with two children. He felt that it was unsatisfactory in this relationship that these two men were treading in each other's footsteps (identified).

Analyst I pointed out that the dream about his daughter and the relationship to the girl avoided the strong feelings and the conflicts that would belong to the dream about his mother.

Patient He said that I must remember that for the last few years he had had no feelings at all about his father. They were buried and distorted, except that they turned up at one stage of the analysis. (He associated the loss of feelings about his father with the absence of the father in the dream.)

Also he said, 'You must remember that what was happening with this girl is an act. It felt natural but it was an act, and the act had come to an abrupt end. Naturally I am in a temporary depression; I feel there is gloom ahead.'

Analyst 'In regard to this act, what has happened is that you have informed yourself as to the hidden meaning in the masturbation.'

Pause.

Patient 'Also in the depression.'

He then went on to say that he wanted someone to talk to about all these things, not the girl nor his wife. He had no friends close enough, and has had none for many years, and in the analysis everything is taken seriously. He needed someone for jokes and games. Some men would drink and feel jilted, and others would work excessively hard or talk around it with someone.

Analyst 'The lack of a close friend is what you are reporting, and it would have to be a man.'

Patient 'Yes, perhaps.'

Analyst 'Also it would be necessary for him to give you his confidences also.'

Patient 'Yes, because only in that way would we avoid one leaning on the other.'

Analyst I asked if he ever had a friend, and he told me about one at college.

Patient He said that he had in fact had no one to be best man and his wife constantly taunted him with the fact that they had to employ a relation of hers. He said he felt the hour was near the end. He would get dismissed, which meant jilted. So it was important not to let anything come up near the end.

Analyst I brought out the full meaning of this word 'jilted', which linked me so closely with the girl. I said: 'There are only two of us here, and if I jilt you, you have no one to be angry with.'

At this point the bell rang and he said:

Patient 'I'm not so sure; there's someone at the door.'

It happened that I had to let in the next patient, who was a man, and as I let my patient out he implied with his looks that he was enjoying playing a triangular game, hating a man who was responsible for his being jilted by a girl.

Tuesday, 22 February

(Five minutes late.)

Patient 'It occurred to me to say that there is an article in *The Lancet* on enuresis, in which emotional diuresis is recognized.' He reported that at one time I had pleaded ignorance on this subject. (This seems unlikely.) He noticed that his own diuresis had disappeared along with the recent progress in his analysis.

Analyst I spoke about my ignorance, which he was pleased about. (I did not defend myself.)

Patient He felt himself drawn between two attitudes, triumph over the analyst and also showing up the physical doctors. There was also in the article, however, a tendency to show that enuresis is frequently caused by a minor organic disability. Probably therefore many disorders which are called psychological are organic.

He spoke of himself as rescuing children from the psychotherapist. He reported this as if reporting a dream which had surprised him. He said it was like saving them from the surgeon's knife. He compared this with his desire for a more rapid approach than psychoanalysis.

It gradually became clear in this hour that he was in a state of resistance; this took the form of sleepiness.

He said he was in a dilemma, whether to be pleased at the attack on psychology or the contrary. The neurologist also implied that cases are labelled functional without evidence. All this implied that there might be a way of dealing after all with the vast flood of psychological cases. *Pause.* He said that he had a curious feeling: there was nothing. It was like any session when he was dealing with his own patients when nothing happens and he passes on to the next case. Here, however, the analyst is stuck for an hour. He cannot pass on. He felt guilty at the way he passes over difficult patients simply because they are not interesting. 'It is rare in medical practice to get a situation like that in analysis.'

Analyst I reminded him of the surgeon 'downing tools'.

Patient 'You cannot get away. The logical sequence is that you must resent this sort of hour when nothing happens.'

Analyst I made an interpretation regarding the neglect of his patients, also drawing in the fact that in some respects I do neglect him, that is to say, between hours.

Patient He said that the analyst puts up with the patient for an hour. He compared it with the claims his daughter makes on him. She really must not assume that because he is at home his two hours are at her disposal. *Pause.* He reported that he was stuck, and claimed that he was tired.

Analyst (*Lost.*)

Patient 'I discovered with the girl that she is shocked by something different from what shocks me.' Any sign of homosexuality shocks her and it appears that she had a homosexual tendency for which she has had something like analysis. 'What shocks me is incest, not homosexuality.' He feared as a child to be kissed by his mother and still dislikes it. Perhaps he had 'abnormal incest ideas'. This filled him with horror.

Analyst I asked him what the horror was associated with.

Patient 'It is not enough to say that it is socially unacceptable. It is not frowned on when a boy kisses his mother.' There was an episode at seven or eight which he reminded me about and which he had reported earlier in the analysis. It had to do with a walk; the whole family was present. The father pushed him over to the mother. There was a scene.

Pause.

Analyst I made an interpretation covering a fair amount of ground, showing his development recently towards a triangular situation, and linking up the sleepiness with anxiety that he is not able to feel but which concerns the new position. I said that I knew that he was really tired but that he would not like me to let this be the total explanation.

Pause.

Patient 'My mind seems to be wandering; it is difficult to concentrate, or to get at thoughts that I want to say.'

Analyst 'My rather long interpretation squashed out these thoughts of yours.'

Patient 'No, I could easily produce nothing at all today.'

Analyst I picked up the subject of undermining and the interpretation which was appropriate at the time, and showed that it had a present equivalent in castration anxiety, father having turned up at least in theory in the triangular situation which was new. I also linked the end of the last hour with the word 'jilt' and with the fact that he heard a man's voice when I let in the next patient after 'jilting' him.

Patient He reported that he was tired.

Analyst 'I think I may have talked too much.'

Patient 'No, I would only sleep.'

Analyst (I was of course influenced by the fact that he had started the hour with a wish that there was a quicker treatment, and I knew that he would prefer me to go ahead in so far as I had material to work on.)

Patient He was concerned at my 'awkward embarrassment'; he said he felt irritated. It was as if he were not accepted. Something was turned down. He felt he ought not to be so put out by his sleepiness. He ought to be able to take it in his stride. He was tired, but there was something else in it.

Analyst 'The sleep therefore is dealing with something opposite, such as aggression, hate, or simply an unknown fear.'

Patient He reported himself to be drifting, very tired, sleepy.

Wednesday, 23 February

He came twenty minutes late. The lateness today was due to an emergency in hospital.

Patient He spoke about yesterday. His tiredness was only part of the story. Afterwards he was only just rather tired, which was quite different. (He recognized tiredness as a resistance.) 'How often I do not remember what happened yesterday. I cannot remember yesterday's session, and I feel I ought to be able to.' He was concerned at his amnesia. Even at the time he was not taking anything in.

Analyst I made an interpretation and linked up yesterday's hour, and reminded him of the suggestion of anxiety underlying the tiredness.

Patient He then reported a fragment of a dream which he had had the night before. He found himself saying, 'It's probably not important but. . . .' In the fragment of the dream the girl friend had MD, MRCP. She took them without effort; hardly knew that she had been in for them; this is really just what she is not like. She is not intellectual or academic, and she is even thought incompetent. She rather makes a point of not thinking clearly. The point about the real relationship with this girl is that she goes to the patient for support. He had anxiety at the idea of not automatically being superior, that is to say, medically. She appeals to him for help. In other words, again he has become the father figure.

Analyst 'This ties up with the girl's dislike of homosexuality.'

Patient 'Yes.'

Analyst 'It's a question, who has the penis?'

Patient 'She is very much criticized by Dr X, unmercifully, and I always defend her.'

Analyst 'But one must defend a colleague, and this seems to imply that she is a male.'

Patient 'There is also a difficulty which I can foresee. We only talk around the medical subjects. If we had not this subject to talk about, we might be left with no conversation.'

Analyst 'The dream gives the clue, it seems. The girl has a fear of homosexuality, and artificially assumes incompetence in a tremendous attempt not to be masculine, and this fits in in some way with your needs. The dream gives the other half of the total situation.'

Patient 'From this I can see all the difficulties that men have with women colleagues. Till now for me girls have always had equal status, and I have been keen on this. Firstly I was angry with men if they called girls incompetent, and secondly it was satisfactory to think of a girl doing equal work with men.'

Analyst I made an interpretation concerning his attempt to deal with the differences between the sexes on a basis which applies more to two men or brothers competing.

Patient 'For the first time I can accept the idea of dominating. Remember that this is one of the chief complaints my wife makes of me, that I will never dominate, make an arrangement for a holiday or anything. I have always felt it necessary, as I see it now, to make sure that she is equally capable.'

Analyst I made an interpretation here and he commented:

Patient 'What you said was just repeating what you said before.'

Analyst I agreed.

I made a further interpretation about his inability to think of a girl as different from a man because it raised his own fears of loss of penis.

Patient 'She is very apprehensive about being masculine. For her, orderliness of thought is masculine.'

Analyst I interpreted that, with regard to the psychology of the girl, we were dealing not just with this problem of his but also with her identification, what her father was like, and so on.

Patient 'But we are not concerned with her psychology. She only comes in so far as it throws light on my difficulties.'

Analyst I reminded him that the orderly thinking of which he was specially capable was masculine for the girl and also for him.

Patient 'The trouble is that for her, being impetuous, which is what I am trying to become through analysis, is a female characteristic, undesirable in men.'

Analyst I said that he was unable to tell immediately whether I would hold this girl's view or a personal one on this subject. I was sure that for him this subject of becoming able to be spontaneous concerned men and women alike. In making an interpretation about girls according to his fantasy, I said, 'It is as if their heads are cut off for you.'

Patient 'Well, that's your fantasy and rather drastic.'

Analyst I tried to link up the orderliness of thought with the special characteristics of his father, but he reminded me that his father was capable of considerable spontaneity and that this did not make him unmasculine.

I then asked him about the female version of himself that went about with him when he was a child.

Patient 'It's very difficult to know, because although I remember telling you about this, I do not get at it very easily. I think, however, that it had a penis.

'In adolescence I noticed that, in my dreams about girls, the girls all had penises. I was not dismayed in the dream but I was dismayed on waking. On the contrary, in daydreaming, which required effort of thinking, I was able to produce girls as they really are.'

Analyst I said that it was a pity we had to have a short hour but I could not avoid this. Nevertheless we had arrived at his adolescent dream in which girls appear with penises, and we had therefore got to the place that the dream was leading to.

I had given him ten minutes extra and now terminated the session.

Thursday, 24 February

I had to keep him waiting for ten minutes.

Patient 'Firstly, I am aware that we were in the middle of something important. I broke off with reluctance. I have only a hazy idea what it was about, but perhaps I could think of it.

'Secondly, I am aware of this matter of speed. How long will the treatment be? How does one know about the end of a treatment? It would help if one could have a target. What about the summer, for instance? How does one know how far to go? Naturally treatment produces a disturbance, so that one would not expect the good effects to show till some time after the end. There are difficulties to do with the arrangement of my future programme, but I won't force the issue. I don't like an indefinite prospect.'

Analyst (I gave details about my summer holiday.)

'I am aware of your real difficulties.'

(Here I recapitulated yesterday's analysis, which ended abruptly on the note of the adolescent dreams of girls with a penis.)

'Your relationship with the girl friend is therefore part of this analysis, valuable just as a dream is.'

Patient 'The girl is firstly not stable herself, and secondly not intellectually a companion for the future. I'm not sure of this. It sounds rather snobbish. We only have in common:

1. a desire for intercourse, for pleasure, and we both use it for the restoration of confidence;

2. as doctors we discuss medical matters; and

3. she has had some analysis.

But there is really no future in the relationship. I don't feel justified in leaving my wife on her account. But the relationship is very valuable. I have found a much greater capacity for pleasure without tension with the girl friend. This is in part due to the analysis. With my wife I make a conscious effort to enjoy things, and it's more like a technique than an instinct. With the girl there is no romance, but it's all so natural. We are relaxed and take things as they come. There are and will be other men in her life, but I don't have to deal with that kind of complication. I have no wish to lean on her, and it would be dangerous to do so. She has served me as an object for me to sharpen my claws on, and it doesn't matter because she herself starts off as unfaithful and unstable (though sincere in her way) and blunt. I also can be blunt and hard without awkward guilt feelings. I contrast this with what happened with the girl I met in hospital at the beginning, when I was ill. She wanted me to lean on, and if I had gone further I could not have let her down without disaster to her.'

Analyst 'It is important all the time here that you feel you can count on me not to lean on you, so that here the only thing is your own benefit.'

Patient 'When I left you before, I thought I had completely left you, and was surprised to learn that you had kept up an interest in me. It occurs to me to wonder whether the same would happen again, whether you would remember me if I left off, and whether you would expect me to come back.'

Analyst 'Yes, I should, if like last time I knew you had left off before ready to do so.'

I also reminded him of war conditions, which hampered me at the time.

Patient 'It's the same again with the domestic struggle.'

Analyst I continued with the theme of being ready for the end.

'There is still the fantasy of the girl with the penis, and if you left off now you would be evading that issue.'

Patient 'Yes. With girls I don't hate other men, I just get annoyed to think of them. My present attitude to women depends on whether or not they take some action indicating interest in me, so that I don't have to be initiating everything. This is partly coloured by knowing my wife's hostility to me, especially on account of my inability to initiate. I am driven into a pleading situation. So I don't allow this again, I don't want to let another girl become a necessity. I don't want to find myself pleading and begging again.' *Pause.* 'Now I am no longer the suppliant with my wife; also I have less urge to be trying to please her all the time. So she gets fed up. She isn't fond of me in any case, and now she has less grounds than ever for keeping things going.' *Pause.* 'It's difficult to say any more now. There's nothing fruitful – only filling in time, talking for the sake of talking, not getting places.' *Pause.* 'I had no dream that I remember; that would set things going.' *Pause.* 'I am aware that there is something to be done. I am reminded here that you used to say that my mother had constant anxiety, when I was a small child, so that she had a need to be perfect. It's similar to my anxiety here. I expect this is in contrast to what other patients are like; they

perhaps have less of a conscious need to get on, and are able to enjoy a
healthy contentment. They might adopt the attitude: "Why say
whatever comes into your head to that silly old man."'

Analyst 'You might feel just that.'

Patient 'I think I have, but I must reassure myself by going ahead.'

Analyst 'You have found out your feelings by indirect means.'

Patient 'It's the same with my chief. I have anxiety about not getting to
grips with a case, awkward about criticism. I feel I shall be disowned,
and I have to take on responsibility; it's like destiny, to be perfect.'

Analyst I made an interpretation which included the following: 'You can
only meet your mother's perfect care by similar anxiety-driven
perfection. Behind this is hopelessness about loving and being loved,
and this applies now and here, in your relationship to me.'

Patient 'I feel conscious of dislike and disgust.'

Monday, 28 February

Patient 'On the way here I was thinking, it's not really useful talking about
reality, about actual things. These things seem less real than dreams.
I am thinking of actual things. Is it worth trying to bring them into the
analysis? They seem less useful than dreams. I was depressed today,
mainly or on the surface, because of home. It's more difficult at home
now. Up till recently I've accepted the situation, been sad, but felt it
would change through the analysis. Now I am faced with having to
make a decision. Logically, I should give up the girl friend. But I'm
unwilling to give up this relationship to go back to the old conditions.'

Analyst 'This feels real and it is real. You really are in a dilemma.'

Patient 'I told the girl about home. It is difficult to get to the girl in actual
practice. I was just planning a summer holiday with the girl – but here
there would be a real need to tell my wife. This would raise the issue,
and either she would understand or else it would bring about a break.
But what have I to offer my wife? Only income and some loyalty, and
if not even loyalty, well, I'm useless. And I have no wish to be spiteful.
Not that I've much sympathy for her, for she won't discuss my
problems, only her problems with her boy friend. There is no place for
talk about me and the girl. I'd like to be able to say it's all her fault.
She might break up, and I couldn't repair the damage. Perhaps she
knows but does not believe, or she doesn't know but all the time
suspects. I'm hoping that there will be some way that I will be able to
start and talk with her. But then, I would only talk to gain a certain
end, and I don't know what that end is, so I don't risk it.

'I might put leading questions, but she knows that trick. There is also the complication of my wife's difficulty, etcetera, etcetera. So I opposed seeing the girl last night, as I don't like to see her too often. But after I felt –' (detail lost).

Analyst 'You and the girl have some overlap of interests, so that when there is overlap you can play, whereas there is no play with your wife.'

Patient 'There is a story of a man whose wife was unfaithful, written by an American author. Eventually this man travelled to Europe and in the end turned round and found himself a girl. Then his wife was no longer able to tolerate herself, gave up her loose life, and went to live with her daughter and became fixed to her and went to pieces. There is the risk that my wife is kept together by my loyalty, and that if I went off she would lose her ability to have a boy friend, and would break up. Do I hate her enough to do this to her? Could I stand it if she is either well and happy or if she breaks up? My wife once said: "I'll never leave you." I feel she meant she could not tolerate the disgrace, etc. She would throw this in my face. At the start she wanted to know if I'd commit suicide. Now I think she may have wanted to ask whether it would be worthwhile her waiting or whether I'd be likely to go off from her if the analysis succeeds. Remembering this makes me think her lack of interest may not be so genuine; she perhaps had to withdraw interest. She couldn't face the situation otherwise. Her disinterestedness may be a defence. I find I have less interest in my work. Work is not a substitute for life. Dr X's pressure would lead me to a life of devotion to work. Here I'm wasting time, just thinking aloud, using the time to clarify my thoughts.'

Pause.

Analyst I said that these real things had not altered the fact that there is very important fantasy in the offing, and anxiety connected with it. There is the fantasy of the girls of adolescent dreams who had a penis. Perhaps the reality situation had sorted itself out according to the fantasy, so that his wife had a penis and presented a problem on that account, whereas his girl friend was being used as the girl of daydreams, who is ordinarily female.

Patient 'Here there is a difficulty in reality. There is an area of play with the girl. I need play in the real situation. Here we have a professional relationship, and the only play is through dreams and the work we do with them.'

Analyst 'Yes, I see that. And you feel me as reluctant to play, as you have said before in other settings. The question is, where is the penis? As there is no man rival yet, there is no one to have the penis, and you expect the girl to have it. In the intercourse dream, in which mother was to some extent the woman, you nearly reached the idea of a man – father.'

Tuesday, 1 March

Patient 'The depression about the dilemma has continued. I had hoped to argue the matter out with my wife, but I did not, and I'm pleased, but at the same time annoyed, at having once again shelved it.'

Analyst 'The point is that you do not know what outcome you wish for, and therefore you feel that shelving it is more appropriate.'

Patient 'What step would make things better? I expect to gain two things by delay: I might get my mind clearer, and something else might turn up. It boils down to the fact that my marriage is a failure, and although I see this intellectually, I cannot accept it. Also, I'm depressed because of the excitement phase, which proved to be short-lived.'

Analyst 'When hopeful, you feel there ought to be changes in your wife as well as in yourself.'

Patient 'I tried that – but my wife was not interested. I'm also depressed because, although with the girl friend it's less of an act than with my wife, still it's unreal. There is some strain and tension. What I really want is a relationship without pretences. Also, though I've changed a lot, there is still the talking difficulty.'

Analyst 'You are using the pattern of your defences as a stable factor, something to catch on to when there's nothing else.'

Patient 'I expected because of the girl to feel colder towards my wife, but that's not the effect. I want her as much. Before, the remedy was to sit at home and be in a depression. I told her I would not be home this evening on account of the fact that I plan to meet the girl friend. Before I told my wife, we had a row over something else. I was annoyed. Here was an opportunity to inform her fully, but I was dishonest – I didn't want to be apologizing; it is better to be firm.' *Pause.* 'Also my wife perhaps sensed what is going on. There are pointers. For the first time for years she put out my pyjamas to warm. There were other details. This was after the row, and before I told her about not coming back. I want to avoid missing these opportunities.

'This confuses my relationship with the girl friend. My wife also talked about the holidays – this is new, she has always pooh-pooh'd this sort of discussion. It would be ideal if I had dropped the bomb at this dramatic moment, that I was planning to go away with the girl friend. But I'm not that sort. I don't enjoy cruelty. That reminds me, on a previous occasion, before I met my wife, I had planned a holiday with a girl friend. Before the day came, we had found we didn't like each other. Here was a dilemma – cancel or carry through the arrangements? I was weak and carried on, thinking we might just possibly enjoy the holiday, but of course it was not a success. It will be – my wife will not accept my letting things go through weakness.'

Analyst 'The weakness seems to indicate a fear of your wife, a fear which you do not understand yet, and which you hardly feel as fear.'

Patient 'It is like eating without being hungry. Weakness means not taking the risk of being abandoned. Heroic people take this risk.

'It's like this with diving, which for me meant breaking from my mother. I was tied to her apron strings.'

Analyst 'It is a question of having no one to go back to. As if you were walking for the first time and there was no father present for you to go to when you ventured to leave mother. Leaving her simply meant going away from her with nowhere to go.'

Patient 'That seems valid, but it is like a new subject. My daughter suddenly stood and walked.'

Analyst 'Your daughter had got further than you, and had already at that time been seen through a stage of development that you are now at.'

Patient 'I learned to ride a bike only by father holding and letting go without my knowing. If I found I was on my own, I fell off. It was the same with swimming. I had to float first; then I could make movements, and at length I could swim. It is the idea of not being held that is important. The feeling is that there is nowhere to go to, or to come back to. Diving was the same. I always tried to cover my anxiety – I just shut my eyes and deliberately dived, but really I remained too anxious to dive. In my work I do find some anxiety when I work on my own. It happens to all, I say, but I fear abandonment – there I am floundering in a state of panic.'

Analyst 'In your series of dreams, soon after the withdrawal moment (the "medium" interpretation), you had one about going for a holiday abroad. It was a weekend, and you came back.' (I made a point of this as it was in the series – 'medium', 'lap', and then the idea of somewhere to come back to.)[1]

He gradually recalled this dream, which he had forgotten. There was a girl in this dream, a hospital doctor.

Patient 'As a matter of fact it was this very girl, before I developed the special relationship to her. This is the same as the end of the analysis – at the end what happens, does it just stop? I feel I would be floundering.'

Analyst 'You feel that the end would be letting go and having nowhere to go to and no one to come back to. This applies especially to the end as a bite – which we have had before. In fact the present phase of the

---

[1] See 'Withdrawal and Regression' in the Appendix to this volume.

analysis is a long digression from the subject of eating me at the end of the hour, or at the end of the analysis. You would be left with me destroyed, and with anxieties about your inside.'

Friday, 4 March

Patient 'Well, there seems to be nothing. Perhaps because I have a sore throat. Perhaps because it is Friday, which means a gap before and after. Friday seems detached from the general run of the analysis.' *Pause.* 'There's a difficulty on account of the break in continuity. I might join it up with what we were saying last time. It's like letting go. A child walks, which means he lets go. But he must be able to hold on. Starting again means letting go again. There seems to be an obstacle here. . . .'

Analyst 'One way would be to say you are thirty, and then two, and then thirty years old again, and the goings to and fro are painful because of the dependence-independence. Or we could say that I have shown I let you down, because of the breaks, that I don't justify confidence for holding on.'

Patient 'I could just lie still (without going to sleep) for the whole hour. I don't feel any tremendous urge today. It may be just that I'm physically under the weather.'

Analyst 'If you are physically ill you know from experience it is more easy to get properly cared for.'

Pause.

Patient 'I'm just planning the weekend; I forgot I was here. I just filled in the time planning and thinking of trivial details of work. It seems I'm lazy; I feel someone else ought to do it for me, talk for me, just as when I'm not well I let the work go and someone else does it. It would really have to be you, I suppose.'

Analyst 'What trivial things, for instance?'

Pause.

Patient 'There's really nothing, only I can't accept the waste. It's unproductive. Why come for just wasting time?' *Pause.* 'There's nothing to get a grip on. I was just thinking about hospital then, and what I'll do this evening.'

Analyst 'What do you plan to do?'

Patient 'Well, I shall meet the girl friend. But what happens depends on how I feel. But that wasn't the thing. I was thinking of my home too, and hospital. It was really a strange coincidence last night, I thought; since I was ill before restarting analysis I haven't taken sleeping drugs, although I have had access to them, though while at hospital as a patient I was sleepless and very much needed sedative. That's a whole year ago now. And then I got this sore throat and had rather a sleepless night. But firstly I had had a very difficult and unusual case, and had stayed up till twelve-thirty to get the notes written up, having to concentrate, and secondly I had this sore throat. I was awake two hours and then went and got some tablets.

Analyst 'Perhaps not such a coincidence; you were already feeling not so sure of yourself?'

Patient 'Well, yes, that's true. In the afternoon, before the case came in, I was not feeling well and I remembered I hadn't slept quite so well for a few nights. Of course it's not like when I was ill. It was simply that I felt that, if I went to bed early, I would not benefit because I would lie awake a little. As a matter of fact I've not felt so stable generally, the last few days. I've had a lack of desire to do the job well, although I have actually done it just as well. There's a paradox here. I was concerned at not having concern. Since I've been with this girl I've had less ambition, or perhaps less time for work, and in the dilemma, work or life, I have chosen life.'

Analyst 'Perhaps there have been dreams during this phase?'

Patient 'No, it's more that I had prolonged consciousness.'

Analyst 'There may be a relationship between the present phase and the break-up of a dissociation – you were not disturbed in your home affairs by the affair with the girl, and then (as appeared in the last session) you began to feel the two matters at the same time and so to suffer the pain of conflict.'

Patient 'Yes.' (Here he went over the ground again confirming the interpretation.) 'It's the same thing as holding on. I don't want to let go of something till I know I have something else to hold on to that is reliable. Last night I felt perhaps I would cancel today's session.'

Analyst 'But you did manage to come, which means that the meaning of cancelling the session can be talked about and you can find out the effect of letting me know . . .' (Here the patient said 'Yes' in a forced way, and I saw he was asleep. After a few minutes I made a slight noise by mistake, and this woke him.)

Patient 'I have a reluctance to talk today.'

Analyst 'While I was talking you went to sleep.'

Patient 'I think I said the last thing.'

Analyst 'No.' (I repeated the interpretation, and he remembered forcing the 'Yes' just before going off.)

Patient 'Yes, it's better that I come, even if I don't talk, so that we can understand it. Not coming would be really wasting it all.

'Also, I was reluctant to make the break bigger still by not coming.

That would be not taking the analysis seriously. It would be unprofessional.'

Analyst 'But what you seek is the impulse, and by not coming you would be making coming more real. If it is a professional matter, you come for other than reasons of impulse.'

Patient 'Yes. With the girl most of the talk is professional jargon. It is very important to me when I can talk with her in a way that has nothing to do with our common profession. Sometimes I feel that rows at home are better than the smooth times, in which I am thrown back on myself. With the girl friend talk is in technical terms and there is some tension, but – this reminds me of one very difficult thing in my relationship with my wife. After intercourse, when we were having it pretty regularly, she wouldn't talk, she seemed awkward or wanted to sleep. It is just then that I feel free from tension, and with the girl friend it is just then that we talk naturally and without use of technical language.'

Analyst 'This period after intercourse is very important to you, for here at least you reach a capacity to love naturally. This difficulty in your wife is therefore a very real one for you. This suggests that there is always some anxiety in your relationship with women, based on an unconscious fear of impotence, a fear of a demand that might be made on you by the woman. For a brief spell, after intercourse, you feel free from this threat, and you are free to love and be loved, which is what you are always looking for.' *Pause.* 'There is also the matter of your having been given a short time twice during the past week; this may have affected your attitude here.'

Patient 'I don't think so, because each time it was due to my being late, and also I realize that I get a full hour, whereas the usual period for analysis is fifty minutes.'

Analyst 'But what about illogical feelings?'

Patient 'Funnily enough, I think I feel resentment more at the loss at the beginning when I am late.'

Analyst I did not go further, but I could see the relationship between this and the demands that may be made by the analyst, and also the lateness was a token 'not coming' which was brought for analysis, and indicated the patient's need to be able to have me on impulse, which is the positive aspect of the anxiety about demands from my end.

Tuesday, 8 March

Patient 'I am wondering whether today won't be able to produce anything, like yesterday. I came to the conclusion that Friday is different because it has a gap before and after. But today there is no gap after.

The only thing I find to say is about home, continuing on the subject of my dilemma. Shall I tell my wife about the girl? The situation at home seems beyond repair. Logically, I should recognize this fact and not try to bring about a reconciliation. Now I see I'll have to decide something soon. The girl has hinted she would like us to live together etcetera, etcetera. Last night at home, when half asleep, I must have put my hand on my wife, she quickly pushed it away. I woke and she was furious. I felt rejected, but I said nothing and turned angrily away. A few moments later she tried to cuddle up to me, and then I was puzzled. What does she mean? This was very awkward, for it meant she was concerned at having rejected me. Again, when I phoned today her tone was warmer than it has been for a long time.'

Analyst 'It was easier to deal with her rejection, but when she seemed concerned you were thrown back onto the dilemma and the conflict in your feelings.'

Patient 'The girl friend has said now that she wants a baby and she would like me to be the father. Since her abortion she has been sterile, and now she feels she is getting on in years and ought to have a baby soon if at all. My feeling more hopeless about home has perhaps made the girl optimistic, but I think my wife is guessing and is beginning to fight back.'

Analyst 'The underlying problem is your two ideas of women, with the girl friend as the woman without a penis and your wife perhaps as the woman with one.'

Patient 'Perhaps the same goes for my wife, too. She has always hated being thrown over into the position of wearing the trousers, yet that is what I have done to her. She has always wanted to be the female.'

Analyst 'The question does arise, what will the girl friend be like in ten years' time should you marry her?'

Patient 'She fears dominating. In the past I feel I would have gradually become dominated by her, but I feel that wouldn't happen now. I used to be so easily dominated. I think I wanted to be dominated. With my wife I find it very difficult to change round to dominating.'

Analyst 'It is always difficult to change a pattern in which someone else is involved.'

Patient 'It's funny that being good-natured, as I am supposed to be, is linked with a willingness to be dominated.'

Analyst 'Somewhere in all this is a relation to one or both of your sisters, with a reluctance on your part to be the one with the penis.'

Patient 'Two things come to my mind here. One, how do you come into this? Are you to dominate me or what? I sometimes fear that I dominate the session.'

Analyst 'Here I am the girl, who has or has not a penis. You wonder what I will feel like being the girl with no penis, when you have one.'

Patient 'True. Then there is the difficulty about the girl friend who regards me as a male to make love to her, and has no very real interest in me as a person.'

Analyst 'From what you say it might be that she could make use of any man, for the man is to represent her male self in her effort to avoid her bisexuality. She may be more interested in your male orgasm than in her own clitoris.'

Patient 'Yes, she is especially concerned with my orgasm. It's rather curious, I often think, since she is a selfish person fundamentally.'

Analyst 'Her drive would be especially valuable to you now, as she needs to make you regain confidence in your potency.'

Patient 'The idea occurs to me that her present interest in having a baby is an attempt to establish herself as a woman.' (Add: implying, in spite of no very strong female orgasm.)

Analyst 'The future is therefore a separate issue from that of the value that you and she are to each other at the moment.'

Patient 'It's funny, but I think I welcome the pregnancy idea out of naughtiness. It would be a challenge to the world, and to my wife. Also there is this, that I feel it would be nice if it turned out to be a boy. I now see that I wish I had had a son. My wife won't want any more children, and so I had lost all hope of having a boy.'

Analyst 'There is also the point that a son for the girl or for your wife is rather like giving them a penis, which relieves you of the delusion about the penis. The important thing in all this is that you have discovered your sadness at not having had a son for your second child.'

Patient 'Yes, I was pleased it was a girl, which was partly a simple denial, and also it made me feel it would be easier to get away from my wife. But I felt I don't deserve to have a son, so I would be glad to give the girl an illegitimate baby. This would be perverse, and this perverseness is important. The only way to make the world acceptable is to challenge it. Somehow the idea is naughty and therefore exciting. That makes it appeal to me.'

Analyst 'Earlier you spoke of your compliant self, and this can be said to be hiding your true self. The true self is in great danger because it is just quite simply a boy child with a penis and important in the family because of this penis. The false compliant self hides and protects the true self from expected danger. However, the true self can be allowed to show if actively antisocial, defiant, naughty.'

Patient 'And what helps is that this antisocial behaviour is unreal.'

Analyst 'Yes, but it is very nearly your true male self.'

Patient 'That reminds me that the present trouble started up when I found myself qualified, and for the first time in a position of responsibility, having to make decisions as a doctor. It was just this that I couldn't accept, and my wife complained of the same in me, that I would never decide anything.'

Analyst 'This applies to yourself as an infant and a young boy with your sisters. There is a complication that must be looked into – this question of your mother's attitude. It could be that as a boy you dreamed of a sexual relationship with your mother and so feared your father. But that is not how you are putting it. Father has not yet appeared in this setting. This makes me think that, when you became a boy with sexual excitement and incest dreams, you found mother evaluating you in a special way, so that you were in danger of getting your maleness bagged. Your mother too may have wanted you to be her penis. From this you retreated, and so you did not get on to the next stage of conflict with father.'

Patient 'I do not remember ever having been conscious of being a boy with a penis, but it would be logical, I suppose, for me to have forgotten all this. Myself as a boy seems remote.'

Analyst 'Your dressing-up as a girl would come in too, as a denial of your maleness. It would seem you couldn't stand the plight of your sisters who had no penis, since you knew of nothing else that they had. I also want to remind you of your thumb-sucking and your need for something to catch hold of. By sucking instead of catching hold of your penis, you avoided the issue of penis or no penis, and what you did made no distinction between you and your sisters.'

Wednesday, 9 March

Patient 'It's not about myself today; something has happened that confuses the issue. Last night I had arranged to sit in at home, with the idea of going to a party tonight with the girl friend, which I very likely will still go to. But my wife came back early, crying. She had called in on her boy friend, and he had taken ill – had gone blind, and had a fit. He is dying (this was inevitable sometime; he has a heart, mitral stenosis and endocarditis). This complicates matters for me. It seems mean for me to enjoy myself, but on the other hand, I can't be of much help to my wife since she won't talk. What point is there in my sacrificing myself for her when I cannot expect thanks? In the past I would have, as a symbol of martyrdom, but now I'm less willing to devote myself to her cause. But I was upset at the news, and she asked my why I should be upset. This was difficult to answer. It was partly seeing her upset about this man. I was annoyed, because she was never upset about me when, in a different way, I was myself ill. Partly I felt all this would interfere with my life. Partly too I was moved by meeting grief in the abstract. I couldn't help being affected, and this was the most potent cause.'

Analyst 'Yes.'

Patient 'After that I was speculating about the future, the probable outcome. On the one hand our relationship might improve. On the other hand it is more likely to deteriorate. My wife will have nothing to occupy her and to keep her happy, and so will tend to resent me more intensely than before when she could hide possible and probable resentment in guilt over her own behaviour. She will be more critical and less sympathetic. Why do I say this? I am only conjecturing.'

Analyst 'You do not know which alteration would be better or worse.'

Patient 'It all depends on the degree to which there might be improvement. If things improve a great deal between us, then I would know which alteration to prefer. I would be thrown back on having to say that it is her lack of affection that drives me away, since there would no longer be the boy friend. This is quite logical but difficult to justify to her. I would so much like to be able to talk it all over with her, as man to man, so to speak, or dispassionately, but that's impossible (apart from this crisis). I want her to challenge me, so that I can justify myself. It is upsetting to find that she says nothing about my unfaithfulness.' *Pause.* 'Did I interrupt? You were going to say something.'

Analyst 'Perhaps you sensed that I was wondering whether or not to say something. It was this, that there might also be direct grief about this man's death, since you knew him.'

Patient 'That is possible, but I had dismissed this. I think it was grief of a more vicarious kind. In hospital I find I am not grieved at the death of a patient, but what worries me is telling the relatives. Is it perhaps watching them react? It was very difficult to tell a mother and a girl of a man's serious illness, and especially to tell the mother of her son's death, though this man's death had seemed no more than a technical matter.'

Analyst 'There is the locked-up grief, about your father's death. Perhaps your indirect reaction belongs to this?'

Patient 'Yes. It is significant that I felt no grief at the time of my father's death. Perhaps I have not felt grief on this account yet.'

Analyst 'There are two things happening at once because of the man's illness. On the one hand you are brought up against grief for which you are not ready, and on the other hand your dilemma is intensified in the way you have described.'

Patient 'Once again outside things have come along and have obliterated the underneath things, and it's not helpful; but it can't be avoided, they have to be gone over.'

Analyst 'There remains the fantasy of the girl with the penis, and it seems likely that your girl friend is felt to have a need for men, while your wife is self-contained and has a penis.'

Patient 'I see the first part but not the part about my wife.'

Analyst I admitted muddle, and said I was not clear enough to continue with this interpretation.

Patient 'I have noticed for one or two weeks that I felt a rather greater wish for intercourse with my wife. What is thought and what is felt are evidently different things. I thought, now that I have a sex outlet I would feel colder, but I find in fact that when in bed with my wife I have a desire for her, though my intellect says "No, there's no need to pester her now." Because I haven't any need now to demand it when I know it's unacceptable, it seems that my desire is less intellectual and more instinctive. In the past I was reduced to saying that if there is to be sex at all it should be with my wife, that's logical, so I approached it as a matter of rights. Now I can ignore my rights, and I find a new and natural feeling comes instead. Of course I could say that there is another explanation. Before I started to have intercourse with the girl I had feelings of impotence. Because I couldn't satisfy my wife I had no proof of my own powers and I had doubts; would it be wise to risk impotence, or to risk not being able fully to satisfy her? After finding I could rely on giving the girl full satisfaction, I could afford to wipe aside doubts.'

Analyst 'It used to be always a test, and now it is more of a natural thing.'

Patient 'Also, I'm no longer in a suppliant position. Now I know I'm able, it's not so much need as that it would be nice. Here I am in a more dominant position.'

Analyst 'This links with being a male in the family.'

Patient 'Yes. For the first time I begin to discover I am a male. That felt like boasting, boasting of sexual prowess, to the exclusion of everything else; here, to the exclusion of progress in analysis.'

Analyst 'The question is, who am I, to whom you are boasting? I might be sisters, or father, or mother or a brother – I think I'm mother just now.'

Patient 'Yes, you're mother. As a small boy I would prove my progress in walking, reading, and then I'd say to my mother: "Look, mummy, I can do it now." She would notice. But this is what happens in my work. If I have an exciting and difficult unusual case, instead of getting the investigation completed and the notes written up, I call in a colleague and I simply must show it off, and can't wait. It's exciting to show it off.'

Analyst 'To mother.'

Patient 'Yes, I'm sure it's mother because I come at it indirectly through a schoolboy story. A boy had a wet dream and rushed into his parents' room shouting "Look, mummy, no hands." You see my direct approach to my mother is buried.'

Analyst 'You could be talking too about motions. First there is excitement about the fact of shitting, and then there comes the pleasure that belongs to saving the stuff up, so that the result is a big motion. If training is imposed, the child has no time to make the natural progression, and there remains a certain degree of need to go back to the excitement over shitting. I could say the same in terms of money, etc.'

Patient 'You may be right, but I still think it's illogical for me to show off a half-finished picture instead of waiting till I can present the whole. I run the risk of looking foolish, and in my work, of putting forward a wrong diagnosis. I jump to conclusions and then try to make everything else fit in.

'This reminds me most of the childhood dilemma of meals. When there was a tit-bit, should I eat it, and then find the rest of the meal dull, or retain it till the end, and usually I ate it up first.'

(N.B. This was the theme of the first period of the analysis.)

Thursday, 10 March

Patient 'I find it surprising that I remember so little. I expected or anticipated this at the start, when I was in a very disturbed and confused condition and when I was not talking much. Now I thought that I would begin to be able to know where I am in the analysis, etc. It is rather like a dream which may be very clear at the time, etc.'

Analyst 'It certainly is very much like a dream. In the analysis to some extent you become withdrawn. We could say that the analysis operates at a layer which is nearer to dreaming than to being awake, especially when you are not talking about actual life, and also after the hour has been started for some time.' *Pause.* 'I could of course remind you.'

Patient 'No, I can see that that's not the point just now. Last time I felt that it was not fundamental. I left with a vague dissatisfaction. I think vaguely that there were some ideas of domination. If I forget what went on last time I might start up a new subject, and this would make it difficult for you. I often feel that I give you a very difficult task. Either you would need to take detailed notes all along or else you would do as I do with my cases, which is to wait until the end and then write a shorter note after I have integrated the material within myself.'

(I did not risk taking notes at this point; obviously the question arose as to whether he had heard.)

He went on to say that this made him very conscious of dependence on me.

Analyst I referred to the matter in the following way: 'It doesn't fundamentally make any difference whether I am taking detailed notes or not; the fact is that I must hear and take in all that you say and all that happens, and have a technique for sorting things out and integrating the material, and this is true apart from note-taking.'

Patient He said that he hoped that one day he would be able to go through his material and to see how the changes had taken place; especially he felt this now that he was all the time so much better and he was unable to understand what was happening.

Pause.

Analyst I went over the material of the last hour. I said it ended with the idea of the tit-bit at meals and he remembered this. I went back further with the schoolboy story and the idea of myself as the mother to whom he could show off in all sorts of developments. I reminded him also that he had said that for the first time he was beginning to feel himself to be a male.

Patient 'When I got married I was very keen to show the world that my wife really was a woman, and took great trouble over this.'

Analyst 'This would fit in with the idea that you had a fantasy of a woman with a penis.' (I noticed that he was starting to go to sleep and it was unlikely that he heard the interpretation.)

Patient 'These things are tied to this idea, and I was thinking this before I came. I get from this girl friend the feeling of being able to take a real interest in work. It is not always true enough. The relation to her makes me feel real, more interested in work, and more masculine. This is also related to the fact that the girl is a doctor interested in the things I do and so on, so there is not an absolute break and, as I have said, this all belongs to the fact that I hate to keep things to myself.'

Analyst 'The positive side of that is that you proudly show off if you can find the right person to show off to. I wonder whether you are not suppressing something about hospital now which you might be telling me.'

Patient 'Yes, in fact I am. In the first place there is a very interesting case, and in the second place I decided to do something today absolutely on my own without exactly knowing why, and I was very pleased with myself. In fact the Registrar would have disapproved, but it turned out good. I let some air into a chest after drawing off fluid, and this made a very good X-ray possible.'

Analyst 'So that made a better diagnosis.'

Patient 'Yes, we were making a diagnosis by default, and now we can make it more definitely.'

Analyst 'And the case?'

Patient 'Yes.' He then told me about an elderly man who had so much fluid that the diagnosis was obscure, probably cancer. There was no proof. Again he had put in air and so had made the contour of the lung show for the first time on the X-ray. 'I did it without anybody suggesting anything.'

Analyst 'You need me to be able to do this sort of thing here.'

Patient 'Yes, I require you to have a technique for making things clear, even perhaps using a stunt.'

Analyst 'There is an identification with me here; you in your job are like me in mine. Or shall I put it the other way round?'

Patient 'I missed some of what you were saying. The fact is that I was getting excited about that case. It may be that as a result the cancer will be found to be operable.'

Analyst 'Have you a good surgeon?' (I did this deliberately, in view of the fact that he had raised the matter of the half-dream state, and also he had mentioned the word stunt.)

Patient 'I had a curious thought then. Your questions like that about work; it happened before; they always surprise me. Do you do it out of interest? In the case? Or what is it? Are you pointing out that I have missed something? I might be resenting this. In any case, it is a great surprise when you do things like that. To some extent I am glad, to some extent resenting it. I feel it is wrong to talk about hospital.'

Analyst 'The question is, who am I standing for? Perhaps your wife who does not know about hospital things?'

Patient 'Yes, or more likely my father, a kind of examiner.'

Analyst 'I knew, of course, that my remark was outside analysis; not within good analytic technique, but you were dealing with the matter of being half asleep.'

Patient 'I welcome it really. I really want anything that could be called a shortcut to psychoanalysis.'

Analyst 'The fact is that I woke you.' (I took account of this warning that he was wanting a stunt, but I did not believe that this was the main reaction to what I had done.)

Patient 'Yes, that is the annoying thing. It is like working in hospital when I get woken up at night. It is not so much the loss of sleep. The irritation comes from having one's dream-life broken into. That rather reminds me of a story of the Chinese of a previous generation. The idea which was taught that the spirit goes away during sleep and that there is an actual danger if someone is suddenly awakened; the spirit never gets back into the awakened body.' (Other material here was lost.)

Analyst I went again over the ground that the analysis has been done somewhat on the dream side of the borderline between sleeping and waking, and that he is evidently just arriving at a position from which he can feel the call to be asleep and the call to be awake at the same time.

(He sensed the end of the hour.)

Patient 'It is the same with not bringing up new material at the end and feeling rejected. If new material is brought forward and there is no time for it to be dealt with, there is a risk and it feels as if there is actual danger.'

Analyst 'I did get the feeling in the last session that you were not expecting the end, and that therefore my stopping was traumatic, as if I were waking you suddenly.'

Monday, 14 March

The patient came late, and had to go on time because of an appointment with the dentist.

Patient 'Well, I feel there must be a pause. There is something to be said about reality, and if I started right away it would seem wrong, like eagerness. When there are real things happening there is no time for dreams and the discussion of them. A dream needs leisure. There is a new development in that I arranged last night to see the girl friend while I was on duty at hospital. She was to come over and see me by ten, but she did not come on time and I started speculating, feeling disturbed, and I was surprised because I did not expect to be upset, for she does not mean much emotionally, just rather useful. Perhaps she did not want to come or had become casual. She arrived at eleven-thirty. So I made love immediately and then was impotent. It was partly her lack of enthusiasm, and also the crudeness of my approach. It is like suddenly starting in when I get here, which I said I couldn't do at the beginning of this hour – it would be crude. I began to have anxiety. Was her usefulness coming to an end? I had enjoyed her because she had restored my confidence, and now it seemed like a new thing. Will the impotence continue? It is difficult to talk freely with her till after intercourse, so here again I missed the value of our meeting.'

Analyst 'You were already angry, and that complicated the issue?'

Patient 'I was not concerned about her, I thought, except when she was there, because she was always available. Now I had to face the prospect of her not wanting to be available at a particular moment. Before, I had no worry about competition with men. If she is not available, however, it can only seem as if she has other interests.' *Pause.* 'There is a dilemma here. Firstly, I find sex very important indeed; secondly, other things seem much more important.'

Analyst 'You did need the experience which gave you sexual confidence before you could come to a "balance" (his word).' *Pause.* 'You needed confidence in your own sexual potency before you could consider the matter of balance.' *Pause.* 'Here you have me impotent, in the sense of being unable to make the interpretation you want, because I do not know what it is.'

Patient 'I want to make sure this is not wasted before I go on to something else and forget it.'

Analyst 'You would have to rely on me to remember it and to meet it at the right moment.'

Patient 'I did not want to be crude, taking the girl before warming her up to it.'

Analyst 'Here you have your analyst standing for the girl who ought to be warmed up. A more positive thing would be to say that your experience last night showed up the fact that usually you do trouble to warm up the girl. If she were excited at the start, this excitement would belong to an experience that she had already had before coming to you.' *Pause.* 'This introduces the idea of the other men.'

Patient 'I was thinking of something else.' *Pause.* 'It's odd. I was really wide awake when I came. I suddenly get sleepy. It seems that after talking to you about immediate affairs I was waiting for you to do something.' *Long pause.* 'I want to start again but I feel sleepy. What I have said would be wasted if I were to start on something else. It must be dealt with first. If I restart it, it will all get forgotten. I have the feeling that you do not want to say anything. It is as if you were withholding something.'

Analyst (I was not at all clear what to interpret.) 'The question arises since I am identified with this girl, what did the girl say? or, alternatively, what might she have said?'

Patient 'I am in a dilemma here, and I can more easily say what she might have said. I was anxious that she did not want me personally. I thought I was involved in a lighthearted way, enjoying a relationship without there being any place for demands either way. I told her that I was upset at her not coming, and this I felt made it sound like a protest. I sounded miserable. I also told her about my wife and her complete unresponsiveness at the present time since the relapse of the boy friend. She cannot be talked to at all. The girl friend said: "What you want is to be loved." I did not want her to know about my emotional demands, my wife being a mother-figure in this respect. I did not want the girl to be like that. The relationship will degenerate into dependence. A satisfactory relationship means equality.'

Analyst 'It appears then that the relationship with the girl has undergone a development. It is now more than biologically satisfactory. The girl has turned up as a person, and you have turned up as a person for the girl, and the impotence came as a sign of this change.'

Patient 'I seem up to now to have shelved the question of her needs. She in fact wants to get out of her casualness. She is wanting a permanent relationship, and I am not sure about her, nor she about me. She would like me to throw in my lot with her completely and set up on a permanent basis. It really is improbable that it would work. I almost lied to her, saying things about the holiday, etc, and I felt that this was just an act. Last night's discovery of a dependence in the relationship sharpened her concern about a permanent relationship. She is twenty-eight and she wants children, but I cannot just let my wife go like that.'

Analyst I continued with the theme of his impotence as a part of a widening of his relationship, and his former potency as something closely associated with a limited type of relationship. The same can be said in terms of feeding and infancy. At a theoretical start there is only instinct, but in the course of time there appears a relationship after which the full satisfaction of instinct is impossible.

Patient 'I feel that a stage has been reached. I cannot now keep up any longer the artificial situation and must consider the doubts as to whether she can offer me more. She has really a shallow personality. The consequence is that I feel hopeless about a further development of the relationship.'

Tuesday, 15 March

Patient 'I can't remember yesterday. I seem to remember that yesterday I wanted to say something and the hour stopped short.'

Pause.

Analyst 'Shall I remind you or not?'

Patient 'I don't really know.'

Analyst 'We did in fact stop early, as you had to go to the dentist. You had wanted me to make an interpretation on your report on real happenings.'

Patient 'Yes, I was trying to help you to interpret. It all hinged round the feelings of impotence which unexpectedly occurred. The question was whether this emotional experience could be productive.'

Analyst 'The anxiety you felt had to do with your feeling that a phase had ended, since the impotence indicated a widening of your relationship with the girl.'

Patient 'These feelings carried on after I had left. After the dentist I went home and I was depressed, thinking that my wife would be inert, and I had nothing to look forward to. Then I had a feeling of generalized impotence, with a total lack of interest in women, which was in great contrast to the excitement of a few days ago. To my surprise, my wife wanted to go out to the pictures (the patient acts as sitter on these occasions), and this gave me pleasure; at any rate this would lessen tension at home, etc, etc. At her request I phoned up the hospital and found her boy friend was not quite as ill as she had thought, and immediately I felt more cheerful. The dilemma would be shelved. When she came back and I told her, she was relieved, and then I became depressed again, more than I had been before. I don't really know why, except that this threw into relief that conflict about the girl. A stage of decision would soon arrive, and I'm not awfully happy about the girl. I hinted to my wife about the possibility of taking a holiday separately and she was more ready to accept this idea than I had expected, so I am up against the dilemma. So I realize I am still attached to my wife, more so than I am prepared to admit, though it's hopeless.' *Pause.* 'It seems the same as yesterday. Will you take up the story, I wonder? I haven't offered you much, I'm afraid.'

Analyst 'I am just wondering why it is that I have nothing to say.'

(I then passed yesterday's session in review and spoke about the dilemma; how to continue to make use of the girl without getting involved in complications that belong to the idea of a wider relationship and inter-dependence.)

Patient 'There is something else, but I delayed telling you about it because I wanted to know if there would be a sequel to what we were doing yesterday. The question has come up, what job to do after this one? The idea has been suggested that I should be Registrar in the autumn in the same group. The advantages would be increased pay, and that the treatment could be continued. This has to be decided. I think I could tackle the job. This is what I was thinking about coming along; I found it exciting, and so I put it into the background.'

Analyst 'This idea indicates real changes in you, especially as the first sign of your illness came when you had to take responsibility.'

Patient 'Also it means not taking more junior jobs, and that it's safe now to aim higher.'

Analyst 'The job comes in as part of the analysis, and you would expect me to be excited too.'

Patient 'It's easier now for me to be offering advice than to do the job myself, because after two years the routine work has become rather boring.'

Analyst 'There will be teaching too?'

Patient 'Yes. The question is, am I mature enough to teach? I was not mature enough before or confident enough to tell people what to do.'

Analyst 'Is it Junior Registrar?'

Patient 'Yes. The man doing it now is not as well qualified to do it as I am, and has had less experience.'

Analyst 'You are saying that a general potency is not annulled by a specific localized impotence.'

Patient 'Yesterday you said about my jealousy of men, that this was hardly showing at all. But it began to become present the night before last when I was impotent, even if it is in the background only. But I have a distaste for it. I don't like competition with men.'

Analyst 'It seems all right to compete when you know you are superior.'

Patient 'On the other hand I do not like to compete when on unequal terms.'

Analyst 'In the analytic room it is important to you that either we are only two – as when you were a small child with mother – or else when we are three the third is excluded.'

Patient 'Now I see that with my wife I did not admit the possibility of a rival. With the girl, even though I knew of the other men in her life, I did not take them seriously. I was amused at the idea of them. I would play at competing. Here in analysis I take the great liberty of assuming that there is no one else, and refuse to recognize there is anyone before and after. I dodge people at the door but only see them by accident and they exist in the abstract. I deny their existence.'

Analyst (Rather off the mark.) 'When you can admit three people you can get the relief that the third can have the rival penis, so you do not need the idea of the woman with a penis.' (Rather loud now, patient going to sleep.) 'Last time you were either angry with me for stopping or else angry with the dentist for coming between us.' *Pause.* (He woke after three to four minutes.) 'You slept, I think?' (He agreed. I repeated the interpretation, and he lost all the sleep tendency as he began to understand what I was interpreting.)

Patient 'It's odd, I thought yesterday that the dentist has a lower status than an analyst, but I have to be more careful to be on time for him than for analysis. The dentist is impertinent, I thought, to expect me to be punctual.'

Analyst 'It is sensible to be on time for the dentist, since you only go occasionally . . . though you probably had to wait.'

Patient 'Yes.'

Analyst 'But the main thing is that our relationship was stopped by a dentist who is imaginatively a dangerous man, who might take out teeth to punish you for biting, for your cannibalistic impulses and ideas – a form of castration.'

Patient 'Yes.'

Friday, 18 March

Patient 'Coming along, I had the feeling that I did not want to say anything; it would be better for you to start off, to ask questions.'

Analyst 'Yes, it's odd this way of throwing all the responsibility on you. Do you in fact remember yesterday? Was the idea related to yesterday's events?'

Patient 'No, I just had this attitude. The last few times I think I have not been productive. I haven't had much to say. So if you accept responsibility you couldn't say I was the cause of nothing happening. Perhaps there's a lot more to it, though. It's a lot to accept responsibility for the way the hour goes, to decide what's of interest, and also what not to say. What a lot has to be turned down as not important! Some things I don't want to talk about. Earlier I assumed that I ought to talk about everything, but with the arrival of more ideas I had to find reasons for suppression. I feel excitement here. It's a question: "Who's to be father?" '

Analyst 'Indeed!?'

Patient 'I feel anxious about being in the father role, concerned what you feel about this. A change is happening, and you are less impersonal, less of a pure analyst. This change is happening in general, too. I have become more aware of the effect of what I say on people, quite apart from analysis. Also there is the difficulty about talking with my wife, when I select carefully because of a fear that I may be just saying something because of its expected effect on her.'

Analyst 'You are just beginning to see that the choice of what to say can be part of anxiety (resistance).'

Patient 'At the start there was no problem of suppression, there was much to say, and then I forgot or went to sleep. These methods are now wearing a bit thin, and so a new method is needed if a subject has unpleasant features.'

Analyst 'I am rather closely linked with your wife here.' (Doubtful as an interpretation here.)

Pause.

Patient 'One more thing, there is the other technique, that there are many details, each obvious, too trivial for singling out.'

Analyst 'Can you think of one?'

Patient 'Well, there was just the idea, a fleeting one, something about counting buttons. The idea came to me as essentially trivial.'

Analyst 'Are there any associations to these two words?'

Patient 'No, nothing here, only that I was discussing with my wife and her mother the number of buttons on a guardsman's uniform. I had no idea that each guards' regiment has a specific number of buttons.'

Analyst 'And to counting?'

Patient 'Well, my daughter is just learning to count and is very fond of games with counting in them, counting objects, and so on. There is also the idea of counting sheep, a practice I have never used when sleepless.'

Analyst 'The idea of buttons has come into the analysis recently, do you remember?'

Patient 'No.'

Analyst 'You spoke of Ernest Jones' reference to a button and this belongs to the idea of cannibalism.'[1]

Patient 'Oh yes!'

Analyst 'And it happens that at the end of last hour there was the dentist who easily gets mixed up imaginatively with the idea of a man who punishes for biting by knocking out teeth. So the counting of buttons can either be reassuring yourself that all the buttons are present, or else accounting for the buttons inside after a cannibalistic orgy.'

Pateint 'Oh yes! And then there is also the idea in my mind of the "belly-button", so-called, which means undressed. At that moment I thought of the nipples. The idea of the nipples came to me before the idea of the umbilicus.'

Analyst 'The question arises, are there two nipples, or is there one twice?'

Patient 'Here is the dilemma. It is difficult for a baby to decide which breast to start to get milk from.' (At this point the patient seemed to be a baby actually reliving his experiences, and he had his right finger at his mouth. His thumb-sucking was left-handed.)

Analyst 'Here surely is the beginning of arithmetic.'

---

[1] See p. 24.

Patient 'Two could mean mother and me.'

Analyst 'There is the problem too, at some time or other the baby knows of two nipples, but at an earlier date (no matter what date) there was only one nipple, reduplicated, so to speak.'

Patient 'With my daughter, I've always taken the trouble to bathe her and to come in early in her life, and this was my father's idea, as I remember it. He said he took part in the care of his infants as early as possible so as to be recognized and accepted as the father, so as to establish his claim as father. I feel guilty that I have done this less with the second baby for various reasons. I wonder: will she recognize me as father, as the older one does?' *Pause.* 'I have an urge to punish you by not talking, by not saying my thoughts.'

Analyst 'The first thing about that is that you need to establish your power to withhold ideas, to find that I don't know your thoughts magically.'

Patient 'In psychoanalysis, if I punish you, you may punish me by being ill or not coming; you have the means for extreme punishment.' (The direct reversal of an impulse.)

Analyst 'This power of psychoanalysis to punish in a crude, talion, way – are you asleep?'

Patient 'I expect to be dominated, so go out of my way to avoid punishment, to avoid withholding. I don't want to punish anyone, except that recently I have become able to some extent to lose my temper a little. There is a kind of acknowledgment of rivalry in this.'

Analyst 'You are dealing with the transition from talion to the humanized conception of a father beating you.'

Patient 'Yes . . . yes . . .' (Sleeps and awakes, probably not aware of having slept.) 'Punishment can take so many different forms. In an ordinary hospital ward, it can be part of a scheme of punishment to keep a patient a long while in one ward. It's like doing lines.'

Analyst 'You have thought of school punishment?'

Patient 'Yes, but I avoided punishment there too. It was a rare feature at the school chosen for me.'

Analyst 'Not finding a rival outside mother in the form of a separate person, father; and having father as an alternative version of mother, you had to find the rival in mother herself; this would sometimes simply be her refusal to play her part, as it would seem to you.'

Patient 'These words "refusal to play her part" apply exactly to what I feel my wife does. This is her attitude, to refuse interest and sympathy. I got to that idea in a roundabout way.' (The patient always feels more convinced when he gets to an idea indirectly.) 'With the girl friend I find it difficult to use her first name, especially at the time of intercourse when I forget her name and usually think of my wife's name. And in general I've gone off Christian names, the use of which I tried to introduce a little while ago at hospital. This could be said to be a denial of intimacy.'

Analyst 'I think you are referring indirectly to your mother and what you called her. Did you perhaps not use her Christian name?'

Patient 'I may have occasionally, but only because of a difficulty over saying "mummy", which is horrifyingly intimate. So I glossed over the difficulty by an avoidance of using any name at all. I gloss over similar difficulties in the same way by avoiding using a name.'

Analyst '"Mummy" is a particularly "mouthy" word. Let me see, what is your mother's name? Is that of any importance?'

Patient (He gave the name.) 'No, probably that's not significant.'

Analyst 'Your father called her by that name?'

Patient 'Well, very occasionally – usually "mummy". With my wife after two or three years I tended to call her "mummy", and rebuked myself for doing so; she would resent it, I felt. It's only logical if the children are there to give her a label describing a special function; it's not recognizing her as a wife. I make an effort to use her Christian name, and I feel she prefers this. She hasn't actually said so. It's a question of function or person. In contrast to call my own mother "mummy" would be all right, but to call her by her Christian name would be cold, or remote.'

Analyst 'You remember how we started; am I an analyst or a person? You have never actually used my name in talking to me.'

Patient 'It is more convenient to use the nonspecific title.'

Analyst 'There is a danger that you sense behind all this. I will put it this way: if you lose the breast you are in danger of losing your mouth as well, unless you keep your mouth free from intimate contact with the breast.'

Patient 'I don't follow that. . . .'

Analyst 'Perhaps I have gone a jump ahead – but . . .' (Here I repeated the interpretation and connected the conflict with the tendency to solve matters by sleeping.)

Patient 'Before I came in I thought: "If I can change my attitude to wanting you to start the talking this will be like the changes that have come through the relationship with the girl friend." Some while ago you were speaking of my acting out masturbation fantasy and I was horrified at the idea. I want things to be real, not acting. I was alternating from pure fantasy to talking about it. I reached an acting out of fantasy that was still unreal. It's now no longer just talking, it's doing.'

Analyst 'In the matter of the use of the mouth you have come to a point where talking, and acting, and fantasy can meet. It seems that your father came into your life very early, before you could count two, or when you could just count two but were still loving by mouth and loving the breast. If he is a separate person, he therefore became linked with the crude talion fears about mouth activity. This means that he is linked with the loss of a breast mouth, which is so serious a danger that you must avoid intimacy between mouth and breast by sleeping and other measures. This interfered with your use of father at a later stage as a human being who could punish and who could become a castrator in your fantasy associated with erection of the penis in your love of your mother.'

Tuesday, 22 March

Patient 'Well, I'll begin by talking about what happened this evening. I had arranged to go out with the girl friend and I did not want to tell my wife. I wanted to, but I knew it would not help. It would only lead to friction. I knew that she rather looked forward to going out this evening (the patient would be baby-sitting), but I phoned and told her I would not be home. My wife became cross and hung up, refusing to discuss the matter in any way. I found myself in a trembling rage, or was it an upset, and this is still there after three hours. I definitely do not want to precipitate a crisis at the present time. The alternatives are extreme: peace means giving up the girl friend; so there is a dilemma now – carry on with endless crises or return meekly although existence at home can only be cold. The relationship with the girl friend is not ideal, but at the moment it is very satisfactory in its own way.' *Pause.* 'The problem is like the one we had before. What can you do about this sort of material?'

Analyst 'For one thing, you are relying on me to integrate two aspects of your life which for the moment you cannot integrate. The relationship with your wife with all its potential, good and bad, and the immediately satisfactory relationship with the girl.'

Patient 'It seems that I am nearer to forcing a break at the present moment than I have been before, so it is more disturbing.' *Pause.* 'There are the two alternatives: one is home which only functions on the basis of complete unreality – no friendship, that is to say, shut off from relationships – or with the girl friend, though with her there is a big imaginative element. I can see it is peppered with romance. It has more reality to it. There is a stalemate in my relationship to my wife, but I do not want to throw it all up. Somehow or other I still cherish a hope, though I have no belief that it can come to anything. I can understand my wife's point of view, but I cannot accept her attitude that lacks feeling, and also there is the fact that I can never discuss anything with her. She has laid down conditions. Undoubtedly I am terribly irritated by her hanging up, that is to say, her refusal to discuss.'

(This took up about one-third of the hour.)

'I have a reason for not saying any more. I do not want this to continue throughout the hour, but I cannot go on to something else without a gap. The affair has cast too big a shadow.'

Analyst 'You are still affected by your reaction to the hanging-up. Possibly rage, you said.'

Patient 'Yes, the hanging-up – I was thrown into a state of impotence. There was nothing I could do. I ought to be neutral or amused and say it's her fault but the rage has to do with anger with myself. Perhaps I am angry at being annoyed.'

Analyst 'You will remember that the antagonism used to be between your wife's attitude and the analysis, and now this takes the form of her antagonism that you feel towards your relation to the girl.'

Patient 'Yes, there is an interference with more fundamental issues.' *Pause.* 'I expected you somehow to be able to find a way of dealing with these things so as to get them out of the way, but of course you can't.'

Analyst 'One point is that here you have a triangular relationship with no other man in it. The potential hate is between two women.'

Patient 'Initially the girl was not concerned with my wife. The affair was not intended to get anywhere. Now, however, she wants more out of it, and she is afraid of being disappointed once again. But we both have misgivings about a permanent relationship. . . . I find her demands exciting and her dependence on me and her direct expression of need, so we get deeper and deeper into a blind alley for which there is no resolution. I am thrown back on the choice between two blind alleys.' *Pause.* 'Also there is something new with my dealing with her side of the relationship. The fact is that she has other men and one in particular. I am beginning to find it exciting, competing and trying to eliminate another man. This is certainly new about men. First, the rivalry is new, part of my development, and secondly, there is the immediate excitement about a fight with a man over a girl. I have never been able to cope with this before.'

Analyst 'In a sense you are all the time looking for the man that you hate on account of the love of a woman. In the long run this is father, a new aspect of father that you hardly encountered, especially as he came into your life deliberately at a very early stage and established himself as an alternative mother to you as an infant.' (At this point the patient put his foot on the floor.)

Pause.

Patient 'There is another factor which I have not really discussed here: there is the aspect of the sexual relationship with the girl friend. There is much more real excitement and satisfaction than with my wife even when things were going well with her. This is partly due to the change in me because of the analysis. The difficulty is that the idea has been introduced that, if I enjoy the results of the treatment, how can my wife keep pace or is it all to be wasted? I was not originally prepared for this. Before, I thought, if I get better I can deal with my wife. Now I have to cope with the feeling that she may become depressed as the result of the changes in me; she may possibly deteriorate. There is so much that cannot be explored directly with my wife. She does not even expect an orgasm, so sex is not desirable from her point of view. But the trouble is that this may be my fault. She may have developed this as a way of dealing with my original clumsiness and inability to be exciting. It would be better if one could talk this over with her. I cannot accept the idea that a sex relationship has to be brushed aisde if I get better. My wife has said that I am not to look forward to sexual experience with her, but this is largely due to its having been so unsatisfactory in the past. She has hinted at feeling superior to sex. It is beneath her. I think that her relationship to her boy friend has been what she would call spiritual. I have a pity for her, but she must reject what I am beginning to be able to give in regard to pleasure and excitement. If I get well, what may happen is that I shall find that there is something wrong with her, and nothing can be done about that as she would be horrified at the idea. All her difficulties up to now have hidden behind the fact that I have been ill, and before that unsatisfactory.

Wednesday, 23 March

(Re-arrangement in regard to times.)

Patient 'The next thing that comes into my mind is that there has begun a curious change in the nature of my problem. At first I was not aware of specific symptoms, and it was just a question of not being able to work or to take responsibility. Now work is not in fact a difficulty, though I don't feel I am yet at maximum capacity – perhaps because of the nature of the job. The issue now hinges round personal and sexual problems. It would be difficult for my wife to understand the sexual and personal as a major problem, that would be a frivolous approach.

But at the moment it's far more important. It comes to me to mention my wife's attitude. I don't know why, but it seems to fit in. Till recently I have refused to recognize the central position of sex but it was probably dormant all the time. Lately I have been more willing to see that the personal are the only real issues. I am reminded that in regard to my inability to accept responsibility, the key was my sexual immaturity.'

Analyst 'You couldn't show a more specific symptom at the start because you weren't there as a person to be having sexual difficulties. It is a part of your emergence as a person that you can now come with personal symptoms.'

Patient 'The sexual with my wife seemed all right at one time, but now I see that at the actual moment of intercourse I was aware of impersonality, I would think of banal things, indulge in masturbation fantasy in order to stimulate myself in order to produce an ejaculation. With the girl friend that's no longer so. I accept intercourse in its own right. My wife must have been aware (perhaps unconsciously) of the incompleteness. Now I am faced with a dilemma, now I know of the possibilities of intercourse. Intellectually and socially I still want my wife. Nevertheless with the girl sex is good, but there are the social complications.'

Analyst 'Yes, you certainly have a big problem.'

Patient 'My wife is not likely to accept a divided relationship – it would be unworkable. The girl would not be willing for this either; she reacted to the same problem by promiscuity, but is not finding the solution satisfactory.'

Analyst 'There are changes in yourself, for instance you are only just starting to meet the idea of men as rivals; also there is the matter of becoming conscious of the fantasy of the girl with the penis and vagina.'

Patient 'It seems likely that I will become promiscuous unless my wife improves or unless the girl-friend relationship matures in the direction of stability.'

Analyst 'If it were not for the ruthlessness implied, what you have needed is just your wife, then the girl friend, and then a new girl to be found for the permanent solution, but you are worried at the prospect of the two women lying around hurt.'

Patient 'I found the girl friend crying and I had a feeling of responsibility – but this may be vanity – though she said she had been helped by my talking.'

Analyst 'There is a value to you in feeling that a girl loves you and so could be hurt by you.'

Patient 'Yes, so I am disturbed about my wife hanging up on the phone. It was not purely annoyance, but also I felt her jealousy. I am only guessing, but I think she knew about the girl and she may have been hurt.'

Analyst 'So she loves you.'

Patient 'I had visions of getting home late and finding the door locked – it was just fantasy. I went home and found her already asleep – this was the same as a stony silence, for she certainly knew when I came in. I feel much has happened to flatter my vanity and I must be careful. I have always been able to help and have been known as sympathetic. The girl said I was the first person she had met who could be promiscuous and yet kind and considerate at the same time. . . . Have I perhaps been too soft and considerate? It occurs to me I have had a feeling of hating to be rejected, as at a dance, upset at not being acceptable.'

Analyst 'In the extreme, you are loved, and so you must hurt if you choose one person. This could be a picture of your early childhood.'

Patient 'It's more that I couldn't choose because I didn't want to miss anything; in fact, it was last night that I was thinking that I recognized that I have little difficulty in making decisions about little things. I believe neurotic people are like that. As I said to the girl, I only have difficulty in making major decisions; where there are genuine difficulties in a situation, and now for the first time in my life I feel I can cope with the future. No doubt there will be a lot of worry and misery and so on, but I can cope. I feel this is the result of two years of psychoanalysis.'

Analyst 'You are saying that you feel you can make decisions, but these decisions involve hurting people.'

Patient 'With me it seems that if I hurt other people that is the same as hurting myself.'

(He implied in his tone of voice that he was concerned in hurting people not so much with hurting them as with hurting himself.)

'I suppose I project myself on to other people.'

Analyst 'It is possible that when the girl friend talked about unconcern of exciting lovers, she meant that they did not identify with her. It would be interesting to know whether they were able to produce satisfaction in her or whether they were chiefly concerned with their own gratification.'

Patient 'Yes, I think that they did include an interest in her sexual gratification but nothing more.'

Analyst 'There is a point that you hurt yourself by choosing any one person. As you have said, you may miss something by eliminating the others.'

Patient 'Masturbation turned out now to have been my need for promiscuity which was solved in that way without social and other complications. The difficulty in stopping was to do with not wanting to miss anything by choosing.'

Analyst 'This seems to me to join up with what we were saying about sums and the beginning of arithmetic.' (I recapitulated about his daughter learning sums and the whole of the interpretation about the one breast reduplicated or the idea of two breasts or a mother and child and so on, going into detail because it was clear that it was news to him.)

Patient 'Funny! I had completely forgotten all that, and yet it was quite clear three days ago. I had no impression left. It was completely blocked out.'

Analyst 'Added to all this was father coming in your life very early, as you perhaps remember telling me, and so joining up with the woman and this being used by you eventually in your difficulty in dealing with him as a man.'

Pause.

Patient 'I was thinking that I feel guilty at bringing too many problems. Why should I feel this to be wrong? I suppose in this I am encouraged by the frequent observation that facts are less productive in the analysis, I wonder whether this is actually true, and whether it need be.'

Analyst 'I can see no reason why it should be true.'

Patient 'Except in so far as real happenings – (at this point he put his foot on the floor) – have less bearing on the personality development than things in the mind. Perhaps they are all impersonal. Immediate things do not get past the impersonal barrier like dreams.'

Analyst 'You are using me in the analysis in various different ways. Today we have the idea of my integrating material for you and so on, but there are more specific ways in which you use me. At one time you will remember I was closely identified with your wife. Later I was identified with the girl friend, and there was an important moment when I made this interpretation after having made a wrong one.' (I reminded him of the details.) 'Now it seems that there is a new phase and I have become the man that you are concerned with in your relation to the girl.'

Patient 'So what I have been saying is boasting. It's curious, for a few days I have been feeling "I think I would like to meet the man", meaning the other man who is most important in the girl's life. I could score him off. Beforehand when I was not aware of sex problems there was not much point in meeting the man behind the scenes and I did not want to talk about you as the man simply because I ought to, but now the whole thing has become more to the point because I can boast and show off.'

Analyst 'In this analysis there has been extremely little negative transference but we are just coming up to it and the analysis has to be able to contain it. There is the fight between the two men who both love a girl. You are coming up to it in a very strong position of the triumphant man who can meet the other man on the basis of boasting of success.'

Patient 'I seem to have been aware of all this in a vague way for a long time but I felt you would be jealous. It has been there the whole time.'

Analyst 'It is not only that you were concerned about me in this way but also you had some work to do about the mouth excitements and the idea of a dentist punishing in a direct way. Only gradually have you come to be able to deal with me as a human being rival. It would seem at first that you are in a position to triumph but this is only true if we consider the girl. I suggest that in regard to the wife it is different. I know that there are real difficulties here which cannot be solved by analysis and which have to do with her ability to change and to recover from the past. Nevertheless, in the imaginative situation while you are triumphant over me in regard to the girl you have accepted in regard to your wife the complete absence of a sexual future. In other words, you have accepted a one hundred per cent ban on sex as if giving me the triumph.'

Patient 'Yes, but there is also an idea here that you are the rival of my wife for my favour, hence her hostility. There is that way round which seems important to me at the moment. I can only come to analysis at the expense of her not allowing it. In this case, you are a woman, a mother-figure, from my wife's point of view.'

Analyst 'Here your mother claims you, and so your wife has no chance.'

Patient 'That reminds me that at the hospital when I was ill a doctor said that I was not in love with my wife and it was as if he had said, "You belong to me", although it did not strike me that way at the time. All I knew then was that I felt very disturbed and in fact insulted, but there seem to be several things all at once here.'

Analyst 'Yes, there are several things all at once, and the relationship between your wife and yourself and me contains many different meanings. It is a kind of portmanteau situation.'

Thursday, 24 March

Patient 'I was thinking on the way that there are no immediate issues, so the way is open for deeper things. But there was something I thought of last night. It's a bit hazy now, I may have given you a wrong idea of the position with my wife. I've done it several times because when here I have a different attitude from my attitude when at home. Here and at work I feel the difference springs from her, and I get a feeling of mastery, that I can afford to crack the whip. She is dependent on me, not I on her. I can tell her to pull her socks up – but when I am at home it's all different. I can't make the start of a showdown. The difficulty appears as I enter the door, and I become paralysed. So there is a contrast in all this with my initial statement; when I was in a dependent state this didn't matter. I just went home to be miserable. Now when there is an alternative I wonder why I should go home to be a martyr. With my wife I only talk about what she initiates, whereas with the girl it's altogether different, and never before have I been free to talk. On the phone I spend even an hour talking to the girl.'

Analyst 'As we said before, there is no play area between you and your wife.'

Patient 'Perhaps an awareness of the existence of a rival would stimulate my wife to be more considerate, but I don't let her know, and I don't really know what I want. A change would only be valuable if it were fairly complete.' *Pause.* 'I'm still not prepared to take the responsibility for a showdown.'

Analyst (I took up the interpretation of the end of the last session.) 'Last time I spoke of my position as the man prohibiting sexuality with your wife.' *Pause.* 'Did you go to sleep?' (Probably he did sleep.)

Patient 'No. I felt then an unusual state of tension. This relates partly to my difficulty at home, where I deliberately avoid the decision which must be made fairly soon now. There is a kind of extended triangular situation, a pentagonal one, two women and three men. The job expires in two months and so I must orientate now towards seeing the girl. Also there is the holiday. I don't want a repetition of the Christmas holiday in which I sat at home. I feel this is actually coming to a head, here and now, at this very minute.'

Pause.

Analyst 'You are showing me how urgent the matter is, and how you want me to do everything I can do in the analysis before you bring about a showdown. The thing is that, if I ignore your wife's difficulties and the question of her ability to change and to recover from the effect of your earlier treatment of her, I can say that you are using her as the nearest you can get to the mother with whom sex is prohibited by father. If I go to your adolescent dream of intercourse with mother, or to your early childhood, I can say that you needed father to say "I know you love mother and want intercourse with her, but I love her and I do not allow it." In that way father would have freed you to love other women. If this thing doesn't get cleared up mother will continue to turn up in your women, and if you were to marry the girl friend the difficulties would appear in that new marriage. Moreover, you have missed rivalry with men and the friendships that come with such rivalry.'

Patient 'This is a new idea for me, that I have missed friendship with men, though I'm prepared to believe it's true. It has struck me that I have no use for games of skill. Cards are more a technical exercise for me, and I have never wanted to watch football. Recently it has struck me, in fact this week, that there are very few things I get excitement out of except sexual intercourse, though occasionally I feel some excitement in reading stories or a few months ago at the pictures. Occasionally music, and in fact it was last week I was excited by a talk on Elgar and the Enigma Variations. Two variations were played. This was the first time for a long while that music has excited me. There was a bit more to it since the variations were written about friends of Elgar, and so represented his friendships, etc.'

Analyst 'So Elgar was capable of love and of warm friendships.'

Patient 'It worries me about the girl friend that her interest is almost exclusively in sexual excitement, though she can be personal, lonely for instance. I could grow out of her limited scope. She finds nothing in music – it's either medicine or sex. Here I feel one thing I might be worried about is that you might not only ban sex with my wife but also advise against further relations with the girl friend. You would be my guardian of moral welfare, so I don't tell you all my proposals for the future. You might become less academic and advise. I like your advice but should not like it if you advised against the relationship.'

Analyst 'So by not prohibiting I am permitting. You can only think of me as in one or other position.'

Patient 'With the girl friend I feel enthusiastic; it's like a wild leap into dangerous waters and I have never been able to do this before. It is of the nature of a good thing, an achievement.'

Analyst 'You never met your father as a man to hate, a rival, someone you feared. Whether because of him or yourself or both, you missed this, and so you never felt mature.'

Patient 'If I never got to father's prohibition then I was left having to find it in myself.'

Analyst 'Exactly, that is what I was meaning.'

Patient 'So that would account for my failure to get excited throughout my marriage.'

Analyst 'It would even have affected your choice of woman to marry.'

Patient 'I married her because of her severity; this appealed to me. She was unfeminine, well-groomed, with a frown, and she has severe features with a narrow face and glasses. She can easily scold, and domineer. Also it is likely that her boy friend was attracted for this same reason. He is rather irresponsible, and he wanted someone who could and would dominate him. He allowed her to make major decisions – whether to leave his wife, and also to start to take care of his health which he had neglected. I was thinking today – what kind of girl do I find attractive? Certainly not gentle or cherubic, but a severe dominating type, and the girl friend is tall and angular and loses her temper readily. It's the very opposite of sweet and unspoilt.'

(Here the patient puts his foot on the ground.)

Analyst 'Then also there is the girl with the penis of adolescent dreams.'

Patient 'I thought that was coming. I feel worried. I might be looking for a man, which would be a kind of homosexuality, which would imply that I'm an effeminate type of man.'

Analyst 'No, I don't think so. The fact is you are looking for father, the man who prohibits intercourse with mother. Remember the dream in which the girl friend originally appeared and this was about a man, one who was ill.'

Patient 'This would account for my lack of grief or of feeling when my father died. He had not met me as a rival and so left me with the awful burden of making the prohibitions myself.'

Analyst 'Yes, on the one hand he never did you the honour of recognizing your maturity by banning intercourse with mother, but also he deprived you of the enjoyment of rivalry and of the friendship that comes out of rivalry with men. So you had to develop a general inhibition, and you could not mourn a father you have never "killed".'

Tuesday, 29 March

(The Monday session had been missed. He had notified me by phone.)

Patient 'Well, I find it difficult to start. Firstly, there are no immediate problems, and secondly, it is curious, but the fact that I have got a bad cold seems to interfere. It clouds things over. It's as if free association and relaxation are a strain like physical exercise.'

Analyst 'I can well understand that if you have a cold you do not feel like the work of analysis, which really is a strain.'

Patient 'It's happened before; having a cold tends to mask the main issues. I feel more like curling up and going to sleep and making no mental effort.'

Analyst 'It would be more appropriate for you to withdraw.'

Patient 'I feel that if I am here I ought to relax and that ought to be easy but it seems like work.'

Analyst 'Yes, so that the limitation of the work to one hour is not only for the benefit of the analyst.'

Patient 'It makes me wonder what is the ideal time for the session and what is the ideal interval. Would daily sessions be too frequent and a less effective use of analysis?'

Analyst 'Perhaps the cold was what kept you away yesterday.'

Patient 'No, it wasn't that; it was just that there was a special case which had to be attended to. The cold hadn't started. I feel that we have talked about immediate problems and it is difficult to go back to the deeper issues. I cannot switch. This reminds me of children being wakened from a dream and being annoyed because it is so difficult to get back to the dream.'

Analyst 'There is something here which does link up with your analysis, which is done in a state which is towards the dream state. It would seem as if gradually in recent months there has been an emergence from the dream state towards last time when one could almost say that the analysis was being done with you awake, that is to say, as a part of waking reality.'

Patient 'I noticed today visiting a hospital because of work that I was able to to talk more freely than ever before, even with strange Residents of the other hospital, and I could take the lead in conversation. I thought this would never happen to me, and it represents a big change not having to wait till I know people intimately before leading off with ideas.' *Pause.* 'Also a few nights ago I dreamed something, and I felt I did not have to remember this; it's an ordinary dream.'

Analyst 'Yes, a dream is an ordinary bridge between inner reality and external reality, and to that extent you were well and not needing analysis because you have your own bridge as·represented in the dream.'

Patient 'This is wrapped up with the idea of not coming here. There seems to be a lessening of the need to come.'

Analyst 'That is to say, not needing psychoanalysis, since the main symptom was that you had a dissociation between the sleeping and waking states and you had partially solved this on the basis of never being really awake.'

Patient 'I wish to make a break here with what we are talking about. I was discussing my future with a friend. The various alternatives to medical specialization and general practice and I mentioned psychiatry. It occurred to me there is one great difficulty here that I am not ripe for at present because I am not yet sure of an ability to avoid identification. I definitely dislike long-winded people with no organized disease and I neglect them. Perhaps I go over a patient hoping to find something wrong because I know I am not interested in the patient as a person. Now in psychiatry I would be dealing with exactly those people. I would have to treat each on his or her own merits.'

Analyst 'You find a relief when there is physical illness.'

Patient 'For a psychiatrist a whole hour of a patient may be an intolerable burden.'

Analyst 'I think you are thinking of me and yourself.'

Patient 'Well, I suppose so. I have sometimes avoided going into this or it has come up but I have not liked to talk to you about my concern as to what you are feeling.'

Analyst 'There is of course the psychiatrist's basic care but within all this there is love and hate.'

Patient 'It's odd, I was just thinking then of two or three other matters. One was what shall I do this evening? The other was almost a dream of a confused kind about a patient in hospital. There were several people concerned. It was a reproduction in miniature of a worrying case that occupied the weekend. I was discussing the case with other people.'

Analyst 'It is important to you therefore that in psychoanalysis there is one person, myself in your case, and no consultation.'

Patient 'That is what I was talking about with the girl friend. Whether it is safe to discuss matters with a psychoanalyst. She said that psychoanalysts are not safe to tell everything to, and yet you must. I took the view that it would be quite possible to withhold an unpleasant detail. She said this would ruin the analysis.'

Analyst (At this point it seemed to me to be important that I should stop taking notes. It was of course possible that the patient knew and needed me to inform him openly. On the other hand he may not have known, and it would be important not to interrupt the course of the analysis at the present time by falsely introducing this idea. I could tell that the patient was very much under the influence of the main interpretation of the last session, and I must therefore sacrifice the note-taking to the work in hand.

(I realized that this man was giving me material supplied by his girl friend, and that I could only make indirect use of it. At the same time I must not waste it.)

I spoke of the discussions around clinical material which analysts certainly do have.

Patient 'I was really only referring to gossip.'

Analyst I pointed out that this matter is of definite concern to his girl friend,

as idle gossip by me would give away details of the private life of the
girl and might reach people she knew.

Patient He spoke about doctors at the hospital where he was ill who
gossiped with him about cases, assuming that as he was a doctor it
would be safe, but this worried him a great deal because he was a
patient and the fact was that he was having to cope with a doctor
gossiping and not with a scientific discussion of cases between
doctors.

Analyst I said that psychoanalysts, like other people, do gossip, being
imperfect human beings. But in psychoanalytic practice this gossiping was recognized as something to be avoided.

Patient He said that his girl friend had discussed the question of malprac-
tice. Would the analyst act if a patient reported antisocial behaviour?
In her case she is afraid to go to another analyst because she would
have to tell the second analyst about the behaviour of her first
psychotherapist which evidently she considers was unprofessional.

Analyst I agreed that she would have to speak of this freely or otherwise not
take up a new analysis.

It appeared that she felt that she would be able to talk freely if she
could assume that the second analyst would not act on her accusa-
tions.

I pointed out that within an analysis a patient must be able to speak
freely, which means not always confining observations to that which
is strictly objective. There must be room for delusions, and there is no
room for these if the analyst is to act, since all the material brought
into the analysis is for one purpose only, namely the analysis of the
patient.

I followed up another clue by saying that it was important for me to
recognize that what he was saying came from his girl friend. He might
want to say something similiar on another occasion and then it would
be material to be brought into his analysis. It might happen in the
course of time that we should look back and find that the reason why
he did not come on the previous day was to do with his suspicion of
me, but at the present time the clear issue was that he had work which
kept him away.

Patient He said that there might be some truth in it in the sense that earlier
in the analysis he would definitely have come. This would have meant
leaving his work aside.

Analyst 'It is possible then to state that earlier you had a fear of me which
you knew nothing about and which you could only deal with by being
good.'

I said that now he was a little bit in touch with his fear of me and therefore could defy me under the cover of using or exaggerating a need for his services at hospital.

I then pointed out to him that he had a reason for the first time in the analysis to be suspicious of me since in the previous session I had come in in the role of the father who prohibits incest. In the previous session he had thought of the father, I reminded him, as avoiding the main issue in which there was hate between him and his son, and therefore the son had no fear of the father. It was this new thing turning up in his relation to me which made him able to bring suspicion as expressed by his friend. It can be said that he was not ready to bring it directly himself.

Friday, 1 April

The note on this session was made four days later. There had been some degree of a resumption of note-taking during the session.

Patient 'Well, I have been put off by something – very much upset by the girl. She has to be in hospital and I am not allowed to visit her for fear of upsetting another boy friend. I am very angry with her and with my wife. The question is whether the man knows about me. She obviously wants both of us but she cannot tell him about me. It's like with my wife: she didn't like to upset her boy friend and expected me to be able to stand everything. . . . Of course I don't really want an exclusive love affair; I'm alarmed at the idea of this.'

Analyst I made an interpretation about the setting repeating itself in which he is angry with the girl for frustrating him and not with the man.

Patient 'It would seem to be all right if I found yet another girl, but that obviously is not the solution.'

Analyst 'It would always come round the same way with you as you are at present, and the reason is that you are all the time looking for your mother and your father has not played his part in coming between you and your mother. Had he done so he would have been a frustrating person; you would have come to terms with him and he would have freed you for all other women.'

(Patient asleep.)

'Were you asleep?'

Patient 'No, I don't think so.' (But it became clear that he had been.) 'I can't see where immediately to go forward. Lately I have been taking it out of others in hospital, losing my temper. In the past I found I have been too lenient, too inoffensive, tolerating everybody; but now I find myself flaring up. I wanted to flare up with the girl but I thought how much I could have lost my temper to a better purpose at home.'

Analyst 'You can see that you did just lose your temper here with me, and to some extent in the imaginative situation I am the person who has prohibited you from visiting the girl. In the previous session you said that you were half expecting me to tell you to keep off her.'

Patient 'I had thought of that, that you might be jealous. I didn't like the girl using the word "ducky". It's what prostitutes use – impersonal. She is probably more intimate with the other man, knowing him earlier than she knew me. I prefer "darling" if it's said right. It all depends. It may be artificial or genuine. . . . Also I tend to forget her name when making love.'

Analyst 'You told me that you sometimes think of your wife's name at that moment.'

Patient 'Oh yes, I had forgotten. I forget things so easily, especially names. I might call people by their Christian names if I know them well.'

Analyst 'What did father call mother?'

Patient Here he gave his mother's Christian name. 'Or he might have used the word "mummy" talking about her. . . . With the girl I felt that I ought to use her Christian name but I was unable to, or forgot it. On the telephone I say, "Hullo, dear", thus avoiding the issue. It's the same with my wife. The use of a Christian name except when adults are talking about children is a bit of an affectation. It's rather a predicament for children at adolescence to know what to call their parents. Their Christian names or "mummy" and "daddy"? Dependence or independence in the relationship? There are stilted words like "mater", but that is clumsy.'

Analyst 'But there are difficulties in your relationship at adolescence with your parents which are reflected in these considerations of names.'

Patient 'Yes, it's all right for a girl to say "daddy", but for a boy to say "mummy" is rather like incest. Society seems to tolerate the idea of incest between a girl and her father more easily than that of a boy with his mother. I think anthropology supports this.'

Analyst 'Are you talking about ideas or about actual intercourse?'

Patient 'I think I mean everything including intercourse. Mother and son is very objectionable. The word "darling" belongs to this intimate relationship. The question is, what is meant by incest? I could have said "love" or an emotional relationship. With the girl, intercourse is acceptable, but love is more doubtful. Today she said, "Of course I'd be annoyed if you weren't upset."'

Analyst 'You are using society's prohibition of incest between son and mother because you cannot find the man who will get in between you and your mother, which means that father did not play his part here, and so you have no hate and no fear of man and you are back in the old position of either being frustrated by the woman or else developing an internal inhibition.'

Patient 'It is the girl who prohibits.'

Analyst 'You are all the time looking for a man who will say "No" at the right moment; someone you could hate or defy and with whom you could come to terms, and you are just a little bit allowing me to be in that position in so far as you got a little bit angry with me.'

Patient 'It just occurred to me that it must be the end of the time and that in a way that is saying "No".'

Analyst At this moment, as it was time, I said, "In that case I am saying "No", which means no more analysis today. I am coming in between you and analysis and sending you off.'

Tuesday, 5 April

Patient 'Nothing seems to come except to repeat that contemporary problems don't seem to produce much, but there are two things about this: one is that this provides an easy way of starting, and the other is that recently contemporary problems have seemed to be much more useful. I am wondering why this should have been so.'

Analyst 'I consider that the reason is that you have been less dissociated, if I may use that word.'

Patient 'Yes.'

Analyst 'It has been less a question of either external phenomena or inner phenomena, and I have been able to stand at the borderline and speak about both because of the changes in yourself.'

Patient 'Oh, I see. Every now and again I seem to want to stand still and take stock. I find that I am much more in the world in my management of patients and the discussion of them. A year ago I felt as if I was two people, and now these two seem to mesh in with each other.

'It may be a coincidence but it has been since I started with the girl friend that I have had less need for withdrawal. Also I am less worried altogether about making decisions. Another thing, I am able to take a genuine pride if things go well with a patient, whereas I used to be just pleased feeling that I had struck lucky. Now it seems that I can realize when I have done something well.'

Analyst 'Going with this will be an ability to allow that I may do well with you.'

Patient 'Yes, you are less of a magician. I had to assume that you were professionally perfect, and now I can see you as a person trying your best to apply skill.' *Pause.* 'I have noticed an ability to get more feeling out of surroundings. Listening to gramophone records last night I found myself excited and at one time sentimental. I have known these records for a long time but have never had this sort of feeling about music. Another thing is a real capacity now to be jealous, emotionally rather than academically. I am definitely jealous of this other man who is in the life of the girl friend. I used to act as if I were jealous but now I really am.'

Analyst 'It is very uncomfortable being jealous but you prefer the discomfort to the former lack of feeling.'

Patient 'Yes, in the past there was a general lack of emotional reaction.' (The patient put his foot on the floor.) *Pause.* 'Sometimes I put my foot on the floor and it occurs to me that it might be important. It is as if I am getting my feet on the ground and just then there was a feeling of mild protest. Why should I stay on this couch? It was symbolic of something.'

Analyst 'In the last few weeks you have put your foot on the floor half a dozen times, and on each occasion I think I have been able to see that it was related to some kind of new relationship to external reality.'

Patient 'I did not know that I had done it before. It's got something to do with what turned up earlier as jumping up or somersaulting backwards off the couch.'[1]

Analyst 'In a way it is the very first step to ending the analysis, and in another way to establishing an equality with me which is the opposite of dependence.'

Pause.

Patient 'Recently I have become less stable, more easily upset, and I feel this to be a development in the analysis. It is a new phase.'

Analyst (Patient sleepy.) I made an interpretation linking my bringing about the end of the hour with the idea of the end of analysis.

Patient 'I was sleepy then. It is difficult to get at ideas. I can get at ideas in a dreamlike condition, but as I begin to wake they seem to be inappropriate. In any case the fantasy is not describable in words. It is more of a kind of action. I seem to be going on drifting.'

Analyst 'It is true that the sleepiness can have two sides to it. On the one hand you are searching for ideas which are not available by direct intellectual effort. On the other hand you are defending yourself against an anxiety when you do not know what it is about.'

Patient 'The things that go on when I am sleeping are not complete facts. It is difficult to make them coherent for reporting. There is less effort in talking about hospital than in talking about thoughts.' (At this point

[1] See 'Withdrawal and Regression' in the Appendix to this volume.

he became lost and he could just say so. He yawned.) 'The trouble is that I have to wake in order to say what is going on.'

Analyst 'Behind the sleepiness at the present time I think is fear of me which belongs to hate of me which derives from my ending the hour as I did.'

Patient 'I feel I ought to be more alarmed. It is more rich to be alarmed; nearer home than just having the idea of a frightening situation. Recently I have been surprised at having the confidence to be alarmed, feeling I could cope. Also I cannot get a definite answer out of you. At the time of being in hospital ill I had no conception of what was going on and I could not be alarmed.'

Analyst I made an interpretation referring to my saying 'No' in terms of ending the hour, getting between him and analysis and his anger with me and his fear of me.

Patient 'I went to sleep then. I have forgotten what was said. There is something about going to sleep in this position. On one hand I can relax here and also I can deal with things when I am asleep.'

Short sleep.

'There is one bit I just remembered. I had told you about a patient and someone else was criticizing me for telling you.'

Analyst 'This reminds me of the idea expressed recently that I might tell about you.'

Pause.

Patient 'While dreaming I was aware of waking but I felt before I woke that waking is less urgent. The treatment of this patient is more important. It occurs to me that this is very strange that I said to you that there is nothing in the immediate situation to discuss today, when actually (he was awake now) I had a bigger row with my wife than ever before, at the weekend. It was very upsetting, as it affected my daughter. I had been definitely alarmed. The thing is that my wife can and does exploit this situation, knowing that I must protect my daughter. She makes certain that we are never alone together and then at night refuses to speak so that there is nothing whatever that can be done about the matter in hand and I am left fuming. This time I was limp with anger, but I can see that I had hoped to make her start a row. But what I have to remember is that with my wife there is nothing that can be said.'

Analyst 'In some way or other in the imaginative situation I am there –' (I withdrew this interpretation as I realized that I had no clear understanding of the transference significance of the row.)

Patient 'My wife and I have no common language.'

Analyst 'You have something in common, which is that on your part there is your difficulty associated with a lack of prohibiting father, and with your wife there is a difficulty in relation to her own parents, and her attempt to achieve independence which seems to be breaking down.'

Patient 'I feel depressed when I recognize that my wife really does not want intercourse; she despises the idea of it and despises me for suggesting it, but I have to remind myself all the time that I may be responsible for putting her in that position because of my original failure with her. The difficulty about quarrelling with my wife is that I do not know what we are quarrelling about. Do I want intercourse with her; Yes, but only if she wants it. It would not be of any value to me if I have to compel her to yield and I know that I cannot make her want it. In this respect she is like her mother.'

Wednesday, 6 April

Patient 'I seem to remember that I was excited about something that arose at the end of yesterday's hour but I can't remember what it was.'

Analyst (After some beating round the bush in an attempt to get at the significant detail): 'There was the relationship of your wife to her mother.'

Patient 'Oh yes, that was it. I felt great anger with my wife because of her contempt of sex which she shares with her boy friend, and despises intercourse, and this is exactly her mother's attitude. This puts me in a dilemma because I am not prepared to accept a life in which intercourse is suppressed.'

Analyst 'The attitude of your wife which you describe gives her an identification with her mother, that is to say, of child with adult, but at the price of a renunciation of actual intercourse.'

Patient 'I deprived her of intercourse, or failed to satisfy her, and so she came to disapprove of it and to despise it.'

Analyst 'If your wife were to become independent of her mother and able to bear the idea of defiance of her mother, you had to make it worth her while, and you feel you failed. So she has reverted to dependence on her mother and a kind of identification. This compares with your own lack of a relationship with your father of rivalry and defiance, which was partly due, it seems, to his attitude.'

Patient 'There is a new difficulty on account of this. She does not want intercourse and is therefore incapable of jealousy. She rebuked me for being late. I said, "You can't complain if I sink to your level", and she (instead of becoming jealous) said, "Oh, you'll never reach my level" (probably meaning high level of idyllic love). And it's true that I have not a really deep feeling for the girl friend and I might get bored with her quite soon.'

Analyst 'You feel doubtful about the girl's ability to create a home.'

Patient 'My wife does not understand this comparison of attitudes – romance with contempt for intercourse, or opposition to intercourse. It's all right in theory but not in practice, and brings unhappiness. Actually what I do really want is to be loyal and faithful to one woman.' *Pause. Pause renewed.* 'I'm trying to remember a dream I had this morning. I did remember it and I felt it was one of those dreams that are not significant in themselves. The dreaming of it was the thing. Mother was in it, driving me in her car. My wife was there too. It's gone.'

Analyst 'What kind of car has your mother?' (I deliberately did not ask about the car in the dream.)

Patient 'Oh, she has a Hillman, but it wasn't exactly her car in the dream; it was older, and decrepit. That wasn't the point of the dream. The point was that it was dangerous, and I had to be exerting control in order to keep it straight. Mother doesn't in fact drive well. But I wouldn't be willing to admit that she could be a good driver. My wife doesn't drive. In the past I would have liked her to drive but now I don't like the idea. I don't like to think she might drive better than I do. I prefer to be superior. At the start I assumed that she was perfect, and now I'm pleased when she can't do things.'

Analyst 'This reminds me of the girl-with-the-penis idea.'

Patient 'My wife started off with a penis, and now she is in process of being deprived of it. At first I wanted her to be equal, but now I want to dominate. I want to make her jealous.' (Some description of interplay along these lines.)

Analyst 'There is a kind of sex play between you in all this?'

Patient 'Yes, but she has this contempt for sex. She may be jealous, but hiding it.'

Pause.

Analyst 'I am not clear what you mean because she might be jealous of you as a male, when you are with your girl friend – as well as the other way round.'

Patient 'Oh, I see. I hadn't thought of that. There is a contrast here with what happened a year and a half ago when I was ill in hospital, and I told my wife of an affair that seemed to be on at the time. She said, "Well, a good thing for you, it may help to solve your problems." Now she's just annoyed. I'm reminded that, her boy friend having been ill, she no longer looks for any quality –' *Abrupt break – pause – sleep.* 'It was something out of a film I went to last night, which is appropriate. A man who hated to be made a fool of. I don't want to be made a fool of.'

Analyst 'There is the problem all the time, that you have to be frustrated by your mother (your wife) or else develop internal inhibitions, because there is no man to come between you.'

Patient 'There was the ending of the hour recently.'

Analyst 'Today there is more than this since this is the last session before the Easter gap. I am soon going to come between you and analysis by saying it's time.'

Patient 'Yes. I was really pleased at the idea of a holiday from you, but at the same time I am annoyed.'

Analyst 'There is room for both feelings at once.'

Patient 'The trouble with psychoanalysis is that so much depends on it.'

Analyst 'So that while you are in analysis I do in fact remain a parent figure.'

Pause.

Patient 'I was talking with my girl friend. She had had some psychoanalysis (I don't know with whom), and she was speculating vaguely about restarting. I ought to say yes, but I couldn't advise her to. It interferes with life, and is difficult to fit in with work. But also it would interfere with her usefulness to me. I felt some of my wife's attitude, that it would be frivolous.'

Analyst 'In the *imaginary* situation I am the analyst the girl will go to, and in that respect you and I are rivals, and you prevent her from coming to me.'

Patient 'Yes, although I know she did not go to you and she would not be coming to you. I feel jealous because analysis would make her want me less, as dependence develops in her analysis.'

BREAK FOR EASTER

Tuesday, 3 May

AFTER THREE WEEKS' BREAK

Patient 'The first thing I want to say is that it seems much longer than three weeks. Mentally there has been a real break. For the first time I feel that I know what it would be like to have ended analysis. For one week I was depressed because of not coming, and then I dismissed the whole idea. The question now arises whether I should stop analysis or come less frequently. I cannot say that the result is perfect but I have come to a workable state. In regard to work I now feel that I can definitely cope. It is now a question, do I want analysis? And I find myself making plans for a holiday in a month's time which I must take if I am to get a holiday with pay. I would never have dreamed before of planning for a holiday at a time when analysis was available. In regard to home life, I have come to an understanding with my wife. There is a relative stalemate. I have come to accept the fact that there is no future in the marriage and so I plan accordingly; there is nothing to be expected.'

Analyst 'In saying this I know you are taking into consideration your wife's difficulties and also the history of the difficulty between yourself and your wife which you have told me about.'

Patient 'Yes, I can see now that it was a mistake our getting married. I feel that it was destined to failure from the beginning and we were never suited. I now find I feel resentment against coming here. It is an illogical thing. I have the idea that you are keeping me against my will. I find I am expecting you to say, "You cannot go", and I will be fighting for my right to go.'

Analyst 'If I have a definite attitude of this kind then at any rate there is something there to defy.'

Patient 'Yes, the decision then is not just simply entirely mine.' (That is, the decision is not based on abstract thinking but on feelings and reactions.) 'I feel I am being hypochondriacal about myself in order to carry on on a basis of need. I have to plead ill-health.'

Analyst 'There seems to be a changeover from needing to wanting, and along with wanting goes not wanting.'

Patient 'And therefore I have come to a position in which I can weigh things up.'

Analyst 'In accordance with this I am changing over from being a therapist to a person, and here the fact of your father's death comes in and my being alive, a human being. You have spoken of the way in which father's illness and death, as well as his general attitude, left you with a burden of personal decisions at a time when you needed a father to identify with and to react against.'

Patient 'Yes, it is also important to remember how my whole attitude has changed since the girl came on the scene. It is this that gave purpose to my life although this seems rather pompous. I have of course considerable anxiety as to what will happen if the relationship to the girl breaks down. Will I come crawling back to analysis? In a way the girl takes your place, because there is an element of bravado both in not coming for more analysis and in continuing with the girl. I wonder how much of life is real.'

Analyst 'The relationship to the girl is related also to the analysis and became possible as you began to exist and to have a capacity therefore for feeling real.'

Patient 'Yes. For instance, coming along today I went to the Academy to look at pictures. I could almost say this is the first time I have enjoyed such an experience. Certainly for the two years I have not been able to manage this. I would always have pretended but it would have been a fraud and a waste of time. I enjoyed the pictures without a frantic search for feeling real. I would always have had to try to think up something to say. I might have been able to manage the cinema or the theatre where there are people to identify with but not going to see a picture exhibition. Pictures require of one a much greater degree of personal stability and independence.'

Analyst 'Pictures do not come to meet you so much. You have to put something into them.'

Patient 'All this makes me wonder, as I see the great progress that has been made in this analysis, whether it is foolish to stop here, because there might be further progress. The trouble is that the decision to leave off might be quite arbitrary. When I first came to you in the war it was an arbitrary decision, and I stopped simply because it was inconvenient. This was unsatisfactory. When I came to you this time there was a definite reason. I was ill and had need of analysis. Now I have gone back to the first state in the sense that as I no longer need analysis it has become like a game and I keep on wondering, is it necessary?'

Analyst 'If you are able to play in this way, that is also a change brought about through the analysis.'

Patient 'Yes, I had a great difficulty about playing and always if I played I wondered, "Is it permissible? Is it not too frivolous? Dare I play?" I had to take deliberate responsibility whenever I was unserious. It always seemed like just playing, meaning that something more serious ought to be going on. I wonder whether my education was too serious and play may have been given too small a part. I was discussing with someone whether play ought to be constructive. I found myself saying, under the influence, I feel, of what we have found in the analysis, that there ought not to be too obvious a constructive element. The Montessori principle can destroy the idea of the value of play. It is as if one is inculcating the idea that play is naughty or immoral. I see that play has a value in its own right and I am aware of having missed something throughout childhood. I played in spite of my parents and also in play was always alone and lonely. With my wife if there is any play it is always serious, whereas with the girl play is spontaneous, and enoyable for itself.'

Analyst 'The pictures also have a value in their own right, I think you are saying, and are not part of the management of external reality or of a direct kind like work.'

Patient 'I would like to go home and tell my wife about the pictures but the very fact of telling her would turn it again into something with a purpose. I would be talking in order to show her that I got somewhere. It would be only valuable if talking about pictures came quite spontaneously.'

Analyst 'I am not quite sure what you feel about your wife; whether she would have been originally able to play or whether she has developed a seriousness in relation to the marriage with you.'

Patient 'She has the same sort of attitude but it is quite a lot of fitting-in with me. She probably could be spontaneous. My wife must undoubtedly have found me very tedious in my inability to play. I am getting away really from the urgent problem which must be solved within a few days. The question of a new job has to be settled. Shall I plan to fit in my job with psychoanalysis, or can I afford now to think of the future and of a career and fit in psychoanalysis with these plans? This might involve coming less frequently or even leaving off for a time. There was a pointer when I was discussing things with my wife and she said about a job, "Don't you think you would find it too worrying?" I am definitely not any longer concerned about work as something that might worry me. I know I can cope. The trouble in the hospital appointment when I broke down was partly that I could not tell what to do next.'

Analyst 'Did you ever feel drawn towards any line of development?'

Patient 'Mostly the answer would be in negatives. I considered general practice, but felt that after the decision the whole of my life is determined. I have the possibility of becoming a casualty officer, which previously would have made me feel anxious. I would now find it exciting. The horizon is clouded by practical considerations. I have considered pathology and anaesthetics, but in these specialities I must get stuck in a small niche. I feel I am no longer in need of the security afforded by the limited niche.'

Wednesday, 4 May

Patient 'I felt yesterday as a challenge. I really wanted an opinion out of you and did not get it.'

(Here followed a long discussion on a reality basis of the general situation, work, private life, and analysis.)

Analyst I included in this discussion an interpretation about the idea of leaving off analysis as a defence against anxiety and spoke about his need to get more clear on the subject of male and female as compared with the combined figure. (During this time the patient put his foot on the floor.)

I then brought in the idea of taking up psychoanalysis, making it clear that, although this had been discussed before, I had no definite evidence from him that he had it in mind. Nevertheless the subject was there as something being omitted.

Patient He said that he considered psychiatry and psychoanalysis only in a ngeative way. His mother and others had suggested to him that he might use the value of his own analysis by taking up psychiatry. He had three objections to this. First, it was a difficult subject. Secondly, the snag is that it involves too much sitting and talking and little activity. Thirdly, there is the amount of work that has to be done with long hours and comparatively little result. Also he had a definite hostility towards psychiatry, knowing that he was always clumsy about this branch of medicine, could not understand it and knew no basic terminology. Only today he had, he said, a patient who needed psychiatry and who ought to have been classified. 'I had no ideas as to an approach. If I used the word "mania" this was simply to impress officials. There is no question of a clinical entity, and to have been honest I should have written "off his rocker". This, however, would not have impressed the DAO. I would like to add that the resistance to any understanding of psychological medicine is very widespread. I find it amongst all my colleagues. Further, I now have to consider how much importance to attach to the social aspects in determining my career. With such an unsatisfactory home it would seem that there are certain branches of medicine that it would not be right to enter.' *Pause* 'I sort of feel I ought to have a more definite objective, but nothing appears. I seem to be waiting for some job to turn up and feel this is a sign of weakness.'

Analyst 'It might be helpful to look once more at your change-over to doctoring from engineering.'

Patient 'Well, that arose out of the fact that, firstly, I did not like the engineering students; secondly, I was not good at engineering as such; and thirdly, I hated the idea of an office job. I felt I must deal with people. It would be more satisfactory and offer more scope. I was in despair about factory work, dealing all the time with inanimate objects. Taking up medicine got me out of this gloomy prospect. There are also other circumstances, such as the fact of my father's illness and something carried over from my father of a political nature. I suppose there is a missionary spirit somewhere and I must find it a worthy occupation. In this way I got tremendous relief at leaving engineering. Here at last I felt I could look forward with pleasure for the first time. It occurs to me now, and I do not think I have ever thought of this before, that my father did not want to be an engineer. He wanted a university career but his father died and he had to run his father's business. He was always dissatisfied as an engineer. He might have been a barrister or a teacher; his subject was maths. Unfortunately he had poor handwriting and was no good at spelling, and I seem to have inherited these characteristics. He longed for something more erudite than what is called for in engineering. He ought to have been a professor. At the start I took up medicine, therefore, because I needed something to justify myself, but now this motive has faded and I feel more that I want to look after my own happiness, and this involves not getting stuck in a narrow groove. I feel now that almost any branch of medicine would do. If someone were to talk convincingly along any line I could probably be led, but not into business or engineering.'

Analyst 'Probably with everyone to some extent there is a dependence on what turns up.'

Patient 'Yes, but I don't like to feel that it is so.' *Pause.* 'Here I feel I want to come back to the question of my wife and her responsibility for placing me in this dilemma so that I have to consider social factors in my career since they are not satisfactory in my home life. How much can I blame on to her? It is probably wrong to accuse her. It is certainly to some extent my fault. I know I cannot blame her but in my marriage I cannot achieve anything.' (Foot on floor.) 'Will it ever be possible or will there always be an incompleteness? In my marriage I looked for friendship without effort but it did not work. Shall I continue the tremendous struggle? Or settle down to life without bother and without friends and without sex? I feel that my wife makes everything seem my fault, and so I react and make it hers.' *Pause.* (It was time for the end of the session, but I had started late.) 'I do not feel I want to say any more; I might say too much and overstep the time limit. My last remarks evoked no response. I feel they did not go down well.'

Analyst 'Firstly, there is myself in the role of a person who is alive with whom you can discuss things on a reality basis, and this puts me in the position of your father. Secondly, there is something left over from yesterday where you had the feeling of myself holding onto you, not wanting you to go. I think that this is the point that you are wanting me to bring into the analysis, and you have been waiting for it and felt dissatisfied when it did not come. You were expressing by having this idea a wish I would hold onto you. From this position you could get away, but you cannot get away from someone who will not hold you because you do not want to be held and accept dependence.'

Thursday, 5 May

(This note was written after some delay.)

Patient 'I will begin by saying that after last time it is difficult to produce further material. If there is only one month more before a new break and possibly an ending, will it be worth while producing new things? I am comparing it with the difficulty that I experienced before the Easter break. This seems to be a potent barrier. I have a feeling that ideas need not come. Perhaps the idea of an ending is based on an unrealistic assessment of the present position. Before I looked forward to an ability in the future to overcome difficulties.' *Pause.* 'I am reminding myself that in the past two sessions we spent a lot of time discussing practical details. There was little actual material of a more personal nature.'

Analyst 'You will remember that sometimes you have complained that real things did not seem important in the analysis, and you are comparing them now with the other kind of material.'

Patient 'Sometimes it seems that the deeper material is not so productive. It might be considered too frivolous, too conscious or something. I seem to be trying to produce the right thing. I often feel guilty that I may be wasting the time or fabricating in a way that is elaborate and meaningless.'

Analyst 'All the time there is myself holding you, and further there are the various methods; on the one hand my general management, and on the other hand the interpretations of material.'

Patient 'I am thinking of my father. Possibly father seemed to reject while mother would hold back. I feel hostile to the idea of mother holding me back, that is to say instead of father.' *Pause.* 'It is just possible that father failed me when I was an infant or a child. It's indefinite. It is an idea suggested some years ago. The idea is there of a child finding his father and being let down but I do not think this is true for me.'

Analyst 'I think that something may come in here which I have derived to some extent from your mother and I have spoken to you before about it. When your mother first spoke about your father before I saw you in the first treatment, she told me that your father was perfect. She obviously idolized him. I think she recovered from this afterwards in her own analysis. I think that you are trying to get to a statement of your feelings about this.'

Patient 'Yes, there is something here. It is true that my father seems to have become less and less perfect as seen in retrospect. His attitude to child education was too theoretical; also in other ways his imperfections and inadequacies have always been shattering discoveries. There is a new idea here of his perfection, that it was mother's idea of him and that it had been accepted by me as self-evident truth. I was amazed in childhood to find imperfections. I can think of an instance when he played cricket at school – fathers versus boys. His movements were clumsy as compared with those of other fathers. On the one hand I assumed perfection and found it very difficult when discovering imperfection. On the other hand there were some difficulties arising out of this idea of perfection. On the whole I suppressed the imperfections that I noticed.'

Analyst 'The important thing would be that this idea of his perfection coming from mother would mean that she did not love him; not being concerned with a real person, she emphasized the quality of perfection. I think that you felt the whole thing as an absence of love between mother and father.'

Patient 'It's really just exactly like this with me and my wife. I had the idea that she was perfect and built her up that way though I was aware of its illogicality. When I found that she did not want me the whole structure broke down, and was no use.'

Analyst 'There is something like this about me too.'

Patient 'Well, yes, at the start I assumed perfection. And again I brushed aside all the little evidence of imperfection. I suppose one has to in this position. I would have to think that if you were imperfect you were not an expert. In the analytic situation if you are not perfect then I have to be doing it myself. I suppose situations arise in which we can discuss things on the basis of equality, jokes for instance. I find myself excited and amused. I feel that you are disappointed or annoyed. The idea of perfection is unsatisfactory.'

Analyst 'The idea of my perfection could be used as a defence when you have an anxiety about a relationship in which there is feeling and all sorts of imaginary possible outcomes.'

Patient 'The alarming thing about equality is that we are then both children, and the question is, where is father? We know where we are if one of us is the father.'

Analyst 'You are hovering here between the idea of your relation to mother alone and your relation to father and mother as a triangle. If father is perfect, then there is nothing you can do except be perfect too, and then you and father are identified with each other. There is no clash. If on the other hand you are two human beings who are fond of mother, then there is a clash. I think you would have discovered this in your own family if it had not been for the fact that you have two daughters. A boy would have brought out this point of the rivalry between him and his father in relation to mother.'

Patient 'I feel that you are introducing a big problem. I never became human. I have missed it.'

Analyst 'I am reminded that you did not consider psychiatry or psychoanalysis as a career on the grounds that you would not be perfect almost immediately.'

Patient 'I have never really accepted not being good at something.'

Analyst 'Your life was founded on a basis of perfection-imperfection which had to turn up and came along as illness.'

Patient 'Imperfect for me means being rejected.'

Analyst 'When I think of what you have told me of your wife I realize that I know nothing at all about her except her perfections and imperfections. I have no picture of her as a woman. I think this is not my fault.'

Patient 'I do not know if I could describe her. I have tended to assume that you are not interested in her as a woman. Also I always have a difficulty in describing people. I never can describe a personality, the colour of people's hair, and all that sort of thing. It occurs to me that others perhaps do describe people in their analyses, and so therefore I felt immediately that you have made a criticism of me. I am always reluctant to use Christian names and I noticed the other day that I used a masculine name that sounds like my wife's Christian name, and behind the mistake was a description of my wife who for me has masculine qualities.'

Monday, 9 May

Patient 'Last time I left here with a feeling of impotence; I mean sexual impotence. I can't think exactly what happened. There was a definite change in what I was like as compared with before I came. The change definitely had a relationship to the session. I had arranged to meet the girl friend and it was the same with her. I was very disturbed. There is the complication that her behaviour has changed. She is cooling off, getting more out of her previous boy friend. He excites her more than I do, so I am becoming somewhat of a nuisance. This produces a dilemma, to fight or to walk out? But to walk out means that I am left with nothing, yet that is not a good reason for hanging on. I explained to her that I did not like acting second fiddle, but I do not know how genuine it all was. Coming here it occurred to me that perhaps I have more need for analysis, that I had been too optimistic about the idea of the end; on the other hand it must be wrong to use coming here as a direct help out of a difficult situation. This is the sort of thing my wife accuses me of doing, and it is a general criticism levelled against psychoanalysis. It is a lazy way out of difficulties.'

Analyst 'You can look at it that there are two of my roles here as analyst covering this subject. In one I am as if your father had come alive, or an uncle, and you have a person to talk things over with. This is not my main function, however, although an important one. There is myself as psychoanalyst in relation to whom changes occur in yourself which affect you in a more general way, and which do not concern the actual solution of problems at hand.'

Patient 'I feel it is wrong to use you the first way; an extravagant thing.'

Analyst 'One does not exclude the other, and it is important for you to find out that I am not rigidly set in one or other role.'

Patient 'The old difficulties have come back, like waking up in the early morning. Has the benefit of analysis been lost? What was it that did happen in the last session? I know it was something to do with father and mother.' *Pause*. 'It was something to do with mother idolizing father and so I could not compete. Why did this produce impotence?'

Analyst 'The first thing we have to consider is this: was I right in what I said?'

Patient 'Well, if it was not right it was reasonable. And I feel the fact that it produced a reaction means that it probably was right. When you say something wrong the test usually is that it has no effect. Right or not, I am worried about the discovery of mother looking at father as a symbol of perfection.' *Pause*. 'I have tended always to expect others to look at me in the same light, and I had no hope of being regarded as perfect. As soon as there was any criticism or evidence that I was second-rate, I became depressed or unduly concerned. There is only one way to achieve anything and that is by perfection.'

Analyst 'All the time you are saying that you have no hope whatever of being loved.'

Patient 'Yes, with other people and especially with girls it is all right at the beginning when there is a prospect of being perfect, then gradually as it becomes obvious that there is imperfection the thing gets out of control and I have no confidence. With this girl for the first time I struggled against this and achieved a more normal relationship; at any rate sexually I seem to be perfect, but after last time I feel I can no longer cope. She did not regard me as ideal but as a satisfactory lover. An illusion is shattered, so I go back to the ordinary position of competing with others, a position I never like. If I am second-rate, then I run away.'

Analyst 'The difficulty seems to be in thinking of men as human beings fighting for a position on account of love for a third person. In that position men have to consider, "Is the third person worth while?" '

Patient 'I think that I only fight if I am sure I will win.'

Analyst 'You are not fighting for the girl but to establish who it is that is perfect.'

Patient 'An important word carries over from last time, which is rejection. Imperfection means rejection.'

Analyst 'You spoke of a reason for ending the analysis being its perfection or your having reached a stage of perfection.'

Patient 'Rejection comes in again here. Do I go ahead to perfection and stop because of obviously having reached this aim, or do we work on a basis in which perfection is not important? In which case I am either rejected at some point or else I decide not to want to come any more. The danger is of adopting the idea of not coming in order to avoid rejection.' *Pause.* 'Just then I was avoiding thinking about here. I was thinking of a minor thing – shall I have a bath tonight? What about washing my hair? The whole point is that I was not being here.'

Analyst 'From my point of view you did achieve going away from me. You walked out and you were able to tell me about it, on account of what we had been saying.'

Patient 'The idea occurs to me, and this is quite new to me, would you follow or not if I walked out? If I walked out I have to turn round and come back, which means tell you about it. The whole thing is, if one walks out, will anybody be upset? Will anybody want to bring one back? It is a very uncomfortable thought to walk out and not to be asked to come back. It makes me think of the differences in child education. What do you do when a child is naughty? My father, for instance – only I think I am not really describing my father accurately – would deal with a child's temper tantrum by ignoring it. No, it's not especially father. It is said to produce results; if a child discovers he is ignored he stops. From the child's point of view I can see that this is an insult.'

Analyst 'It leaves him with the thought that if he goes off he is abandoned.'

Patient 'As a matter of fact I remember father was the opposite. If his children were naughty he said "They are unhappy and need sympathy" and he acted on that principle.' (NB Analyst remembers having been told about this in the first part of the analysis). 'He neither scolded nor ignored.'

Analyst 'This would surely produce a kind of paralysis in regard to ordinary rivalry. I can see the value in saying that a child with tempers is unhappy, but I think that your father avoided the ordinary clashes that belong to the father–son relationship.'

Patient 'I think he was like me. A clash was allowed by him only if he knew that he would win. In this context about fighting, it seems senseless to fight if one knows one will lose. I fail to see how in the old-time duelling, honour could be satisfied by being killed. It seems pointless.'

Analyst 'The subject is from your point of view one which can only be spoken of in terms of actual fights. You are not at the present time able to employ fantasy or playing or the easing of the situation which is shown in the touché of the duellist. You can only think in terms at the moment of actual death of one of you if you and your father were to fight, and therefore you have to make quite certain that the prize is worthwhile.

Patient 'This is connected with my wondering whether the hour is near its end. It is part of the same thing. If I go on I may get stopped, and that means losing or being thrown out. If I am lying on the couch and it is time, I feel that you order me out.' (This occurred seven minutes before the end of the hour.) 'We effect a compromise in that I gradually come to an end and have no more to say and then you say it's time. I am prepared in advance but, even so, get an unpleasant surprise.'

Analyst 'It is not usual for you to deal with this matter several minutes before the end.'

Patient 'I usually keep quite about it but I feel uncomfortable. It is very difficult to be stopped in midstream.'

Analyst 'I know that the expression "stopped in midstream" is a metaphor but it is the nearest you have come to the idea of castration. I would say that it was as if you were stopped passing water in the middle of doing so and it brings to mind three degrees of rivalry; one in which there is perfection and the only thing you can do is to be perfect, too. The second is that you and your rival kill each other; and the third, which has now been introduced, is that one of the two is maimed.'

Patient 'I accept the idea here of being stopped in the middle of passing water; it is also very much as if one were stopped in the middle of intercourse.'

Analyst 'We thus come around to your using the word impotence in describing your feelings after the end of yesterday's session. I would like to join up the idea of your being interrupted in intercourse with your own impulses as a child to interrupt your parents when they were together.'

Tuesday, 10 May

Patient 'I was agitated last night. I suppose there were several reasons. One was the deterioration of the relationship with the girl friend which has rendered home less tolerable. There was also what happened here. I cannot quite make out why. Is it something real or is it just wishful thinking? There is certainly an element of wanting to feel disturbed by the analytic sessions. I feel that it is the only evidence I have of something happening. I feel very disappointed if there is no disturbance which to me means no progress. The distress of the last two sessions has been satisfactory from this point of view.'

Analyst 'Shall I speak about what has been happening?'

Patient 'Well, yes' (doubtful), 'I think it would be a good idea.'

Analyst 'The idea of rivalry with a man which has been so difficult for you to arrive at seems to have turned up in the relationship to me. You felt impotent after the session before last, and in the last session you came round to the idea of being cut off in midstream so that in fantasy the idea had been introduced of two men, one of whom maims the other. Previously there had only been killing and this meant that the rivalry situation was not worth taking up.'

Patient 'I cannot quite explain why with girls I have a special difficulty in regard to flattery, which after all is part of the technique of love-making. It feels unreal. About girls I do not seem to be able to build up words in praise. Is this stretching things too far? It seems to me that there is a link here with the avoidance of rivalry.'

Analyst 'One link would be that the girl must claim you without being won.'

Patient 'Yes, so that has been the experience – that the girl must come and get me.'

Analyst 'You are referring to rivalry in the process of love-making.'

Patient 'It seems to me intolerable that there should be rivalry over love-making about a girl.'

Analyst 'If the girl does not choose you, then you feel abandoned.'

Patient 'It has happened with regard to my wife and also with the girl. Now that I have become a nuisance she can only pity me.'

Analyst 'There is something of this kind that could be spoken of in terms of yourself as a small child with your parents and rivalry with father in regard to gaining mother's affections.'

                                        Pause.

Patient 'I do not think there is any connection of that kind.'

Analyst 'Perhaps you had something else in mind.'

Patient 'Yes, I was thinking out what to do in the future. It was suggested by the girl friend that I should do a Casualty job as there was one available in her hospital. I had never thought of it till then. Now there is a Casualty job available in "X", non-resident. I am wondering whether to apply. There are some advantages. For instance, I could come here and manage to keep on with the analysis if evening times are available; also there are practical things, I would not have to pay a resident fee and I would save a pound a week. It would be strenuous; mean getting up early in the mornings; also I should be home more and would have to face up to home difficulties, but I feel attracted by the idea. The Casualty job would not be leading on immediately to a career but it would be a satisfactory way of postponing a decision.'

Analyst 'Included in all this is the idea of wanting to continue the analysis.'

Patient 'Yes, psychoanalysis bites into free time and makes it difficult to have time for friendships, but I am wanting to continue with it.'

Analyst 'How far will it interfere with your relationship with the girl friend?'

Patient 'That has now become unimportant. It has gone by the board. I cannot seriously weigh it in with the other factors.'

Analyst 'What are your prospects if you apply?'

Patient 'I have already telephoned the present Casualty officer and discussed the job with him, and there appears to be a good prospect except that I have done no surgery before. At any rate, I can apply and see. This means psychoanalysis for another year.'

Analyst 'This gives you time to come round in your own way to your idea of the final aim.'

Patient 'Yes.' (Theme developed.) 'Also there are perquisites in the job. There is a further point which is very curious. I am attracted geographically; it is on the other side of London and I know "X", of course, on account of the hospital. Perhaps this is not very important but it makes the job more attractive. It probably is nearer to here.'

Pause.

Analyst 'Something has happened. You have walked off and you found that I have not abandoned you. You walked off by definitely considering stopping analysis, and also, a few months ago, by having thoughts that were not obviously in the line of what was going on here in this room.'[1]

Pause.

Patient 'I feel a certain amount of general excitement. The idea of a new job partly, and this providing a way of getting round difficulties about stopping analysis, but this excitement makes it difficult for me to get down to anything else just now. Is not this rather common, that one comes round to something absorbing and for a limited time it is difficult to get on to a different subject? Now I want to get up and take action immediately. I feel a strain as if I were on a leash. I want to deal with it.'

Analyst 'How much easier it is to have something like this that you can actively deal with than this business of psychoanalysis where you have to wait for things to happen.'

Patient 'I feel guilty about the way I have got jobs during the last two years.

---

[1] See 'Withdrawal and Regression' in the Appendix to this volume.

They have come without my taking any active steps except going once to the British Medical Association. Everything else follows. I do not want to drift on any more. It is disgraceful. I am ashamed. I have a feeling of weakness, drifting with the tide, and in any case I am not decided on a career. Even with getting a girl I cannot go out of the way to start but drift along. When I went to college after school I hardly applied but drifted into it, and even doing medicine the decision was to some extent mother's. She pushed me into it a bit. I feel very much sympathy with my wife, who complains when I am shopping that I can never decide on anything. I can never choose a present. My wife despises me. So I am excited at the idea of going and getting which has now come my way. My wife also criticizes me that if I go out with her she has to choose where to go.'

(The important thing in this session was the recovery from hopeless-ness shown in a general change of mood as compared with the previous hour.)

Friday, 13 May

(He arrived ten minutes late, which was unusual; this meant that at the end of the hour there would inevitably be a sense of 'being cut off in midstream'.)

Patient 'There is really nothing to say, except that I've continued to feel slightly better. The tension and the anxiety seem to have passed. This is in part related to the ending of the affair with the girl. The end has brought relief. I'm aware that there was a good deal of pretence in the whole thing.'

Analyst 'Intellectually you have all the time been prepared for this ending, but emotionally it is a matter of experiencing. Perhaps you are sad?'

Patient 'Not so much sadness. It's more like desolation, despair, a feeling of "never again". As I look back, I see I was aware that I was playing a game, and the game was to keep up the illusion; that in itself is a positive thing for me since formerly I could not play.'

Analyst 'Playing with enjoyment.'

Patient 'Yes.' *Pause.* 'Something has happened over the last few months; I have certainly more ability to be frivolous, or lighthearted, though still self-conscious about it. But the game was to be frivolous, and it is as if all the time I disowned this being frivolous even while it was on. I was lighthearted in disguise. Of course there are times when I get tired or depressed and when tension returns, as if it's too much effort to create this other person that is me being lighthearted. So I'm not really quite spontaneous.'

Pause.

Analyst 'What about you here, with me?'

Patient 'Well, that's different. There's no point in having an artificial self here, or in being frivolous either. I can discard all that here and be my own self. Sometimes I have to drift away from here to get deep, and so I'm somewhere else, as if I leave my body and wander in my mind.' *Pause.* 'This drifting is hard to put into words.' (Compare previous withdrawals.) 'I have an image, and part of me wants to say it but another part says "No, you can't", and the result is silence. Just now I'm in that mood, and in danger of going to sleep because there is nothing pressing to be said. So I wander, and forget I'm here.' *Pause.* 'There's a curious analogy that occurs to me. Those men clearing the wall opposite in painters' cradles. I pictured myself doing the same, lazily swaying in and out of here as if in a painter's cradle. I can't help feeling there's something I want to say but fear to say. Last time felt satisfactory, because of the anxiety of the tension – now, however, I feel better and I don't seem to want to risk something fresh. Also, it's a curious idea, but I feel just now that I'm an assistant in here to help advise about someone else.'

Analyst 'That's true in a way, as you often can be said to bring yourself, and at one time we used to talk about you, and you yourself hardly came at all.

'You are wanting me to help you to see the way in which your present difficulties are related to the idea of rivalry that has come up recently. You first arrived at a recognition that there could be rivalry with one or two males getting killed, and the fight was not then worthwhile. Then you felt near the idea of two males in a clash, and one could be maimed and survive, and then there is the other theme of being abandoned.'

Patient 'I can say about that, that if I bring myself, the part that is due to be brought is reluctant to come. I have to keep on bringing it back.'

Analyst 'This self cannot stand the idea of possibly being abandoned.'

Patient 'Yes.' (Unconvincingly.) *Immediate sleep.*

Analyst 'You did actually sleep then.'

Patient 'I can't think why because I'm not tired.'

Analyst 'There is something really dangerous about me, and it was the word impotent that you used and meant to use a few days ago to describe the state I brought about in you. The affair with the girl friend happened to end at the same time, and I now wonder whether it was not as much brought about that evening by the situation here as by the change in the girl.'

Patient 'Yes.' *Sleep, momentary.* 'I have a difficult task avoiding sleep. If I keep awake I keep back my thoughts; if I release control I go to sleep.'

Analyst 'So that on the whole sleep is the more productive of the two alternatives.'

Patient 'I feel that for the first time for some weeks there is no immediate problem, no distraction, and therefore my reluctance is shown up. I would like to know what it is that I fear.'

Analyst 'That if you yourself come, and get into contact with me here, you will be maimed.'

Patient 'Who will be maimed, me or the other?'

Analyst 'You.' *Sleep, momentary.*

Patient 'There's an analogy between leaving the girl and leaving here. I fight to go on here, and run away from the idea of being maimed.'

Analyst 'Soon the end of the hour will come, and then I shall be quite literally in the position of someone who is maiming you. I say this while you are still here and before the moment for stopping has arrived. I think that the holiday was experienced by you as a serious maiming of you by me.'

Patient 'Today is exceptional in this matter of going to sleep. It must have something to do with the topic of father being perfect, and my not being able to compete, and all that.'

(As if the patient had not really heard my interpretation in spite of his just managing to say yes before going to sleep each time.)

Analyst 'Yes, father and you in rivalry brings dangers, especially if you include actively making love. I am not sure if you feel father could make love?'

Pause.

Patient 'I've nothing to add, only to say the same in different words. It needs much more work to adapt oneself to diverting a woman's attention. The phrase "I'm not ready for it" occurs to me. It's all very vague.'

Analyst 'It seems you kept your penis and your physical potency partly by giving up all making love and active diverting of attention.'

Patient 'And I would add to these negative things like not being at ease, or lighthearted, because it's curious how I'm lighthearted heavily, with great effort.'

Analyst 'There seem to be these two alternatives, and if you now begin to be able to make love actively instead of being passively chosen, you find you have a new fear – impotence.'

Patient 'I had a curious idea then. This all seems futile because father is dead. I've never come up against this before. If it's a matter of rivalry, well that's academic, since father's dead. I feel his death affects things in two ways: one, I recognize he's dead, and the other, the matter has now been talked out.'

Analyst 'It seems a funny thing to say, but at this moment I think you are forgetting that in fact I am alive. And it's now time.'

Tuesday, 17 May

Patient 'Really there is a lot to say today but I will start with what you said last time. You said you were alive. It had struck me that in the last session you were not doing any good and it seems to me now that it already symbolized that you were not alive. Your being alive is the same as your doing things, making a difference. It had occurred to me that I had no feelings about you at all, neither admiration, love, nor hate. It is as if I felt that you were not alive.'

Analyst 'So when I said I was alive it did not cut much ice.'

Patient 'No, I don't mean that, because it brought the subject to the fore. It brought something into sharper relief which arose out of a discussion that I had with my wife. I forced her to talk and forced admissions. I got her to talk about the idea of her seeing yourself at an earlier date when she decided not to do so. She has always refused to say why she decided not. She even said, "I never will tell." At the same time I guessed that she was thinking about my liability to commit suicide if she left me. She has now admitted that she wanted to ask you what would be the effect of her leaving me. She did not take the matter up, however, because in her own way she decided not to leave me at that time, in spite of having a boy friend. Also a few times ago you said you did not know what my wife was like because I never described her as a person. I felt that you implied that you had wanted to and that you deliberately did not see her. At the same time I had an idea that you had been in communication with her behind my back.'

Analyst 'What would you feel if you found that I had been in communication with her?'

Patient 'I should be shaken, whereas earlier I did not mind the idea that mother spoke to you without my knowing it, because that was reasonable. I was incapable of managing my own affairs, but now I would be very annoyed. My wife tried to persuade me not to go to the hospital, not to give up work, and not to go to psychoanalysis. She has given a new reason for not wanting me to go into hospital as a patient. She feared that because of her boy friend she might no be able to resist the temptation to leave me. At that time I was powerless. About not going to psychoanalysis her hostility was partly based on the fact that

I had always told her that I was opposed to psychoanalysis and she was horrified at my weakness. She regards psychoanalysis as an expensive form of quackery. This raises the question, how much progress really has been made here? Would I not have made just as much progress if I had not come at all? I certainly have some sympathy with her point of view. I am now continually reminding myself of my illness three times a week, and that is what my wife says, and the implication is that I had better not come and that I had better go on developing normally. I suppose you can't provide an answer. Naturally you would not say, "Yes, I am a quack", and if you were honest you would have left off the treatment if you thought it was not doing good. If my wife had concluded with a promise that she would stand by me if I left off analysis, I might try not to come any more, but she didn't. Moreover, if she did promise, would she be able to keep it up? I wonder what has been done here. The trouble is that I always try to force others to make decisions for me. I would like to make you say something, but on the other hand if you make a decision that makes me feel childish.'

Analyst 'I think that in talking about these matters you are leaving out of account the whole matter of unconscious cooperation. If you were to be coming here and I were to be failing you, I think you would have reacted by leaving off before now.'

Patient 'I am always expecting a stage at which you will say that although there is more to be done we have come to the end of what you can do.'

Analyst 'Yes, that could be.'

Patient 'Last time I certainly had doubts during the hour, "Can Winnicott cope?"'

Analyst 'There are two ways of looking at this. One is the rational, which you have talked about. There is also the fact that there are certain very big anxieties in the offing. These have to do with the new developments belonging to recognition that there can be rivalry between men, and the further point that in the clash between two men one could get maimed instead of killed. Incidentally, last time you came late, which is unusual, and this meant that I knew all through the hour that the end of the hour was going to feel to you like cutting off in midstream.'

Patient 'Lately I notice I am much less fussy about arriving on time. This is Tuesday, when you often keep me waiting. Previously I would have run the risk and been on time. Today I was a few minutes late and it was my own fault. It is just a matter of altered emphasis.'

Analysis 'There certainly seems to be a lessening fear in regard to this business of being on time.'

Patient 'I feel I have gone as far as to dare to be very late. A few minutes today that I was late really symbolizes being incredibly late. It was a silent protest. I do not seem to have dealt with this before, that I never let myself know the exact time during the hour. I never look at my watch. I feel I must not. The fact that there is no clock visible must be part of the technique inducing relaxation. Occasionally recently I have looked at my watch surreptitiously but felt I was being rude, but I cannot see any reason for all this.'

Analyst 'Incidentally by this means you avoid checking up on me to see whether you get your money's worth.'

Patient 'Well, by the present arrangement I sometimes get overtime and then I feel you have given me a present. If I were to look at the watch I would feel I ought to remind you that it is time.'

Analyst 'In these different ways you are engaging in rivalry situations with me in token form.'

Patient 'I would like to go back to where I was about my wife. I certainly do not know what I want and I don't know what I ought to want. It seems it would be unrealistic to make her go back on her decisions, to drive a bargain with her. It would not be worth it.'

Pause.

Analyst 'Your wife is still against psychoanalysis?'

Patient 'Yes, probably, but she does not say so openly. If she did she would have to offer something in exchange. What she would say is that she would like me to be standing on my own feet. The trouble is that she has never believed that I was ill or needing help, and the consequence is that whatever happens now from her point of view is the fault of the psychoanalytic treatment. Also I have just been offered the job of Registrar. This excited me very much. It means increased status and pay, but then I came to realize that it was very dangerous. The question is, can I do it? And also, am I burning my boats making an academic career inevitable?'

Analyst 'Which would mean, of course, never doing a surgical job.'

Patient 'No, that's not important. The important thing is that this job would give me too much opportunity to be undisciplined. In my present job I am kept at it by the patients, and their needs. As a Registrar I could get slack. In many ways I demonstrate to myself a lack of self-discipline. For instance, I decide not to smoke but then I smoke and this is in part weakness, but also it is being naughty. I have to smoke in order to defy my own discipline.'

Analyst 'Something that controls you from within is so strong that you feel liable to be paralysed by it and must defy it to retain freedom.'

Patient 'When I have time to spare I cannot make myself work sometimes.

Otherwise this inner drive would make me inhuman. Always there is the feeling that I do not want to miss something, and everything may be missed if I get into the power of this which disciplines me from within.'

Analyst 'When you can wait until you actually want to do whatever it is, you feel in a better position about it.'

Patient 'But I want so many things. For instance, there is the desire at the moment but I also feel a need to be good. The primitive desire is not the main thing. There is this feeling of a need to be good which is based on fear. Also I do not wish to be good from fear as this makes me more lonely. In this job as Registrar, if I do it well, I become remote and the prospect is terrifying. At the end of the day I will just go home and life stops. I notice that I do not want to be alone with my wife because in this way I feel cut off and she has practically no friends. In a way this is an opposition to growing up, to being a parent. If we are children we are all children together, but parents are lonely. Also it is the same thing in regard to my difficulty over talking to people. I fear that I would dominate from above, and so, as a subterfuge, I have nothing to say and then they start the conversation and I come in amongst them and thus avoid loneliness.'

Wednesday, 18 May

(On this day I personally was very tired and it was with the greatest difficulty that I could keep going. Evidence of this is clear. On this occasion the patient was not sleepy.)

Patient 'Yesterday we left off in the middle of something. I can't think what it was. I know that I said something about looking at my watch and the techniques to avoid being interrupted.'

Analyst 'I cannot for the moment say what happened at the end of the last hour, but I will let you know when I remember it.'

Patient 'I can't think what it was. I feel that my forgetting is a definite protest against something. There was something about my wife's attitude and you spoke about unconscious forms of cooperation.' *Pause.* 'There seems to be nothing in the bag today.'

Analyst 'It is coming back to me now that we spoke at the end about your feeling that if you were to be in the parent position you would be lonely and if you are in the child position you have others with you.'

Patient 'Oh yes, this fits in with my wife's criticism that I am childish and complaining in my talk. I feel that unconsciously, so to speak, I do this deliberately.'

Analyst 'This is a kind of playing. There seems to be a very sharp distinction in your mind between being in the parent position and being in the child position, as if the two were mutually exclusive.'

Patient 'Also, there is a fear of talking things out. The question is, will what I say go down well? I feel my talking is artificial and stilted.'

Analyst 'In the two extremes you either tell and direct or else you are told.'

Patient 'No, it's more the feeling that others will lean on me. It's not quite the same. It's the same idea said in another way. I ought to say that the anxiety about the new job is not only from the deep unconscious; it's also a conscious wondering, have I the ability? Something happened pictorially at that moment; someone came in from outside the house. There are unknown factors outside, but inside anxiety is dealt with, so I shut the door to prevent outside factors interfering.' *Pause*. 'I seem to be getting away. I thought for instance of a film I went to last night. It seems that I am choosing to run away. I could make the observation that if I produce ideas, that is work, but relaxation which seems to be demanded of me here is the opposite and no ideas come or I wander off.'

Analyst 'Where in fact did your getting away get you? What film?'

Patient 'Well, I went to *Carmen Jones*.'

Analyst I remarked that I had seen the film.

Patient 'A caricature of *Carmen*. This has to do with the hospital problem where the negro nurses are gradually replacing the whites. The film features all negroes and this in itself is abnormal. Even in the USA you would never find nothing but negroes. So the film was remote because it was different from real, so that the negroes and the negro nurses did not fulfil the role of friendship.'

Analyst 'You went away expecting to find children to play with but there were no brothers and sisters suitable.'

Pause.

Patient 'One thing comes in here. I went to the cinema with the girl friend and she told me that she had had an Egyptian man as an experiment, so the idea occurs, have I just been another experiment? It all becomes very impersonal. Also, could I bring myself to try the experiment of a negress woman? There is a contrast here to do with my wife who, in spite of the fact of her boy friend, still has a horror of infidelity. She would never discuss infidelity even in the abstract. She feels very uncomfortable about her boy friend because in her mind she cannot allow the idea of two at once. The idea of absolute fidelity seems to me too abstract and therefore not important. My infidelity does not matter as long as one is faithful ideologically. I think this was a reason why my wife thought she would leave me because she could not stand the idea of infidelity.' (Notes not clear at this point.) *Pause.* 'I cannot think why I cling to a hopeless situation in regard to my wife, leaving out for a moment the matter of the children. One reason is perhaps that I look at my wife as a parent. It is as if I were clinging to a mother-figure.' *Pause.* 'I seem stuck.'

Analyst 'You seem to be able to be a child in relation to mother but if you become a child there are no other children.'

Patient 'About that there are four things to be said. Firstly, in clinging to my wife I am an only child. Secondly, clinging to one's wife in this way is abnormal; society does not accept it even if my wife were willing, which she certainly is not. Thirdly, I know my wife has contempt for this attitude. Fourthly, I despise it myself. So I leave her to carry the weight of decisions about coming here. It was all right when I was ill. I could ignore her judgment then, but now I feel that her ideas offer a real challenge. By coming here I degrade myself. I am looking through my wife's eyes, and she can see that my mother and sister who have had a great deal of analysis are not normal and each in fact has gone back for more analysis. Mother is still extremely inconsistent, and this emphasizes the idea of psychoanalysis as a quackery.'

Analyst Here I tried to give the two sides of the idea of leaving off analysis. One, the rational, which he was describing clearly, and the other, his fears belonging to the development in the analysis of a triangular situation and a rivalry and castration. My interpretation was not given clearly because I was tired and also because I was not certain before I started exactly the interpretation that was called for.

Patient 'I have been off again thinking about hospital.' (At this point I myself was finding it very difficult to pay attention.)

Analyst (This interpretation was given more to keep my own attention going than for any other reason.)

'When we come to ideas of rivalry between yourself and myself you find yourself in difficulties. For instance, you have never referred to our relationship in the sense that you employ me.'

Patient 'My wife despises me and I share her feelings. If I depend on you and on her for a decision, as I do, I cannot decide myself about staying in analysis or stopping. Two nights ago she said about her boy friend that the thing that was important to her about him was that he decided to leave his own wife. This was the first time that she had made this clear. She was then in a position to decide what to do about him. He certainly did not say to her, as I feel I am doing, that if she would live with him he would leave his wife. He made the decision on his own first. My wife would need me to make a decision about psychoanalysis and not drive a bargain by saying that I will leave it off if she decides to stick by me.'

Thursday, 19 May

Patient 'I have forgotten again what happened yesterday. I always do tend
    to forget, but this has been especially true the last two times, and
    again I feel sleepy although there is no cause for it in the sense of my
    having a right to be tired.'

Analyst 'I think it may be best today for me not to try to remind you but to
    let things come. I would, however, like to say that yesterday I was
    very tired and this may have affected you. I will mention the fact that
    at the end you managed to make a criticism on the subject of there
    being too much white around here when I pointed out that the house
    opposite was being painted.'

Patient 'I should like to take the last of those points. I really had liked the
    yellow of the house opposite and I had thought that it was the natural
    colour of the stone but I see now that it was painted. The point is that I
    feel you have a deliberate policy to make everything colourless to
    provide a neutral atmosphere.'

Analyst 'Yes, there might be some truth in that. My pictures, for instance,
    are not very striking.'

Patient 'The question is, is it a policy or is Winnicott really like that? Is that
    your outlook? For instance, sometimes you have a small vase with one
    flower in it. It seems to me mean or impotent, as if you can't produce,
    as if you are barren. I have a fear that I should be left at the end of
    analysis with a barren outlook. For instance, I have no photos in my
    room. Nothing of my family. I don't want this to be true for ever. I
    read a novel, the significant part of which was that a nurse on a ship
    had no feelings. In order to convey the fact that she was hard, it said
    that in her cabin there was no ornament and no photos. I don't want
    to find this is really me.'

Analyst 'So there is a risk, if I am like that, that the analysis will leave you as
    you are.'

Patient 'Yes, in a sense depersonalized. When I was in Switzerland I
    noticed how clean it was, but characterless. The Swiss people seem to
    me to be an uninteresting sort of people. There is no evidence there of
    great culture. There is another aspect of the same subject. I noticed in
    a recent Italian documentary film – it showed electric trains, no soot
    or dirt. Efficient, but nevertheless there was a lack of the powerful
    engine, which is a romantic symbol. There will be a loss of the
    dramatic if steam engines are to be abolished.'

Analyst 'This reminds me of something which happened last time, which
    was to do with my having said "I am alive".'

Patient 'That was two times ago. Also, I am discovering the things about

you which cut across the idea of the perfect psychoanalyst. I used
to think of the psychoanalyst as always in command. I wonder if
you can carry on if you are tired. I must be boring, and all that sort
of thing.'

Analyst 'By thinking of yourself as boring just there you are bringing back
my tiredness to something coming from yourself, and getting away
from the idea of my having a private life.'

Patient 'For the first time I recognize jealousy here, that you are seeing
others.'

Analyst 'This reminds me that you said that if your wife is in the maternal
role you think of yourself as the only child. Last time there was also
this about your wife, that she talked about her boy friend's attitude,
how he had not tried to strike a bargain.'

Patient 'Oh yes, I remember all about that; certainly I feel I must be
cautious; there must be something available before I give anything
up.' *Pause.* 'I seem stuck here.' *Pause.* 'I remember about last week that
I said I could not stand on my own feet, and you said that I had to
stand on my own feet too early. This seems to fit in with the idea that I
have to make sure that there is something there before I let go.'

Analyst 'The phrase "standing on your own" reminds me of the actual
picture you gave me once of finding a baby on mother's lap and
straining to stand on your own, which produced pains in the lower
limbs.'

Patient 'It's all really a part of the picture of a child walking and holding on
to things.'

Analyst 'If people fail to hold a child in the early stages, then the child has to
take over holding himself up.'

Patient 'After last time I was thinking that masturbation fits in as a buffer
against not having sex relationships. It is something to hold on to. I
cannot tolerate the idea of no sex relationships, and one of the ways of
overcoming that difficulty is to pretend that there is no need. And it's
literally holding on to something too.'

Analyst 'You might also be speaking about thumb-sucking.' (I was aware at
this point that the patient and I were communicating without direction. Almost for the first time I felt that I as the analyst was
floundering, simply dealing with the immediate points raised, and I
was wondering how to get back to the patient's own process which I
felt I had interfered with at some point not exactly known.) 'I suppose
you are telling me that masturbation has come back.'

Patient 'Yes, and it never went altogether. Somehow I used it as a yardstick
of progress. Failure to get away from it feels like a symbol of
uncompleted progress. The idea was that a relationship with a girl

would make masturbation unnecessary, but this was not true; and in fact it ought not to be, since it would mean that the point in the relationship was simply to get away from masturbation and not something positive in regard to relationships. In any case I regard masturbation as a harmless addiction.'

Analyst (I noted here in my own mind that there would be found a relationship between the masturbation and castration fears, and that it was important that he had now told me about the return of masturbation. I thought this was not the right interpretation to make at this point.)

Pause.

Patient 'I recognize here a contradiction. I am trying to achieve independence, and yet by coming here I am more dependent. My wife does not understand this, and in fact I don't either.'

Analyst (I thought that this was the moment to try to gather the whole thing together, and I made a long interpretation which was possible because he was very much awake.)

I said that at the present time there had been a return to the type of relationship which belonged to two people, himself as an infant and his mother, the sort of thing that started with the word medium and which went right on until there appeared a third person.

Patient 'My wife's criticism of psychoanalysis has to do with the dependence.'

Analyst 'It is very painful to you yourself to be dependent, especially now that you are getting better. You run the risk of being abandoned and, in any case, developing dependence just for this analytic hour when you are independent in everyday life is a strain on you.'

Patient 'I certainly feel abandoned when you do not say anything after I have made a remark.'

Analyst 'There is also to be taken into consideration your girl friend's attitude, which must be felt by you as a rejection not only by her but by me, since she represented some aspect of me. I mentioned that I was tired last time because I felt that you would feel it to be a rejection as you are sensitive on this point.'

Patient 'As a matter of fact I didn't notice it. I was not fully there.'

Analyst 'Yes, I think it possible that you didn't notice it but I could not tell. There was also the matter of the negroes in the film and at hospital and the experiment. The question arises as to whether analysis is an experiment, and the neutrality of the psychoanalytic atmosphere seems to link up with the feeling you had that the negroes could not provide a relationship for you.'

Patient 'I recognize the fact that psychoanalysis cannot guarantee success.

At the start I had to assume that the analyst's failures, which I recognized intellectually, could not apply in the case of my analyst. I see it is a great gamble, this assumption that great progress is bound to be made.'

Analyst 'I think that when you came to me it was essential that I had to look for you and therefore to take all responsibility. You were ill and you easily accepted this, but now that you are comparatively well you find yourself having to make the decision to come to me and to take all the risks, and this is very painful.'

Patient 'It is a difficult question to decide. When is it safe to try letting go? I cannot tell till I try. It's like learning to skate; as long as you hang on to the side you can't skate. So I see that one day it won't be a transition, but a sudden breakaway. There must be a dramatic decision by me, unless you suddenly tell me to stop coming. It was the same learning to swim or to ride a bike. Father's attitude was to give support and then suddenly to let go, so I'd find that I thought I was supported but actually I was not. It worked, but I fear the same thing here. You might suddenly say: "Well, you *are* on your own now." Although it worked with the bike, it would be a shock to me here.'

Analyst I said that there have been certain difficulties since the appearance of the third person, and the course of the analysis was affected by a retreat from anxieties belonging to rivalry. Incidentally relief provided by a triangular situation was something that he could not obtain because of his retreat from it. The question therefore was at the moment one of dependence and independence, or alternatively the fear of being abandoned.

'If you were to leave off at this moment you would be establishing independence or avoiding being abandoned, but this would be breaking off in the two-person relationship and, in your case, would be avoiding the new features that belong to the triangular situation. In the triangular situation you have the chance to win or lose in the dream of a fight with father, and the fear changes from one of being rejected to one of being killed, or maimed. The important session was the one which made you go away feeling impotent, and it was as if I had damaged your potency and ended your relationship with the girl.'

Monday, 23 May

Patient 'Again I haven't any clear idea, except that I can say that since last time I have been more in the frame of mind in which I feel I could do without coming here, though I can see that there is more to be gained by coming. I mean I could manage. This ability to manage depends partly on external factors, but I have to consider what would happen if external difficulties recur. I have a great ability, however, to cope with adversity. The main bit of adversity is loneliness, and this I find less worrying than it was. About loneliness, I am mostly lonely when there is the smallest number of useful people, and now I feel a gradually expanding number of people I can use.'

Analyst 'If you can stand loneliness, then you are in a better position to make contacts, because if you fear loneliness each contact is spoiled at the beginning by the way you go at it.'

Patient 'People only enjoy your company when you are not particularly concerned whether you meet them or not. But I am making less demand now on others. And also I am very much less tense. Talking to people is not altogether easy; it requires effort, and I am all the time conscious of the feeling that I must be boring them.' *Pause.* 'There is something I thought of at the beginning of the session about not talking. That is something that happens here. I am almost obsessed with the idea that I must produce something interesting. I remember in the Queen Anne Street days (the first treatment), that I kept on saying: "I have nothing worthwhile saying." If I talked of ordinary things it was silly, frivolous, but here I do not say things sometimes because I feel they are not worthwhile saying. Outside, I find other people talk about minor things, so I have to assume that that is the normal; so I make an effort to learn how to chatter. Here I do not feel self-conscious about it. Perhaps I could talk about what I see and odd things like that; if you take these things seriously, then it is as if you are patronizing, like dealing with a rambling delirious child – "There, there, that's all right, dear," etc. Only apparently taking the thing seriously. There is an inherent difficulty in psychoanalytic situations. You put up an atmosphere of formality. You pretend to be serious and so on. Perhaps you are avoiding laughing. I feel that all my prattle is immensely valuable, but you might be laughing. If you were to say that something was rubbish I would feel very crushed.'

Analyst 'There are two elements then in your talking, the prattle element and the content. There is the prattle which is apart from talking and which is derived from babbling, just something a small child does as part of being alive.'

Patient 'But I sort of feel that I need convincing that the unserious is acceptable, although I know perfectly well theoretically that for the analyst it is acceptable. The only way left me is to force myself to be frivolous and then to disown it quickly, especially if it misfires.' *Pause.* 'I seem to be casting around for a place to start. How can I express the difficulty I have in regard to prattling or talking lightheartedly? I can come to a sudden stop. There are no more words. It is an absurd situation. Stopping means that I am showing that I am ashamed.' *Pause.* 'Again I have the idea of waiting, hoping others will talk. It is a method of avoiding responsibility. If the other starts he cannot object. And at any rate one can avoid that way being laughed at.'

Analyst 'It seems very likely that once or perhaps several times in a certain period you were prattling and then laughed at, and that this was traumatic and you made a mental note "never again".'

Patient 'There might of course have been a specific instance. It's like a lack of achievement here that there are no specific instances discovered – it gives it lack of drama.'

Analyst 'In this instance there may be a specific point. This thing relates to the question of whether you are loved or whether you are loved under certain conditions. The second is only any good to you if the first has had an innings. I am reminded also of the words "cut off in midstream". The idea is there of damage having been done to you.'

Patient 'The idea came that it is intolerable to think of talking to someone and then they are not there and one is talking into an empty space.'

Analyst 'There is always the problem for me whether to take up what you say or to concern myself with the fact of your talking.'

Patient 'The question is whether you bother to listen or not.'

Analyst 'There are two possibilities. One is that the other person goes away in fact, and the other is that the other person is preoccupied.'

Patient 'I meant the second of these.'

Analyst 'There can easily have been times when if you prattled the other person went off but if you talked in an interesting way they would stay.'

Patient 'That must happen very often in childhood.'

Analyst 'Perhaps it is the first time it happened that we are concerned with; someone who was preoccupied with you suddenly became preoccupied with something else, and to illustrate this I can take you to your own preoccupations that occur every now and again and which you sometimes describe now as going away from me here.'

Patient 'Perhaps I tried to *attack*, I mean *attract*, mother's attention and got snubbed and felt ignored. So I decided to give no more opportunity for snubbing.'

Analyst 'Probably you felt that you had snubbed me by going off.'

Patient 'No, it doesn't strike me that way. When I come back I am not concerned about that. I can come back to continue the analysis. At times it would be nice here to be able to talk trivialities, not having to work hard.'

Analyst 'You hardly believe that I could find you childish and still allow it, and in fact you have never been able to do this here.'

Patient 'A patient at the hospital described an interview with his analyst in which he had nothing to say, so he talked about the opera. He did not believe it was right to do so, and did it out of contempt for the analyst. "You are no good, so I will take you literally", but he was surprised to find that what he said was taken seriously and something came of it.'

Analyst 'As far as you bring yourself to analysis it cannot be expected that you will prattle, because when you come to report as you do, you can report content "in the other aspect of talking".'

Patient 'In a sense it is an absurd position, because I come here to be able to do the thing that I cannot do in order to be able to do this very thing which in a way you are expecting me to do.'

Analyst 'We are talking about your inability to hand over to me the care of the infant so that you could be the infant.'

Pause.

Patient 'It is rather difficult to go forward. I have got to make use of any absurd situation but that is the only way. I feel as if I have tried to be spontaneous but it has misfired.'

Analyst 'I would like to remind you of the mistake you made earlier when you said *attack* instead of *attract*.'

Patient 'Oh yes, I remember.'

Analyst 'Possibly this is the one significant word of the session, the word "attack".'

Patient 'Yes. Also, if I am spontaneous, I feel as if I will not be accepted, so I attack in order to restore the situation. This implies the idea that my temper attacks represent the destructive impulse directed at my mother because she would not listen to my prattling.'

Analyst 'You may be speaking about a very high degree of anger.'

Patient 'Again there is the risk of the end of this session here; this reproduces a situation in which mother or someone is not prepared to listen any longer.'

Analyst 'By thinking things out in advance you protect yourself from intolerable situations. Intolerable partly because they produce rage.'

Patient 'It is the same thing as plunging into water. If I am not heard it is as if I jumped in in vain and I drown. Self-control is necessary unless I am held.'

Analyst 'It is as if you were speaking about actually jumping onto someone's body and finding that they were not really ready for you because they were thinking of someone else. It would be no good if father let go the bicycle not because he intended to help you to learn to ride but because he became preoccupied with someone else.'

Patient 'This reminds me of a game of hide and seek. As a child I found the game of hide and seek very dangerous. If a child is not found the people are preoccupied. There is an intolerable sense of being abandoned.'

Tuesday, 24 May

Patient 'Again I have nothing in my head. There might be an hour when nothing comes. If I were to talk nothing but trivialities, that would be the same as nothing. I am reminded that you said yesterday that perhaps there was one significant word in the whole session, so everything else might just as well not have been said.'

Analyst 'In a sense I fell into my own trap here by dealing with content and for the time being ignoring the prattle element.'

Patient 'It is very rarely that things occur which are valuable, and they are more important than hours of discussion. Dreams and mistakes are so rare.'

Analyst 'The mistake was evidence that you exist apart from yourself reporting. It was evidence of conflict within yourself and of there being a contact somewhere.'

Patient 'I feel I ought to be trying to avoid the censorship but it is too difficult.'

Analyst 'One thing we know is that you have a tremendous fear of being laughed at and of being cut off in the middle, and you protect yourself from these dangers. Something I note is that we are again talking about your direct relationship to your mother, or to one other person who may frustrate you. Somewhere or other you are near the idea of being stopped in your relation to mother by father.'

Patient 'In that connection I remember that father was in the habit of teasing. He would leave me inwardly very cross, and out of that I think came a destructive wish, so that I wanted to kill him. I was so annoyed that he would go on teasing.'

Analyst 'We have to deal here with something in your father who avoided the direct clash with you, and yet his antagonism came through in the indirect form of teasing. There is a magic in teasing which has an effect beyond the meaning of the words.'

Patient 'There is something here which appeals to me very much. It is like satire, or sarcasm, which I use to counter teasing. It can have a withering effect. It is a powerful weapon. Satire appeals to me much more than a direct assault. If annoyed, I express myself through sarcasm, which may be very subtle and which need not be recognized by the victim.'

Analyst 'So through sarcasm and satire you have the power to wither your opponent, and it is very important to you that you take for granted that I will not be sarcastic.'

Patient 'It occurs to me that, when I wonder whether you are effective or not fully alive, it is because you are never angry; you never tease; you never are sarcastic, and never dogmatic; you will even be apologetic and ready to withdraw, to fold up in a profuse apology. If you are alive you must dominate more. On the whole you wait before making an interpretation. To come alive you would not wait. Also you never direct me. It is all negative.'

Analyst 'This means that I am dead.'

Patient 'This is in complete contrast with my father. When alive he did all these things that I have mentioned; took a strong line; so you are always mother who was not the sarcastic one, etc, etc.'

Analyst 'So it is easy for you to have a relationship to mother here.'

Patient 'It occurs to me that if you are going to be my mother that is no use because I have got one. It is father I have not got.'

Analyst 'You will see that always I am either father or mother, so that there is never more than two of us. You are therefore concerned with mother becoming preoccupied so that you feel abandoned or else with father who is dead. The idea of father interfering between you and mother does not occur, unless we think of father being carried around alive inside you somewhere, stopping you from prattling.'

Patient 'Yes, father plays the role of censor. I only succeed by the game of pretending that what I say does not come from me.' *Pause*. 'One of the things about sarcasm and satire is that there can be a double meaning which the other person does not see; I visualize people hurt, actually wounded by sarcasm. It is more effective than a direct assault, so I try to hurt that way.'

Analyst 'It is important that it can be all done in a hidden manner.'

Pause.

Patient 'One thing which is difficult to express is that if I want to praise because of love, it is harder to find a way to do it indirectly. I cannot find the equivalent of satire. When I cannot give presents, it is because I am not there when I go to get a present in the shop. If I could do it in a veiled way it might work. For instance, if I want to buy my wife flowers, in part that means that I want to show affection in a hidden way but there is a danger of being laughed at. The offer may be turned down. Somehow or other I have the picture of a small boy proud to present his mother a motion, and then it is ignored and he suffers a crushing blow. This situation comes to my mind as an idea of what psychoanalysis expects and says: The child presents his mother with a motion and is very proud, and it is ignored and disdained or disliked. That is my interpretation in psychoanalytic terms.'

Analyst 'I do not want to lose the importance of the same thing in terms of babbling, prattling, and talking. Possibly also passing water.'

Patient 'Passing water does not occur to me in the present context. All the things that I am saying could be expressed in the word "lazy". I know that psychoanalysis does not accept laziness as something existing in its own right, and that laziness is an expression of hidden objections, etc, but a lot of my difficulties can be explained on a superficial basis as laziness. Playing tennis the other day, for instance, and not doing well. One reason was that I was lazy. I did not run towards where I knew the ball would come. Instead I substituted the idea of being in the right place. But then I would find that I must do and not only know.'

Analyst 'In some way or other this avoids the risk of failure.'

Patient 'I thought: "If I go to hit the ball, that is all right if I succeed, but if not, that is silly. If I think the idea that I ought to be more to the left but I don't actually move, then I can explain the failure." The end result is ridiculous when I hit nowhere near where the ball is, but I avoid in this way a more subtle danger, and avoid some kind of blaming of myself. Also in serving, if I throw up the ball in the wrong place and I know that it is wrong, I do nevertheless hit it. After all, it might be all right. The alternative is to show that I cannot even throw the ball up.'

Analyst 'You could be saying all this in terms of talking, couldn't you? So that you avoid making the mistake like the word "attack".'

Patient 'It is back to the same thing. I don't want to let go. I don't want to move to where the ball will be. Moving means letting go. Standing still with the idea of movement is safe. Moving means letting go the place where I was. Talking freely means taking a risk. Everything is out of control.'

(At this time he was playing with a rubber band and started flicking it, making a noise, and this kind of behaviour is very unusual with him during the sessions.)

Analyst 'There seems to be a live father who dominates and who prevents you from being a child with spontaneous movements.'

Patient 'The idea of carrying around father seems to me to be just about right. He is always ready to pounce if I make a false move or an indiscretion.'

Analyst 'Which means that you cannot be your real self.'

Patient 'It's odd. It's as if I have a father instead of a superego. Or perhaps that's what a superego means.'

Analyst 'Well, there can be a pathological superego.'

Patient 'At times I do feel almost aware of carrying father round with me. When I say I am angry with myself, I mean that this father is angry with me. When I say I am discussing something with myself, it is this father and I who are discussing. Sometimes I feel almost as if I am father.'

Analyst 'The difficulty is that in your memories of your father you are not able to think of him as entering into your world and not even sponsoring it either.'

Patient 'Mine is a valid criticism of my father. He could never enter into anyone else's world at all. People simply had to go into his world.'

Friday, 27 May

Patient 'The question is where to start. How far can I get by conscious effort? At first here in analysis was the hope. Now too little happens here.'

Analyst 'I think you are wondering whether to get up and walk around while here.'

Patient 'That would make what goes on here less important. The ideal is when the subject is about sex – sometimes I feel like not bothering about sex, to wipe out all that. But shelving is not solving.' *Pause.* 'This is incidental. I might talk about abstract ideas and aims but that is unproductive. It is especially difficult at home when I talk and my wife does not answer and I get angry.'

Analyst 'There is a contrast between talking about things and discussing problems.'

Patient 'There is a barrier somewhere. I need to have some way of tearing down the barrier. After the break the barrier seems to be bigger.'

Analyst 'You were, I know, disappointed last time at the end. You expected something suddenly to happen. We are looking for the reason for the barrier.'

Pause.

Patient 'I had an idea then. I was in a dream world and I was presenting a written abstract or report. If I had to write everything down that would be very difficult because I dislike this sort of thing. I was to leave the report on your desk. The report was illegible. I am in a dilemma here. If I do not talk I feel frustrated in the treatment. This is a matter for rage. The abstract idea occurs to me that a perfect sexual relationship depends on someone else entering into my world. I need not talk then or wake. It is the same here. You ought to know what is in my mind, and what I am feeling.' (Probably asleep.) *Pause.* 'I am toying with the idea of sleep to see how far you can get without my saying anything. In practice this is silly.' (Material not recorded.)

Analyst 'I am reminding you here of your father's inability to enter into your imaginative world.'

Patient 'Oh yes, I had forgotten. He talked a great deal. It was his pet hobby.'

Analyst 'Which means that you all listened.'

Patient 'I am trying to get away from my father's intellectual approach. The ideal is to be able to play. This is still unattainable for me. Tension in myself is part of the effort to get away from the intellectual talking about play. The more I try, the less playful I become. I know I am boring because I talk instead of playing. I am not able to effect the use of substitutes for the actual. I had an idea then that talking about hitting you is like hitting you. I am not certain what I am hitting you for.'

Analyst 'This is an example of the sort of sudden action that you fear.'

Patient 'It is as if your are the obstruction. You are not lifting the barrier. Hitting you would be to force you to do something.'

Analyst 'In that case you had the fear that you would find you had suddenly hit your father.'

Patient 'I cannot recollect having actually done it. I certainly wanted to. He was difficult to hit because he showed no resistance.'

Analyst 'He was opposed to the idea of opposition.'

Patient 'If you hit father he would fold up. He would just not be there. It is different in playing where aggression might enter in.'

Analyst 'In the playing with me that you describe we were bashing without aim.'

Patient 'I am tempted to remember a discussion at the hospital about relief of tension by finding ways of expressing aggression. It is of no use. Aggression is not there.'

Analyst 'That is about father, I think.'

Patient 'Yes, he really was a pacifist.'

Analyst 'And at the same time you had no brothers for mutual loving and hating and pushing around.'

Patient 'I feel that that is what I am doing to you, pushing and pushing. I feel though that you would be damnably peaceful, limp like cotton wool; nothing firm. If I hit you, my arm would be left there; it would not come back, but I had a respect for my father's strength. With you, hitting would be out of place.'

Analyst 'You never seem to be able to find anyone to match your strength against.'

Tuesday, 31 May

Patient 'Two things occur to me. The first has to do with realizing more what you mean about my true self not coming, so that I censor everything before speaking. This makes it all impersonal, and there is no excitement or anger or elation, and I do not want to get up and hit you. It is only what we talk about, and nothing is felt or demonstrated. Others are personal, angry, and avoid getting worked up. This is a shortcoming but it cannot be manipulated. The second thing is about last night – well, it's hardly worth talking about. It doesn't add anything to the situation, but reproduces the present state of affairs. It has to do with my wife and her boy friend. In a dream my wife's mother was to blame for everything. I refused to see her. I have felt like that sometimes. In the dream she was all remote and impersonal. I have not much feeling of dislike of my mother-in-law – just annoyance.'

Analyst 'In the dream you and your mother-in-law come into a clash. Here is someone real and external, playing the part which you cannot easily give to your father.'

Patient 'I am thinking of my feelings here. The only emotional expression seems to be sleep, which is going away – negative expression.'

Analyst 'You remember that once you had the idea of brushing past me and rushing out.'

Patient 'My attitude then was the same as my wife's. I don't want to get involved. Here I am dependent and I find I need to come.'

Analyst 'One part of you is in the way between your true self and me.'

Patient 'I often wish I could add something to psychoanalysis so as to get dramatic responses. The idea is to break through the barrier of lack of feeling. My mother-in-law tries to be friendly, but this makes me shudder and I keep her distant. She irritates me. I keep picturing the idea of breaking down the barrier. It is like breaking a dam; there is a flood pent up behind; a flood of water. When I first came back I said I would like to be able to cry. It is all part of it. I need something outside to break it down. I have no courage to do it on my own. There is a need for dynamics. For emotional situations. To bring on the crying. But it only happens occasionally and always away from here. We ought to plan to break down the barriers. I picture you either unwilling to do something to unleash the forces or not able to do it.' *Pause.* 'I am still thinking the same, like walking on the edge of a wall exploring the perimeter.'

Analyst 'You have always said that you dislike the idea of the transference.'

Patient 'I am not quite sure how genuine that was. Or was it just a phase? The girl friend had some influence over me then when I said that. She despised homosexuality. So my hostility to the transference was part of a need to demonstrate to her that I was a man not needing a positive transference to a man. You see, I had to take her point of view into account.'

Pause.

Analyst 'You have described a great deal of pent up feeling and that behind the dam are tears of grief.'

Patient 'And also love. My wife would not be able to help. She can only patch up the wall which leaks. My wife would try to oppose the idea of breaking down a barrier. She would rather have me bury what is difficult to get at. She is not concerned with getting it out. The question is, will it happen and also is it necessary?'

Analyst 'The barrier is between you and me, and one of the things that it avoids is the idea of my loving you.'

Patient (Sleepiness.) 'Only odd fragments which are difficult to bring out. A feature was that there was less control, and so things were much faster.'

Analyst 'We must assume that that the lessening of control produces water, peeing, and crying.'

Patient 'Also slowness of speech belongs to the control. This explains my causing everyone to be bored.'

Analyst 'It causes an even rate of talk, because no impulse comes through.'

Pause. (Probably asleep.)

Patient 'Thought there is completely lost. Something was dramatized. Something to do with the attitude that the talking has to babbling. My mother-in-law is the opposite to myself in this controlled thinking. She talks fast all the time without worrying what she says. A lot of it is obvious nonsense. She says the first thing that comes to her head, and so I dislike it because I envy her. It is stupid, but people stop and listen, whereas with me they get bored.'

Analyst 'I suppose what she does comes straight from herself, like your prattling that you described as a feature of your early childhood.'

Patient 'I feel restless, as if I have something to break through, or is it that I want to be restless? Or is it just the idea of wanting to be restless?'

Analyst 'By this time everything is impersonal, and this has been a feature all your life.'

(Here I referred to Wordsworth's 'Ode on the Intimations of Immortality from Recollections of Early Childhood' – 'Shades of the prison-house',[1] etc, but to my surprise he was not acquainted with this.)

---

[1] 'Shades of the prison-house begin to close
Upon the growing Boy . . .'

Patient 'Today I was playing with my daughter. A child has easy spontaneity. At the start I envied her ability to rely on herself. So my
mother-in-law has retained something of childhood.'

Analyst 'It can be annoying when adults retain something of childhood.'

Patient 'When father did all the talking, it left no one any scope. I felt
hemmed in. No one had any time for me when I talked, and so it was
best not to say anything.'

Analyst 'I am reminding you of the changeover from prattling to your need
to think first, so that the content would be appreciated and people
would not laugh and you would not feel ashamed. It is rather like a
stammer, this deliberate talk of yours, which holds people.'

Patient 'Even now there seems to be hidden excitement. It is touch and go.
Will the barrier break through? When I am safely out of sight?' (Here
the patient put his foot on the floor.)

Analyst 'You put your foot on the floor, and I think that you feel at this
moment that you could act, as for instance walk away. That is an
expression of your true self.'

Patient 'Yes. It is part of the restlessness. This is the crucial moment, the
chance of a lifetime, and it is missed.'

Analyst 'Lying on the couch has to do with your attitude.'

Patient 'Yes, lying is symbolic of being controlled. It is peaceful, and that is
not what I want. I picture your suggestion that I should get up and
play a game.'

Wednesday, 1 June

Patient 'For the first time I feel that I am here myself. That means that I was
unaware of time at the end of last session. I got carried away.'

Analyst 'Your true self has its own time, in contrast to your false self which
keeps in touch with clocks.'

Patient 'When my daughter wakes, I notice that she has no idea of the time.
She imagines it is day in the middle of the night. Also I have been
waking less regularly lately. Usually I know exactly what time it is. I
had no idea of the time today and was awakened by chance by a noise.
After I left here yesterday I felt excited. The barrier was almost
broken through. The question still arises about occupying time by
talking, but there is no longer the same pressure. In the train I had
nothing to read and it was difficult to know what to do unless I slept,
but I noticed that most people are not worried by this and they are
willing to sit an hour or more with no problem in regard to the
occupation of the time. There is some progress here in that I am less
worried. At the hospital where I was a patient I was preoccupied with

the difficulty of filling in time. However could anyone live on his own, I felt. How could one cope with this problem of time? There is no question of idle chat, which is sufficient for most people.'

Analyst 'You are telling me that for the first time you might be able to be alone, which is the only satisfactory basis for making relationships.'[1]

Pause.

Patient 'It seems a bit of a pity to have stopped yesterday when everything was in full flow. The problem is how to get back.' (Here the patient had his pipe in his hands, playing with it.) 'I wonder how long it will take to break through the protective barrier. Is it your fault or mine that it takes so long? Also, is the treatment just beginning or just ending? How does one know? I do not.'

Analyst 'This matter of the barrier and its removal is not something suddenly happening now. There has been a gradual development in the course of your analysis which has brought you to your present position.'

Pause.

Patient 'In that pause I had confused thoughts. It was abstract and could not possibly be reproduced.'

Analyst 'This unintegrated state that you describe at any rate is your true self.'

Patient 'In this confused thought is extreme annoyance, aggression, some-one lying down in or on a bed, I don't know who it is. The idea came from a patient admitted today into hospital without my being told. I was dramatizing the scene. I fantasied that I went into the ward in a temper, removed the clothes off the bed, and pushed the patient out. I could see that it might also have to do with this couch here. I might turn up at the wrong time and you would be annoyed and turn me out. In a way that's what you did at the end of last hour. I was thrown out. Something that fits in here is the annoyance that I feel when I get home late at night and find my wife already gone to bed. I never complain, of course, but somehow I feel she ought to wait up.'

Analyst 'The centre of all this is the reaction you had to being thrown out at the end of last hour just when you yourself had turned up. You were in a vulnerable state.'

Patient 'Something fits in here. I had to turn my daughter out of bed this morning. My wife never gets up till I call her twice. This annoys me, although I am awake anyway. I always hope that she will get up and get the breakfast sometimes, but it's no good making a fuss; that doesn't get one anywhere. Also at hospital this morning I was in a

---

[1] Cf 'The Capacity to Be Alone' (Winnicott 1958).

mood to discharge patients. I felt annoyed that they were there occupying beds. At the time it seemed quite reasonable, but now it is obvious that this was related to the feeling that I was turned out from here.'

Analyst 'There is also the question of the end of the treatment and your feelings about this.'

Patient 'Also there is the whole question of discharging patients. What is the basis for turning them out? Is it for my sake or for theirs? Do we want them to be well or become independent as soon as possible, or to be rid of them?' *Pause.* 'There is also the feeling of wondering whether I shall change dramatically, so that others notice it. Will there be results? Others must be affected by differences in myself. How different am I for others? At the hospital where I was a patient people asked: "What is wrong with you? Why do you need analysis?" I could never explain. Would people possibly notice an easing of tension if I were easier to talk to? The crucial test is, will my wife notice? Probably she won't. She has made up her mind that I am no use. I can't expect her to change. It's too late.'

Analyst 'Your daughter would be the one who would notice.'

Patient 'About her I feel I had to wait for her to start playing, and I found it difficult to follow her. I kept on feeling, "I don't want to play or read", and was irritable, but now I feel less pressed and I can even enjoy playing. I don't know if she has noticed.'

Analyst 'I think she must notice it if you enjoy it a little.'

Patient 'I find I can now begin at last to enjoy my younger daughter. She has not come into the picture before. Her existence was only of academic importance. I never felt that she belonged to me. In a way, I would have been really pleased to have found that she was not my child. Nevertheless, I can just feel able to anticipate a change here. I am not sure I can attribute this to psychoanalysis. It may be just an intellectual process. I don't want to decide to take her on. A change in my relation to her must happen to me emotionally.'

Analyst 'To decide to take her on would be operating from the intellectual, which for you is the false self.'

Patient 'This applies to all relationships. It is a matter of deciding, and then it's no good. This reminds me of another person, which is mother. I feel guilty at having neglected her recently. In fact I have not thought of her. Why should I? But of course she pays. She is a supporter, and to that extent I can't cut her out. For a long time she did not seem to be a mother-figure to me. I blotted out the idea and did not even want to call her mother. I don't know what to call her, and this fits in with the idea that she is not a mother-figure for me.'

Analyst 'The mother-figure for you has been your analyst since a certain point in the analysis.'

Patient 'I would like to know when mother ceased to be a mother-figure. Can you help me?'

Analyst I picked out various samples, such as when he went to his mother and found a baby sister on her lap and strained to stand on his own, and also when at some point his prattle was not accepted, etc.

Patient 'This suggests to me that father was not able to play and he took everything too seriously, so I had to try to be grown up. I have occasionally speculated about orphans. Have they the same difficulty when they have no parents of their own? This is an academic point.'

Analyst 'When you have parents that you can take into yourself, a lot depends on whether these parents were rigid in some way or other, or whether they were adaptable. If you have only rigid parents to take in, you are rather in the position of orphans who have lacked some human aspect in their early care. You have been using me in the analysis to displace your mother and your father at various times.'

Thursday, 2 June

(Patient quarter of an hour late.)

Patient 'I find myself in a quandary. I ought to be able to start in a different way, since two days ago I seemed to find a new way of working. I don't like to go back to the old way of having nothing to say, and the formal opening, etc, etc. I ought to start out directly. I know this is not a realistic feeling, etc. I had the idea that it is important to break through the barrier problem, to find the the quickest way. You said the more formal approach has achieved something of itself, but nevertheless it must be slower. One thing I noticed this morning was that I was more aware of having dreamed. I forgot the dreams soon after waking but not immediately, and I was conscious of a lot having gone on. I had the feeling "this is more like normal".'

Analyst 'You felt there was life going on in you while you slept, so that the dissociation we spoke of the other day was less complete. So part of the function of the dreaming was achieved, the formation of a bridge between the inner world and waking life.'

Patient 'I suppose I could have tried, I could have written down the dreams, but it seems to be a part of the psychoanalytic technique to dismiss any form of aid except just talking – it's easier to believe in work done by other methods – especially as I distrust talk as something that father was good at, you might say to the exclusion of other things. I remember the recent discussion when I turned down the idea of my being an analyst; this was more a feeling of hostility to the idea of talking.'

Analyst 'It does seem that, if a conscious effort is made to help the analyst, there can come about new defences, but I would not say that there is no place at all for conscious effort.'

Patient 'I would like to find another way, for instance to find that you know what's happening, something less laborious than my writing things down and then reproducing them.'

Analyst 'The bridge provided has to allow of two-way traffic. I am not sure at present whether I am talking to your true or your false self, using the language of recent sessions.'

Patient 'It's the false self. People hear in two different ways – one might say two aspects of the personality, like intellectual and emotional. It's feasible to be distracted and yet to be talked to at the same time – one part takes the emotional, and the other takes this intellectual aspect of the same sentence. When things go well, both recognize the situation, both work together. In a way I feel concern about lack of emotion can only be intellectual.'

Analyst 'At the start when you talked, this talking had its own importance, as I have said, apart altogether from content. It meant you were alive, awake, eager.'

Pause.

Patient 'I felt anxious just then. One difficulty is that a breakthrough might release so much, and then I would become changeable with each emotional facet as it presents, so I keep busy talking, and this gives no time for me to take in what you say. I have a vision of being careful not to do all the talking, so that you might not bother to listen.'

Analyst 'What would happen then? This would be one-sided, like the alternative of waiting for you to provide all the talking.'

Patient 'If I were to talk without inhibition there would be no point in my coming here. I could talk to myself. I had a thought about last night when it was difficult to talk with my wife. The thought was that there was no reason why I should stop if I were talking without inhibition, going over the same things and not progressing with an idea. There would be no point in stopping. I would get no pleasure. There is no emotion in it.'

Analyst 'I would remind you here that you were late and I am not sure whether this had any meaning to it today. It could be something that is more nearly related to yourself than your talking is.'

Patient 'No, I think it was not significant or perhaps it was just rude. I can see that I could have saved a few minutes but the important thing is that I could have been more worried about being late. In that way it does come in. I felt coming here, "I wonder if Winnicott is offended?" This is a new departure. Previously I have been only concerned with the idea of being punished. This time it was less the effect on myself and more the effect on you. Would you be upset? Today, therefore, there is some point in apologizing. Previously if I apologized it was only to cover up what had happened.'

Analyst 'You seem to be less under a compulsion.'

Patient 'My feelings are less remote than they were two years ago when it was simply intellect. I felt I ought to be concerned. Now I do not think about it, but if I am late I am concerned about upsetting you.' *Pause.* 'I was thinking then, I wonder if others will notice the change that came over me in the last few days.'

Analyst 'You would like this. It would feel more real.'

Patient 'Especially if my wife noticed the change, that is what would really be the acid test of progress, she being so unwilling to recognize psychoanalysis as useful.' *Pause.* (Right finger to mouth.) 'I was feeling then that I recognized there is a danger in being concerned about others' feelings. Previously when I had a more intellectual concern I could afford to ignore what others thought. I could say "be damned" to everyone else. But if I share with others, then I become more concerned and must expect to have my imperfections noticed. I used to dismiss all this by saying I am ill, but now that I am not ill any longer I have to face up to being imperfect if it is me.'

Analyst 'There is something perfect because unused or unexperienced that you wish to preserve as perfect in yourself, and if you are not ill then what you fear is that you will be found to have failed in the preservation of this perfection.' (This interpretation was almost certainly wrong at this point.)

Patient 'I do not seem to be concerned at the moment with the idea of breaking something perfect. I mean that I cannot use that just now. I was thinking of something else and I only clocked in halfway when you were speaking. I was remembering that this afternoon I started to read a book about the eighteenth century in USA. The characters were dressed in the style. I remembered that I had forgotten to bring this book back with me from the hospital and so I shall not have it tonight, therefore, and this is the thing, I shall have to plan what to read. This is a minor catastrophe. It is a story of a tall and thin man who studied at Harvard. He gets drafted into army life which changes his whole career. My own job is due to end. A change in my life is therefore coming through the agency of forces outside my control. I have the same difficulty here sometimes about abrupt changes.' (Right index finger to mouth.) 'Also I was forgetting the important point is escape. Reading provides an escape for me, especially at the present time because there is something to escape from, the environment.'

Analyst 'What do you feel would happen if you were well this evening and if your wife were to respond?'

Patient 'Firstly, I would talk more easily. Secondly, she would be more interested in my hospital affairs. Thirdly, I would be more interested in her doings. Conversation would flow. We would be happy. We would sit and chat for one or two hours. But what will happen is that we will talk with strain and tension or there will be silent tension. For me I feel silence like an active denial of talking. It is a deliberate act. If I reprimand her she will have nothing to say. It means I do not want to talk. I have gone away.'

Pause.

Analyst 'You think that we are near the time for stopping and you do not wish to embark on something new.'

Patient 'Yes, I was thinking if my wife saw a change in me how important it would be.'

Analyst 'But here, as you are implying, is the one place where you cannot act. I would say this, that the one thing you cannot do is to act not-acting.'

Monday, 6 June

Analyst I announced at the start that I would need to go out for ten minutes towards the end of the session.

Patient 'Ten minutes ago I can say that I did not want to come. Coming is a nuisance, and your demand, not my need any more. Now that it has become less urgent I only come because of the job being incomplete. There is less motivation, and then I have the thought of the time that my job ends in ten days so that alterations will have to be made in the times, and it suddenly came over me how soon this is. It will be convenient if I can stop instead of making alterations. I do not feel prepared to discuss them just at the moment. Last time it seemed that the stream of excitement dried up, so that I am now not sure whether or not I am on the brink of a change. This gives me a reason for wanting to go on. I think I unconsciously am alarmed at what was happening and so unconsciously I dried up. It was a good example a couple of nights ago showing me that I have still a long way to go. A garden fête at the hospital, and I felt out of place, but I could see everyone else being gay. When I returned to the small room with two or three others in it I felt safe again. Again I seem to be drying up.

There seems to be a picture of myself lying down and finding words coming out but in fact nothing was happening. Today all the time I am feeling I would like to be liberated from here but the question is, would I be able to enjoy the liberty?'

Analyst 'The question of liberty here does not arise at the present moment.'

Patient 'I seem to be aware of an ending.'

Analyst 'An important thing comes into that, which is that the operation of time is traumatic to you. When your true self appears, then the only meaning for time that you can endure is if you begin and end something yourself. This would be one of the blocks in the way at the moment that you realize that your true self is in danger of being affected by my time which goes by the clock, and this danger is very real.'

Patient 'This gives some relief. Even as a patient at the hospital I see now that I was very much affected by my dismissal at the end of the hour, although at the time I was not aware of this. Now I realize that I experienced fury at being stopped; extreme annoyance, and I was even aware of this when my sessions were cut from three to two.'

Analyst 'You are telling me then that this rage has been going on inside you all this time but that it never shows.'

Patient 'It makes me think of a situation in which my father would set a timetable for playing. This was useless. I could not play when he said it was time to play and stop when he said it was time to stop. My father would sometimes say "You can't play now."'

Pause.

Analyst 'There is one thing left over from last time and I am wondering whether it was important. At a certain point you took your right finger to your mouth. I am not quite sure when it came but it might have been significant. I think that it was your left finger that you sucked.'

Patient 'No, I think it was my right finger I sucked. I know about this because there is a scar on that finger and I remember that I cut it and used the fact that it was difficult to suck it while it was bandaged as an artificial break to the finger-sucking.

Analyst 'I do not know of course how you came to hurt your finger but in a way you describe what seems to stand instead of a threat that it would be damaged if you did not give up finger-sucking.'

Patient 'I do not remember the accident but it fits in here that I have been smoking less for a week. I have often intended to reduce smoking but never with success. Whenever I set myself to stop, something else said to me: "Why stop?" But for the last few days it has been different. Much easier to stop. I allowed myself to run out of cigarettes and I did not find it distressing and afterwards was able to control smoking. There seems to be a logical association between smoking and finger-sucking; both come in response to stress. Also when you said that you would be breaking the hour for ten minutes, first of all I felt, "Good, that's something novel. Now I will be able to have a smoke." Now it occurs to me that the first reaction was to deny that I was alarmed at what you said. Your going out of the room would leave me with the problem, what shall I do?'

Analyst 'One can say that the cigarette is half symbolic of me; something that can be used instead of me, but half of it is an indication of stress. Something used compulsively. So it seems possible that what you did with your finger was significant. And also that my breaking into the hour cannot possibly be good from your point of view, although you seemed to accept it very easily. It makes you look round for ways of dealing with strain.' (At this point he was playing a game, banging his little fingers together.)

Pause.

Patient 'I cannot remember when your holidays start. The question is, will it be worthwhile fitting in something, making new arrangements, when I start to do the new job, as this will only give a little while and it might not be worth the bother. I shall know whether I have the job on a permanent basis by September when you return. I have a feeling that it would be good not to try these four weeks, so as to make a longer break in which I might be able to find out if I want to come or not. The question is, is this honest? Is a long time away really a help in making a decision of this kind? I remember that you once said that all the years between the two treatments I had kept my development in abeyance so that from the point of view of a treatment they were wasted years. There is also the thing that coming along means a constant probing into the private life.'

Analyst 'Included in all this is the idea that you might really be able to come to your own conclusion about this matter.'

Patient 'Yes, but I am not clear about whether I just do not want to come or whether I am trying to avoid something.'

Analyst 'There is one thing that we have been talking about which you may be trying to avoid which has to do with fury which is going on inside you and which is not felt at the appropriate moments.'

Pause.

Patient 'The idea occurred to me then that I might have thoughts that belonged to me. It would take time to explain it. Something *could* be kept to *myself*. It is not absolutely necessary to bring Winnicott into it. This is all part of a gesture to not come.'

Analyst 'Not coming would seem to indicate that you cannot be sure of the right to keep something secret.'

Patient 'Earlier on I used to talk all the time and try to say everything. It never occurred to me not to want to say something. So this is a novel idea of having secret thoughts. In the relationship with the girl every detail came into the analysis. It always felt to me that it all belonged to Winnicott. Now I seem to want to do something for myself. Talking here about things is a deterrent to freedom outside.'

Analyst 'So this is really what you mean about not coming. It is part of your wish to find out what you are like.'

Patient 'Previously everything was talked out and I had no desire for privacy.'

Analyst 'I think the point was that you had nowhere to put it.'

Patient 'The intellectual was simply an area for discussion; not a place where anything could be hidden.'

Analyst 'So it seems that you have turned up and you have an inside and an outside.'

Patient 'If I were to change my analyst I have always felt that all would be wasted, but that has to do with my intellectual self. The only place in which I had to hide was in someone else that I would confide in. I am reminded that as you went out of the room, though I was prepared for it, it came as a surprise. I was at a loss. I rationalized it by noticing that I had forced you into offering me a cigarette. I was amused because of the way in which this indicated loss and deprivation.'

Analyst 'The cigarette that I offered really got in the way of your fury.'

Patient 'Yes, I nearly refused as an angry gesture.' *Pause.* 'It's difficult to decide what to say next. Now I have dealt with the mechanism of interruption, I now have to deal with the interruption itself, which is more difficult. I have to start all over again. I can resent the idea of being compelled to talk.'

Analyst 'The idea of being compelled to talk seems to rule out the idea of your talking because you want to.'

Patient 'Also whether I want to stop or not. The thing is, will I find myself in a situation in which I need to come; something to do with time? I never really enjoy myself because it is dependent on my coming here.'

Analyst 'It becomes more and more clear that not coming has to do with your discovery of yourself and of your capacity to keep a secret, and it is only from not coming that you can discover a spontaneous wish to come.'

Patient 'That seems true but it is not real for just now. I cannot recognize that I might just want to come; something I am not used to yet.'

Tuesday, 7 June

Patient 'Nothing seems to come. Having found a possibility of talking differently there ought to be another opening and I feel disappointed.' (Here the patient put his right fingers to his mouth.)

Analyst 'I feel that you do not give yourself time. If you are communicating from your intellectual self, then of course there is no point in waiting and it is natural for you to engage immediately on arrival. If, however, it is your emotional self that is here, then it is unlikely that you would have the impulse to speak exactly at the same moment as I become available.'

Patient 'Yes, it is a kind of protest about there being only the three sessions in the whole week. If I am operating emotionally then I must have the right to come when I want, so that to be expected to start straight off is an adjustment to try to meet an unsatisfactory timetable. What I fear is that I will protest by not talking at all for the whole hour.'

Analyst 'It is like letting me know that you want to be away but coming in order to let me know.'

Patient 'If I do not start I have a definite fear that I won't be able to begin. Each second provides a mounting difficulty and I also talk because I can't bear the time wasted, though of course trivialities may be a waste too. This applies in my relationship with other people. I have a need to find something to say, though I probably feel like saying nothing for hours. I would like a relationship in which it was not necessary to talk or there could be a jumble of words and phrases and that would be no use. This happens with my wife. I try to say what comes, try to be natural, but there is nothing but a jumble of ideas. This seems artificial, glib. I am talkative, trying to be lighthearted, but the result is confusion. This is why people lose interest in me. At times that could happen here and you would not be able to take in what I was saying because it would be too confused. That is why I edit everything.'

Analyst 'But editing produces annoyance in you.'

Patient 'I really want to talk like a child; like my daughter, for instance. It is sometimes difficult to follow her but that of course is common with children of her age.'

Analyst 'With you as a child I am not sure that there was anyone who recognized that it was natural for your conversation to be difficult to follow.'

Patient 'Possibly I was rebuked for nonsense. Probably by father, who would call me long-winded. There was some special time at nine or ten, but it may have happened earlier as well.'

Analyst 'You see how concerned you are about my attitude if you should talk like a child. And child talking is really more like acting or doing, whereas in the conversation of an adult the content is more important.'

Pause.

Patient 'Now as before I am trying to get away from the intellectual approach, which is a barrier, but in doing so I am in danger of falling asleep. I am not sure if I can afford to neglect this intellectual compulsion if I am to keep awake.'

Analyst 'Going to sleep, however, is really you.'

Patient 'But it blots out everything else. If I were to sleep the whole hour –'

Analyst 'Even that would be something. You would not sleep anywhere. It is because you are here.'

Patient 'Perhaps I would sleep anywhere and I have noticed a tendency both with my mother and with my mother-in-law. However, here there comes the social need for me to be awake. I feel I do not want to bother to be sociable. I have gone to sleep in that way and it has annoyed my wife who says it is bad manners.' *Pause.* 'One difficulty about sleep, I risk wasting the hour and feeling guilty about letting you down, so I can keep awake to some extent for your sake.'

Analyst 'But you cannot take it for granted that I am here unless your intellect is active –' (Here the patient slept and snored, and then was suddenly awake.)

Patient 'It does seem not only guilt; also a challenge to you expressing contempt.'

Analyst 'That is you and is real.' (Renewed sleep.)

Patient 'It seems as if you are challenging me to go to sleep if I want to, as if you are giving permission, but it won't get us anywhere. Talking is the medium of progress.'

Analyst 'This reminds me of your father.'

Patient 'Yes – um – um –' *Pause.* (Probably asleep.) 'Especially disconcerting that I keep thinking of things about hospital and wasting the short time I have here asleep.' *Pause.* 'Sometimes I think about hospital problems to avoid something else because I can say about them that I need not discuss them, but if it is not about work I feel I must tell you.'

Analyst 'You as editor have strong views on what is suitable for publication here.'

Patient 'Like yesterday when I said I don't want to come and I feel guilt about it. It's rather subtle but it's not the same thing showing that it is not worthwhile coming.'

Analyst 'In regard to your intellectual self there is the editor, and I am interested in what kind of editor he is, and what does he think important?'

Pause. (Momentary sleep.)

Patient 'I had a dream then that as an alternative to saying nothing I was talking too much and people were annoyed at the liberty I was taking, expecting them to listen to me going on talking.'

Analyst 'You are therefore talking about curbing a compulsion just like stealing.' (Probably asleep.) 'You have a claim on me to listen to you and a claim on my time.' *Pause.* 'I would add, a claim to be able to waste my time; as a symptom this makes sense and indicates that you feel you have been deprived in all these ways.'[1]

Patient 'In spite of all this there is a deadlock. It is either hospital problems or sleep. What I am concerned with is the present, and the question that I am asking is, how does this sleeping join up with now?' (By this time he was fully awake.)

Analyst 'At this point I can remind you of the fury which you found exists in you and which does not find expression and which is likely to be underlying the symptom of sleep.'

Patient 'It's funny, I was just thinking that I was protecting you from an outburst of temper. I was thinking, I have shown very little temperament here. There has been a half-hidden feeling which I now see as extreme fury. I fear a violent outburst. Perhaps I may find myself expressing tremendous anger which ought to have been expressed perhaps with father at an earlier date. Somehow I missed the boat.'

Analyst 'I can now speak to you again about father standing between you and mother. I would remind you of the cut finger which you produced as an accident and used for breaking yourself of finger-sucking, being as it were unable to fight father coming in between and threatening you, although in fact you felt the threat. Father missed the boat as a strong person coming between you and mother and between you and what was symbolical of mother.'

Patient 'If he got in between it was in a way that was not recognizable at the time. I feel restless now. I really do not want to lie down. That means falling asleep. I would really like to turn over on my face.'

Analyst 'Evidently you have taken it as assumed that I have prohibited your turning over on your face.' **(This is what we have been leading up to for years.)**

Patient 'I remember that at about twelve to fourteen years old lying on my back meant death. It was when I was at school. It seemed that it

[1] Cf 'Psychotherapy of Character Disorders' (Winnicott 1963b).

meant being helpless, lying in a coffin. It was all right if I was awake, outdoors under a tree, but in bed dangerous.'

Analyst 'Did it perhaps get connected up with the woman's position in intercourse?'

Patient 'No, I don't think it's that at all.'

Analyst 'Then we look at other things. I would like to remind you, as I have done before, that in the first analysis you had a very important symptom which was the inability to lie down, and that the end of that analytic phase came when you were able to lie down and to tolerate the anxiety associated with it, which at that time had to do with having been satisfied as an infant by a perfect mother, the satisfaction producing annihilation of the object. In other words, you had no knowledge until the analysis that if you waited there would be a return of desire and therefore a return of the object of your desires.' (On previous occasions when I have reminded the patient of this he had been vaguely able to remember but the reminder did not produce any new material.)

Patient 'It had a special significance then because it was so near to my actual fear of lying down which persisted up to that date from the twelve-year-old period.'

Analyst 'I wonder if you are able to tell me anything about the twelve to fourteen years.'

Patient 'At that time my father began to be ill but he did not know. The first time was at a fête when someone was making a lightning sketch of him and I suddenly saw that he looked old and tattered. I remember that I was completely shaken. He did not look well and I realized that I could no longer take his being alive for granted. Soon after he became ill (the beginning of the long illness – cancer of the lung). So I see now that I did not see then that subconsciously I had reason to doubt his immortality for the first time at that fête. I had no way at that time to explain the whys and wherefores. This might be all wrong, but it is how I remember it today.'

Analyst 'From that time onwards, therefore, you had to protect father from your fury and at an age when defying your father would be quite natural and part of the process of growing up. About adolescence I would say that, although father has won over you in regard to your early childhood relation to mother, he now comes along as someone you can defy when investigating relationships with mother substitutes. I would say that at the time it threw you over into an exaggeration on the homosexual side, although this did not develop into anything.'

Patient 'I don't think I remember about that.'

Analyst 'Well, at the time when you first came to me you were dressing in a way which was quite different from the style which you adopted when you left me. For instance, you wore a pink tie.'

Patient 'Yes, I remember the flamboyant ties, but it was also an act of defiance. I was not really at ease with them but I mistrusted myself. I would say that all the time I was afraid of what father would say.'

Analyst 'You have probably heard the term, the return of the repressed. The rage and your defiance of your father were not available but they turned up in this way.'

Patient 'You remember, don't you, that at the time I came to you first he had already died?'

Analyst 'Yes, I know, but you had not accepted his death and indeed it was in this phase of the analysis about a year ago that you accepted this fact.'

Patient 'As a matter of fact I am only just beginning to accept it now.'

Analyst 'It is impossible to accept the death of your father unless you are able to encompass your anger with him and the death of him in the dream in which you kill him. He, being ill, had to be protected, and your protection of him has kept him alive all this time.'

Friday, 10 June

Patient 'I have been to my daughter's school open day, and found it very bewildering. I had to make the effort to be interested but after an hour I became agitated. It is impossible to be normal there, and this is in marked contrast to what I feel at hospital. In the classroom I did not know what to look at and meekly followed the others. I felt I ought to be fascinated. I was upset at not being affected. The building I found more interesting. It reminds me that at one time I nearly was a teacher and I am horrified at the thought –

'In contrast I have been excited and even fascinated to realize how much children of five and six are capable of thinking, the way they manage abstract ideas like learning to read and write and various skills. I seem to be finding out for the first time what adults take for granted, and I was able to picture myself in the school as a child although unable to take part as an adult.'

Analyst 'I would like to remind you that yesterday you were speaking of difficulties starting at the time of your father's death when you were adolescent.'

Patient 'I am reminded that you said that it was only recently that I had allowed my father to die, and I said, "Has it happened yet or perhaps it is happening now?" Now it is as if I have accepted this, and that has taken me back to the period earlier than the age at which father died when things first seemed to be unreal. Probably at the time of learning to read. The sort of age that my daughter is at now.'

Analyst 'So that as a child you felt unreal at school learning to read, etc.'

Patient 'It was difficult to work with children. It is the same difficulty now fitting in with what others are doing, though I missed joining in. I want to be social but something gets in the way and I cannot be. This has to do with the age five or six, the time when I started to be on my own and I never got back into line again. Today I ought to have wanted to go but I didn't.'

Analyst 'What about your memories of five and six? For instance, about the first day at school?'

Patient 'Only vaguely, but I was seven then. You remember that mother ran a school and it was not until seven or eight that I went to a prep school. When I was five I went to mother's school with the two sisters and the children of neighbours.'

Analyst 'So that the other children at this school run by your mother were intruders in your home.'

Patient 'For a long time, in fact, I refused to take part. One motive was resentment and this is a new idea to me. Resentment that the other children moved into my family. Quite simply, I moved out.'

Analyst 'You remember having withdrawn at some sort of date, as when you found your baby sister on your mother's lap.'

Pause.

Patient 'Now I feel a tendency to face the situation, to look forward but not accept. This has to do with my going to sleep. It is the same as not going to school, and the same as withdrawal at the age of four or five.' *Pause.* (Probably asleep.) 'I have difficulty in keeping awake here. That is the same as running away from school. I never reach a dilemma but run away.'

Analyst 'You are protecting everyone from your rage, and thus saving the world. If you do not go away everyone will die.'

Patient 'Why?'

Analyst 'Because of the rage we were talking about.'

Patient 'Occasionally I wonder if I had feelings at that time of destroying the other children that came to mother's school.'

Analyst 'By withdrawing you do two things. You keep omnipotence, and also you save the lives of the children.'

Pause.

Patient 'Just now I feel the obstacle is so great that I will not be able to get over it.'

Analyst 'We have found that in adolescence you had to protect father from your fury, but at the age of four and five in a sense there was no father to save the situation because he avoided the role of the strong father.' (During this interpretation the patient quickly went to sleep.)

Patient 'I seem to have been going to sleep several times today. This must be important.'

Analyst 'I think you did not hear what I said. I spoke about father being ill so that you had to protect him.' (I repeated the interpretation.)

Patient 'It occurs to me that it may be a pointless observation, rather abstract, that the difficulty here is that there cannot be an ordinary withdrawal as in a social gathering in which I do not have to talk if I don't want to. Here I have to go further to escape from a situation. Not talking is too well understood.'

Analyst 'Not talking is equivalent to killing.'

Patient 'Part of silence is a need to keep some feelings away from here. I have the right to not say things but I am not aware of the deep feelings. I can only take for granted the word fury.'

Analyst 'Yes, we do not know yet for certain.'

Pause.

Patient 'It seems also as if from an early age, say four or five or six, I substituted an intellectual for a real emotional self, because the latter was not able to make itself felt.'

Analyst 'And the latter is consequently inexperienced.'

Patient 'It is more difficult to concentrate and to keep awake today. Does that mean that there is something especially dangerous? This is partly related to the fact that by changing the job I am uncertain how long I will be able to come at the usual times, though of course if I need to come I will be able to.' *Pause.* 'There is another idea about silence. That it is unproductive. You said that it can be useful. Today I seem to be challenging you. All right, you say it is useful. Let's see what happens if I do not speak. Prove yourself! Probably there is some anxiety about the idea of your having been able to make use of the silence. When challenged, then, there is no escape from not coming. There is no way of bringing not-coming.'

Analyst 'I think here I am mother and you are four or five years old.'

Patient 'It is very important that mother did not know my feelings because there was something I dare not tell her as it would involve her destruction.' *Pause.* 'My only hope in those days was to grow up suddenly and so avoid a great deal of unpleasantness. I tried to become an adult from the age of five. I wanted to be sociable but to do without the intermediate stages between early childhood and being grown-up. That was the only safe way that was possible.'

Analyst 'The whole period which people call latency period seems to have been wiped out. Father's death at a later age seems to have been a version of its own during that period.' (I felt from the failure of response here that my interpretation was probably not right. The patient was nearly asleep.)

Patient 'It occurs to me now that, two weeks ago when I was suddenly able to talk freely and was unaware of time, this was to some extent artificial, a trick. The point is that it hid the idea of not talking at all. I am starting to discover what is behind the not-talking in the past. I have always thought of this symptom as just a nuisance, though you have spoken about it as potentially valuable. I believe that it was concealing something, only now I mean what I am saying, that the silence itself is the significant thing.'

Tuesday, 14 June

Patient 'Last time I slept a lot. If I let myself go, then I would sleep all the time. I feel this may have been very important, an avoidance of something, unconsciously, perhaps something was getting near that was dangerous. There are two things: first, today I am more tired, but second, I feel that there is less risk of going to sleep, because being really tired I'm not likely to get to dangerous things. It's a curious position. I don't feel externally that I have made progress lately, that is to say I don't feel better, but nevertheless I wonder when and if I should expect to reap the fruit of the work done here. If I have to stop, will all the recent work be wasted, or can it be consolidated? Psychoanalysis while it goes on produces an area of disturbance, I know, so that I cannot expect to feel well while I'm coming.'

Analyst 'Do you remember about last time, and the work we did on the subject of silence and its positive meanings?'

Patient 'I only vaguely remember. I don't talk with my wife because she will not argue and so offers no struggle. We talk only about minor things. I have given up trying. It's not urgent now and experience shows its fruitlessness. It isn't worth trying. She's deliberately not talking and I am forced to play the same way. Not talking is an active thing.'

Analyst Here I collected together all the recent work we had done on silence.

Patient 'It's curious, all we had talked about had disappeared. It still seems remote.'

Analyst 'So you are referring to the need you have for me to remember, even when we agree.'

Patient 'About agreeing, I feel I'm only too likely to agree. I tend to accept unless I definitely reject. I willingly accept and seldom flatly disagree. I hardly ever argue.'

Analyst 'I would remind you that you said I would be like cotton wool, if you hit me your arm would go right in and it would get lost.'

Patient 'I had a mental picture then – a fight with you, I kept you at a distance. This would be the ideal if you would not be aggressive all the time but would be in an aggressive state – a kind of boxing match, but the blows would bounce back off you. There is some dislike of you here. You adapt completely and produce a negative atmosphere – this is too much like my father. I have an abstract picture of a mother who adapts too easily, trying too hard to be perfect.'

(This is the mother's exact description of herself at the time of the patient's infancy, given to me before I started the first analysis.)

'The result is soft and distasteful.' *Pause.* 'I remember a striking difference between the desire to be silent last time and the desire to get away from chattering. Chatter has limitations. It has an edge to it even if it has no meaning. I like the idea of chatter, but pure chatter has no edge, no purpose. Chatter is talking to no person. The effect is only a temporary amusement.' *Pause.* 'I was silent then because I recognized it as a good thing in itself sometimes not to talk. Not to talk for talking's sake. In the past I made too big an effort to try and say everything.' *Pause.* 'I feel that if I don't talk there is a danger of never talking at all, and then going to sleep. I can't trust silence.'

Analyst 'Did you sleep just then in the pause?'

Patient 'No, not really.'

Analyst 'There is something real here, in your silence, that it is you yourself, whereas talking for talking's sake means you are not sure you exist, or me.'

Patient 'The difficulty is that if I don't talk or don't want to talk this needs an interpretation. In general I don't like talking.' *Pause.* 'Tiredness has something to do with not talking. It provides an excuse, so that at the moment I don't have to talk, nor do I have to explain why.' (Patient yawns.)

Analyst 'You are needing an interpretation from me, and I will say that you are making a claim on me.' (Patient asleep.) 'I think you wanted to hear my interpretation but you went to sleep because you were afraid of it. You perhaps fear the right interpretation.'

Patient 'I assume that the interpretation is right, if it is made. The fear is of what I might find to be true. I had not thought of the possibility of your making a wrong interpretation (it would then be only an opinion, which I would accept as an opinion by not accepting it as an interpretation). So it's not so much the interpretation that I fear as discovery of something, as if I were to be hit over the head.'

Analyst 'You recently said that silence could be hitting.'

Patient 'I had a curious idea then, that somebody was eating something, like eating ideas, so if you produce something (an interpretation), you are vomiting. Therefore, accepting an idea from you is distasteful. There is the danger that I don't recognize these ideas till they are half consumed, and then I find out and vomit. For a moment I had a very clear picture of all this, of you sitting at a meal, with a plate of food which you eat, and while you eat the food increases, which means that you are bringing it all up, slowly.' *Pause.* 'It seems very difficult, this not talking, it's dangerous, nothing happens. Can you make use of it? It's only too easy never to talk. I remember now, as I left yesterday, I wondered, is it worthwhile to carry on if not talking is life?'

Analyst 'This connects with the idea of being loved with sanctions, or being loved meaning having your existence valued.'

Patient 'I feel about that that I can try to believe and assume that I am loved, but what if it isn't true? I almost find myself in water without being able to swim, and no one to support me.'

Analyst 'Exactly, you've said it – that's what happened to you.'

Patient 'There is a big difference. I ought to try (although it's impossible) not to do things myself but to make others do things in abstract, *without* their actually doing them. This is a contradiction, it can only happen by magic.'

Analyst 'What you miss is the fact of mother's identification with you, her baby.'

Pause.

Patient 'Sleep is not purely negative or avoidance. It provides an element which gives you a chance to come forward.'

Analyst Yes, my only chance.'

Wednesday, 15 June

Patient 'After I left yesterday I was thinking about our conclusion. I've been a long time facing the problem, to find a hopeless prospect of being loved or wanted for myself rather than on account of what I do or achieve. I had discussed this before, when we were on the subject of perfection. I did not recognize the possibility of being wanted or respected for myself, so perfection was the only alternative, and anything less meant complete failure. So when I first complained that I was ill I was appalled at the dilemma, as I felt so far from perfection, which meant absolute failure. Before that I avoided the direct onslaught by retiring into myself, and so avoided problems of being wanted or loved, or of being perfect. I did not believe in being loved, and so the talking difficulty arose, because there was no point in demanding what I wanted to get without demanding it.

'Then I wondered, having discovered this situation, what was the next step to take, what would solve the problem? No practical step would help because, by the nature of things, I could not take action. In this dilemma, is it possible to get over the fact that for so many years I have missed something, missed or failed to recognize being loved if it was there? Also it struck me that mother might have suffered from the same disability, if she had no hope of being loved for herself – hence perhaps her desire for perfection.

'Also, what role did father play? I cannot picture him in the same category. He seemed to have no problem.' *Pause.* 'At the start I wondered whether to talk about yesterday or not; it is difficult to talk about without making it too intellectual.'

Analyst 'This is where silence comes in, if it is understood.'

Patient 'But how in silence can I demonstrate how important it is? Also at the end of yesterday I was impressed by the discovery, perhaps by its drama more than by the truth of it, that is to say its definiteness, rather than by its subject matter. It seemed very important but too simple to explain everything.' *Pause.* 'It seemed to follow (I have recognized it for a long time) that I have been obsessed with a need to try to please everybody, this being all part of perfection and of the drive to find love and respect. I have been concerned not to upset people, more than with the positive aspects of relationships. If I said something definite, I was disturbed if this was not accepted. There was an example today, discussing a case over the phone with a GP. He wanted advice about a child, and he argued with me instead of taking what I said for granted, and I was very upset. It was simply a case of a three-months-old baby that possibly has rubella, and the GP was critical of the diagnosis. I felt I was being shouted down. He was more definite than I was, and I felt wrong, uncertain, and then annoyed. I could have been firm.'

Analyst 'Yesterday, when I made my simple interpretation, there was the content of what I said but also the firmness of my attitude and statement. You were affected by my feelings displayed by the way I did it.'

Patient 'I enjoyed the categorical nature of your statement, because I can't be like that. Often you seem cautious, you don't commit yourself, you are reasonable and admit when you are wrong, but I find that less satisfying. It would be better for you to be gloriously wrong than vaguely right.'

Analyst 'Well, I was definite and that was satisfying. We now have to consider, was I gloriously wrong?'

Patient 'It's difficult to remember things, but what you said fits in in the back of my mind. The meaning is vague but the memory is of something definite and decisive. My own not being decisive is not only a fear of being wrong. It turns up in the taking of case-histories, and in my not remembering people's names. There is a definite reason – as an excuse I am vague. There is an obvious thought here – being decisive is father. Part of my distrust of it in myself is that I do not want to be identified with him. If I am too much like father, then, if I am loved, it is on account of my being like father, not because of myself.'

Analyst 'Do you know of mother's early history? Had she childhood difficulties?'

Patient 'My own memory of mother's mother is coloured by the fact that she was elderly when I knew her, but she was a difficult person. This is not the representation of what she might have been in mother's childhood. There is also what mother said, and this is her subjective account – I might have the idea now of making my difficulties go back to my grandmother – but she had an anxiety drive. As I see my own difficulties now, they arise out of the fact that mother was a more powerful personality than father was. I am aware that father was too perfect – this doesn't ring true. If father was decisive I was happy, though I disliked it. I respected it. Now if mother starts to be definite I am irritated. It's not right coming from her. About mother I can speak of contemporary feelings, but in regard to father it all dates back to the time before I was conscious of the problems we have found here.' *Pause.* 'I had an idea here, about father. His being decisive had one disadvantage for me. It left no room for play.'

Analyst 'So that –.'

Patient 'I am trying to pick holes in father, trying to find a chink in his armour.'

Analyst 'What was later good in father may have been bad from your point of view when you were an infant, especially as father took a motherly interest in you from early days, as you have told me. But I would say that eventually father's human decisions would be preferable to mother's rules based on the idea of perfection. You could be defiant with father, but you can't do anything about rules.'

Patient 'I feel there is one thing to be avoided, not to accept anything too readily, since so little can be done.'

Analyst 'Also to avoid a positive relationship, both ways, between you and me.' *Pause.* 'I think you slept?'

Patient 'Yes, the first time today. I was aware of getting sleepy. It's difficult to face up to the situation, I mean the content of your interpretation.'

(That is to say, as opposed to the decisive manner in which he felt it was given.)

'I still feel, "also I'm trying to avoid". I cannot get to the not-wanting-to-talk as a positive thing.'

Analyst 'When you sleep you drop me. You never had mother and so could not drop her.' (Patient sleeping?)

Patient 'I feel at the moment that what goes on in my mind is far away from what we are talking about – a vague daydreaming – difficult to get hold of – it's about children playing.'

Analyst 'Father didn't give room for play.'

Patient 'And mother didn't know how to play, so she was unable to.'

Analyst 'So it is very important I don't drive you to the point by being decisive.'

Patient 'Also I am speculating about my perhaps not being able to come after next week because of the change of job. I might not want to come because you have become the nasty man who discovers what I don't want to have discovered. So I get sleepy and express my disapproval. It's childishness, that way of putting it, but it's important that you have become the ogre of childhood play.'

Analyst 'So you have been able to reach play with me, and in the playing I am an ogre.'

Friday, 17 June

Patient 'I used to think it important to discuss how I was feeling; now it seems relatively unimportant. Feelings and moods are variable, transient. They depend on variable factors. More important is to get at the things behind the moods.'

Analyst 'Yes, you are saying something I hadn't thought of before. Your mood was the nearest you could get to your self.'

Patient 'One thing that emphasized the unimportance of my mood has been the fact that I find other people are not impressed by how one feels.'

Analyst 'When people say, "How are you?" they definitely don't want you to say you have a pain in your elbow. It is not appropriate to follow up the idea in the question.'

Patient 'This has to do with things my wife and I have had rows about, and I have rebuked her for not asking me how I feel. She says, "What's the point? You are always miserable." There is something else. Before I came I felt some confusion as to the reason for my difficulty or reluctance in talking. There are two factors: the fear of the fury, and hopelessness about being loved. I suppose if one is right the other must be wrong. In the last two times anger has disappeared.'

Analyst 'There can be a connection between the two. You must have some
hope in order to be angry. To be angry you have to be able to keep in
mind that which you hoped for while reacting to its absence.'

Patient 'In that case the idea of my being completely hopeless is an
exaggeration. One exaggerates to get a simplification, to find one
cause for all one's troubles.'

Analyst 'We have often found that when we clear up a point that leads on to
the next.'

Patient 'I am really aware that one thing cannot solve everything.'

Analyst 'There is a difference between the fury and the deprivation. You
reached theoretical fury but real deprivation in the past weeks.'

Patient 'Yes, the fury was somewhat theoretical, except that I felt vague
annoyance. I felt there might be anger somewhere. Another thing
about anger; it's always a temporary mood, never lasting long. Is that
what it is like, or must there be buried anger that I cannot sustain?'

Analyst 'We see you going to and fro from anger, which produces its own
dangers, and hopelessness, which is not so much dangerous as that it
makes you feel life is futile.' *Pause.* 'In the analysis you came to certain
dangers, associated with anger, and so you went back to hopelessness.'

Patient 'Anger is more productive than hopelessness, which is negative.'

Analyst 'You feel more real when you are angry, even if the ideas that belong
to anger involve a sense of danger.'

Patient 'Anger involves an object, but hopelessness – well, there's nothing to
pursue. So anger entering into discussion today might possibly be
more useful. I feel excited at the idea of reaching to hopelessness, but I
seem to have come to a dead end, so for two days the anger has got
lost. I feel I'm getting a bit repetitive. The idea occurs to me that I
might be boring by constantly going over the same thing. Socially, I
know I'm boring by being monotonous, but I can't help going on
doing it. The alternative is hopelessness, silence, absolute.'

Analyst 'There can be anger at realization of deprivation, when you feel
hope and hopelessness almost at the same time.'

Patient 'Hopelessness is only relative because if complete it isn't recognized.'

Analyst 'Yes.'

Pause.

Patient 'I find now that I ought to be starting thinking about the next stage,
making use of these discoveries. I notice that in contrast with the past
few weeks I am no longer sleepy. This is disappointing if sleepiness is
evidence of something emerging. If I'm awake I start thinking clearly
about the future, and this can be unproductive.'

Analyst 'The new situation comes from the idea which is the opposite of deprivation, that to some extent, here and now, I have love for you – a new version of the series of events in your analysis that started with the fluid medium.[1] Here I mean love with no ifs and no sanctions, nothing more nor less than my capacity to be identified with you.'

Patient 'It occurs to me that I've just arrived at the situation that I was in when I first started to come to you, that is, for the first analysis. I could not think what the devil to talk about.'

Analyst 'That is to say, that had I known about you (and I would have had to have been a magician) I could then have made the comment I am making now. I could have said, "The only way you can start is by my coming to you with love, and you cannot say this because you don't know it." This was dramatized at the start of the second analysis when you had no idea of wanting me, and you would not have come to me had I not come and fetched you. Of course I do not alter the fact of the first deprivation, that of your early infancy, I only offer a token of loving.'

Patient 'I feel that I could not start because I had nothing to work on. I never had the idea that things ought to start from you.'

Analyst 'So we come to a positive meaning for silence – the expression of the idea that the start must come from me.'

Patient 'This is not new. I remember before feeling hopeless about producing anything, but I thought it was that I would *like* you to produce something first. Now I see it is more than just convenience.'

Analyst 'If you like me to start, it is already no good for me to start, because in doing so I only follow your wish. To make adaptation to your *need* I must come to you with love before you know about the need.'

Patient 'This reminds me of my relationship to women, which only starts when the woman takes the initial steps. I feel hopeless about making a conquest. If I try, I start with the assumption that it will be hopeless. I don't see why it is important that the drive should come from outside, except that at an early stage it didn't.'

Analyst 'From your point of view, whether true or not, your mother was unable to surrender herself to an identification with you, her baby. You will see what I mean if you think of the word confined, which implies that the mother, like the infant, is caught up in a process, and which shows the mother's temporary identification with her infant, which is almost complete. In the same way I am caught up with you in the process of your analysis and of your going back to infantile dependence and your emotional growth forward again. Only if I am

---

[1] See 'Withdrawal and Regression' in the Appendix to this volume.

caught up as you are in these processes can you start to exist.' *Pause.*
'This leads to a consideration of the analyst's motives.'

Patient 'Yes, I was actually thinking, "I wonder in broad terms what you
are out to do, what faith you have in your ability to do something." A
friend, a doctor, was recently talking about his future, and he said he
thought of trying psychiatry; he said it might be profitable. He had no
belief in its being any good and he said, "It's a waste of time really." I
was annoyed about the waste of time idea, but I too had doubts as to
whether or no there was any truth in it. I wondered, "Do you regard
psychoanalysis as an experiment, not knowing the outcome?"

Analyst 'I might be doing it for money and I might be doing it without belief
in my ability to get anywhere, but what concerns you is: Do I suffer
with you if the analysis is a failure?'

Patient 'Yes, because it's so easy if you decide psychoanalysis is a good line
to take up. You might not believe in it but you might carry it on as a
technical exercise, and be prepared to jettison the work if you find
something else more promising.'

Pause.

Analyst 'In comparing the analyst's job with that of the doctor you are
noting a difference. The doctor deals with illness, and if he cures the
patient of the illness he has finished. The analyst, on the contrary,
needs to have a positive feeling, something in his relationship with the
patient that does not end with the cure of the illness. This concern for
the existence of this human being underlies any wish the analyst may
have to cure the patient of illness.'

Patient 'We came to this once before, I remember some months ago, soon
after I restarted with you, after we had talked over the immediate
causes for tension. This was all tied up with the question, "Why have
psychoanalysis at all?" Since if relief from symptoms is all that is
required, I needn't have come. This answers a problem I have never
answered before: how to decide whether anyone does or does not need
analysis. It hinges round whether it will be discovered that the
symptoms are the important thing or whether they are a minor
problem as compared with something else. I had one thought this
morning, before I came, how much ought I to be ambitious, to
struggle, or have a I reached a stage at which the best policy would be
to live within one's limitations? I wondered whether, once having
given up one's ambition, would one then be satisfied, or at least find a
workable existence?'

Analyst 'You are getting to a position from which you can consider these
matters.'

Patient 'Is there a state of trying too hard, so that one does not exist at all?

There is an analogy, if I look at a picture and do not enjoy it, should I go on trying or just pass on to one that I enjoy and get pleasure from, and ignore the idea that I was supposed to get something out of the other?'

Analyst 'The idea of yourself existing just comes in here, in contrast to the idea of your living up to someone else's expectations.'

Patient 'Expectations can come from inside.'

Analyst 'Yes, surely, from people inside who are to some extent built on outside people, such as father, that you have wanted to please. But you have had to maintain these introjected people because of your own lack of sense of existing in your own right.'

Patient 'That summarizes it, in trying to achieve being myself I have had to use artificial props, and these are no longer necessary. I feel just now aware of a much more positive hope. I can visualize a situation arising, a foreseeable future, not so remote, it could be that it will be possible to say this has occurred. I used to feel there was no prospect that I would *actually* start to exist. It was like a challenge to you – do your worst, but I had no belief that something would actually happen.'

Tuesday, 21 June

Patient 'You might start by asking about my new job. I have a feeling of dislike of the idea of that, I don't know why. It's the idea of being congratulated by you. It would be the same with my mother and my sister. It seems that it would be an intrusion. You would have no right to make a comment. It would not matter if it came from people who work with me or some casual acquaintance, that would not be actively intruding.'

Analyst 'There is a link here with the theme of being loved without any ifs. The idea would be conveyed that you would be loved because of your success, which for you is the negative of being loved.'

Patient 'Yes, in general any remark you make about outside things here is out of place, undesirable. Mother fits in here because she is partly responsible for my coming to analysis, but I don't see how my sister comes in. I mean the sister who is having analysis.'

Analyst 'How does she seem to be just now?'

Patient 'She is fairly well, working. I find talking to her a strain. Her treatment is incomplete; her behaviour is unreal.'

Pause.

Analyst 'You are inevitably comparing your sister's condition with your own. If you were to make a deep change you would be concerned as to whether your sister had made the same change.'

Patient 'I'm not sure; it might be. I'm just thinking about it. I was thinking
before I came today, there was a demonstration of cases at hospital for
postgraduates; it happened to be a demonstration of mental cases.
There was a discussion, and one thing that came up reminded me of
my anxieties when I first went into hospital myself as a patient, that is
to say, before the second analysis. Was I a schizophrenic? Whether
the unreality feeling was part of a true schizophrenic? These unreality
feelings were discussed in the case demonstration. I thought I had
dealt with this, but now again I have to consider this part of my
problem. The doctor doing the teaching said that psychotherapy was
of very little use in the treatment of schizophrenia. You once said that
I had a psychosis rather than a neurosis, and I find the idea
disquieting.'

Analyst 'Yes, I did say that.'

Patient 'I am anxious about the natural history of the illness. It might imply
that there is worse to come; there are natural remissions in schizophrenia and I must perhaps anticipate relapses. The relapse rate is
high, even when patients have improved through physical treatments. So perhaps we are only delaying the final breakdown; because,
though I feel well at times, I have moments of unreality. I have
avoided putting a name to it because I regarded schizophrenia as a
pretty hopeless proposition. On the other hand I find myself arguing
against the assumption that schizophrenia should be treated by
physical methods. It seems wrong to treat a thought disorder by an
empirical method. A few of the doctors argued even that schizophrenia was an organic illness with a physical pathology. The basis of the
argument was that certain drugs produce schizophrenia attacks. So I
feel anxious that I might prove untreatable.'

Analyst 'You are faced with two alternatives, and these involve pretty big
issues. On the one hand you can be treated, in which case all these
doctors are wrong, and the official view of schizophrenia is wrong; or,
the psychiatrists are right and you are untreatable.'

Patient 'Again, in a discussion with my wife, she would have helped if I had
not had psychoanalysis. One argument originally used was that I
might get much worse, but she would not accept blame if I got worse
through not having psychoanalysis. Again I remember at the time I
was in hospital I had a fear that I would get so out of touch that no
treatment could possibly be effective.'

Analyst 'When you were so very ill, you were dependent on the fact that I
and your mother and your sister held views about the psychological
nature of your illness, and it is this that joins us three together.'

Patient 'Another alarming feature is the feeling that a breakdown might occur if I were to meet any new stress, so I wonder if I must be careful in choosing a job, avoiding the danger of emotional stress. The disadvantage here is that this produces a state of boredom.'

Analyst 'Boredom itself is a form of stress, too.'

Patient 'Yes, but the anxiety is about the shelving of the problem. I'm worried at the idea of going on shelving the main problem. I offer as an excuse that I've got to justify being irresponsible, which comforts at the moment and gives relief from the alternative of recognizing that I have a schizophrenia symptomatology. So frank schizophrenia is a variation of normal behaviour. Therefore schizophrenia episodes are in fact nothing to worry about.'

Analyst 'If schizophrenia is related to the normal in this way, that would rule out the theory of an organic illness.'

Patient 'That would be comforting.'

Analyst 'So in the psychoanalysis of yourself you are finding out the answers to this vast general problem of schizophrenia illness.'

Patient 'Also, I wonder if I'm not too much of a burden on other people. My wife, talking about my breakdown, implied that if I were schizophrenic then she could not tolerate still living with me, if I was so ill as that. So I have a conscience about my burden on her being so very great. Also some of this anxiety about others comes into it, especially if there is a possibility of my doing psychotherapy in the future. If I have to accept the idea that the majority views on schizophrenia are mistaken, then it would be immoral for me not to do anything about it. Here is an immense task, needing missionary enthusiasm, which I've just not got. If I find a lot of people doing something wrong it's not comfortable to be doing nothing.'

Analyst 'You are dealing with an abstract problem of the general theory of schizophrenia, when the true problem is your own self and can you get well?'

Patient 'It's not easy to accept that that's fair.'

Analyst 'The first two others, after yourself, would be your mother and your sister.'

Patient 'Yes, if one assumes that my illness is schizophrenia, then theirs is also, and after all there is the family element too (I mean familial not necessarily inherited). There is implied here an anxiety about the state of my own children, though I have assumed that it is not likely they are affected in the same way, though I have no rational grounds for such an assumption. It just seems unlikely.'

Analyst 'There is the question of your wife. For instance, would you say she is accessible or inaccessible, on the whole, to her children?'

Patient 'She's inaccessible to me, when she suddenly disliked my illness, but she is not so with the children. I wish she was therapeutically more stout.'

Analyst 'Perhaps you chose your wife because she was different from your mother in an important way.'

Patient 'Yes, she has a large amount of common sense, which is absent in my family. Although she is prepared to plunge into the unknown, nevertheless she keeps her feet on the ground. She knows what she wants, and she goes out to get it. So I recognize that I chose her because of the contrast relative to my own family.'

Analyst 'So the children are not likely to be affected, although it is difficult for you that you cannot get from her what the children naturally derive from her sense of reality.'

Patient 'Suddenly then I remembered a quotation from a paper I read three days ago: "People wrapped up in themselves make a very small package." That is myself, or what I am trying to avoid. I am able to despise myself for my limitations. It occurs to me that a reason for my distrust of psychiatry is part of my whole attitude to psychological medicine and to schizophrenia. It is based on a wrong attitude. This is something I was subconsciously aware of before the breakdown. If I accept the idea of working with the majority, then I have to accept what is wrong along with all the rest –.'

Wednesday, 22 June

Patient 'Feelings continued after last session. I had anxiety about what is likely to happen, having arrived at a label; what will happen in the future? The implication might be that the treatment must go on for a long while. Anxiety was mixed up with some relief and even amusement. Relief because a name to the illness makes it less obscure, easier to deal with, so I felt more confident; but amusement at the idea of the fools who argued that schizophrenia can't be treated by psychotherapy, and at the idea of how many are not aware of the nature of schizophrenic illness. It's amusing to see what expression they would have if told that I myself am schizophrenic. I managed to get so far in medicine as to fill a resident post. They might even be horrified, people I have worked with recently and medical colleagues, especially those who interviewed me at the beginning and who wanted a report from yourself. They would have forgotten by now.'

Analyst 'If all goes well, people forget; if things go badly, they remember?'

Patient 'I feel anxious now, insecure about my new job, and so on. I've no means of knowing.'

Analyst 'You are also wondering about my capacity in my job here.'

Patient 'Of the six or seven consultants I work for, only one is on the selection panel. I still feel I need to be helped on a bit. In my work I've still to be dependent on being pushed forward. To compete on equal terms makes me feel insecure. I've not had to, except in the first job (when I broke down). Also at this present stage there is the disadvantage that one does not apply for a new job till one is out of a job, so I might be unemployed, in which case it would be very difficult being at home all day. Finally, I'm still worried about the question of the future. I'm up against practical problems. I'm not in favour of being a GP, but there seems to be very little alternative prospect. A reason why general practice does not appeal is that the GP is self-dependent.'

Analyst 'People tend to ignore this aspect of general practice, the GP's isolation.'

Patient 'Yes, for instance, it is all right to refer a hospital patient back to the GP but not thought good for the GP to refer a case back to hospital. This makes a paradox. One thing that alarms me about being a GP is this measure of security, that is, as a permanent job. It is in any case distressing to be committed. It is the insecurity of hospital appointments that is the attractive feature. One need not make any decision about the future yet, but one can go on temporizing. But once a GP, it's GP for keeps.

'To revert to the topic of yesterday, there's something I forgot. It escaped me at the time. It has to do with what would happen if I had an easy steady monotonous job; then I should suffer from lack of interest. I'm worried about choosing being a doctor because there are difficult problems to be tackled the whole time, and no regular hours. I wonder if I'm right to choose medicine at all, because I have to face perfect security, long hours, inadequate pay for the responsibility taken; but there was no alternative at the time of choice. You've got to have missionary enthusiasm to be exploited. There is also the problem of how much administration is to be done by medical personnel. A doctor hates to be told what to do by lay persons, but doctors would hate to do the organizing themselves. I seem to like to have a perfect administration as a background. I feel I despise myself over this weakness of dependence, while resenting interference.'

Analyst 'Your dependence on the administration is a dependence on people.'

Patient 'This is part of my dispute with my wife. I like to regard her as the administrator, who sees I do the right thing at the right time. She expects me to do all that. My organization would break down if she were not there to look after it. She resents this.'

Analyst 'In regard to your present job, is that more administrative?'

Patient 'I'm not sure yet. At first I found it somewhat easier being in an advisory capacity, with less day-to-day anxiety about direct responsibility. I worry if a consultant says, "See this patient is admitted to the ward", because the task falls to me to arrange it. This is worse than a medical problem.'

Analyst 'This is like the problem of environment and of yourself in an environment.'

Pstient 'I don't think I'm clear about what you said. I feel anxiety about administrative work – like looking after children – you can't just let things go. If you've got children they've got to be dealt with. You can't say one afternoon, "Well, I've had enough." This is the awful thing about administration. I wonder if this is an expression of my mother's feeling of inadequacy as a mother, that she herself is insecure, so that I am more insecure as a father. In the same way that administrative problems are like children, so is chess. It is difficult to tackle chess problems, it occurred to me a long time ago, because you decide on a move, which is difficult enough, but the next move depends on what someone else does. It is therefore a living problem. In tennis it feels different to me. Before I can confidently tackle a problem I like to have the situation tied down, so that there is no urgency – no dynamic insecurity.'

Analyst 'This could be carried over to the analytic situation, with analyst and patient.'

Patient 'Yes, and someone with whom what you do affects his whole future. This is the most worrying but the most interesting thing about psychotherapy.'

Analyst 'You are hoping to integrate the two aspects which are at present not integrated in you.'

Patient 'At the time that I felt most acutely ill I was like someone in a bog, or trying to climb up a cliff of sand or gravel, and each step losing ground, surroundings being far from static, a dramatization of dynamic insecurity. But I knew even then that I yearned for a basic security, I was aware of never being happy, so I wanted the ability to deal with the dynamic situation.'

Analyst 'You wanted a basic security, and longed not to need this same thing, basic security.'

Patient 'It was an intellectual awareness. Now it is more that I *feel*; it's not just knowing, or of being in the direction of knowing. Still it seems too much like a gamble, in which the risk if I fail is too high. This is not my idea of desirable excitement. It was often said that father used to tease me because if I had to make an answer giving choice I always said "Both." I was always horrified at the idea of missing something. That fits in with my inability to cope with dynamic insecurity. Gambling is an unsatisfactory solution to that problem, not a sensible decision, a wrong method.'

Analyst 'Your alternatives are to be an individual taking the environment for granted, or to be environment-minded, and to lose individual identity. You are telling me that you cannot solve the dilemma of these alternatives.' (Patient asleep.)

Patient 'I feel bewildered, out of my depth. Yes, I slept. Sleep is one way of getting round a dilemma.' *Pause.* 'One thing occurs to me, associated with sleepiness. It has to do now with bewilderment, when I'm faced with being unable to cope, desperate, hopelessness that I can ever get better – then I go sleepy.'

Analyst 'You have an intellectual understanding that for a solution of the problem something depends on me, but in fact your problem has not been solved, and you are left in a state of bewilderment.'

Friday, 24 June

Patient 'I find it difficult to start today. I seem to be in a stationary condition. There is no prospect of something happening. It strikes me that, broadly speaking, in spite of the ground covered, I feel the same as when I came two years ago, though more confident and less depressed. I feel just as unreal as at the start. A factor may be that the stage in my work is unsatisfactory. I have less contact with patients now, more time to spare, with no definite place to be. Living at home now may make it less easy to keep up contact with the other doctors, whereas as a resident this was easy. At home it is a little easier. We don't fight or struggle now, but it's no more satisfactory, and it means I have not progressed if I can't deal with my present situation better.' *Pause.* 'Also I felt after I got here, it would be nice to lie and say nothing, and see what happens, but probably nothing would happen. You would sit there and accept my silence, and this would leave me unsatisfied.'

Analyst 'There is something you want, but you feel hopeless about whatever it is happening.'

Patient 'I find a link between this and the topic we have recently discussed about being hopeless about being loved. In a way I can bear this out in practice; in situations outside here if I were to take it easy and wait nothing would happen. So I can't just leave it. The outlook would then be hopeless.' *Pause.* 'Also I could add something about being hopeless about being loved. I feel hopeless about my being able to cope with the situation should love arrive.'

Analyst 'You would not be sure you could accept it.'

Patient 'I never have been able to accept it and have feelings, and so I have doubts.'

Analyst 'If I loved you, then the test comes as to your personal difficulty, but while none is available you are untested and you can then keep the idea that it might just possibly be all right. You are saying you have no experience in this field, that you just can't know.' (Patient sleepy.) 'You are telling me about this deep split in your nature, so that your impulses make no contact, but your acceptance of reality is with a false self that does not feel real.'

Patient 'Yes, if that is the situation, what can be done about it? Will recognizing it alter it? It is easy to understand, but how is it possible to deal with absence of feeling?'

Analyst 'Let us say, then, that this is where you are, and you see no way out.' (Patient sleepy.)

Patient 'But this sleepiness is not directly related to what is being said. It is more the general situation, a reaction to the hopelessness of the situation.'

Analyst 'By the nature of it, you cannot see any possible outcome.'

Patient 'For two years we have uncovered interesting ideas and all that, but we are no nearer tackling this all-important problem.' (Sleep.) 'I had a curious impression then, almost a dream. Someone was trying to get into touch with me about hospital matters. What would you do if this happened? If the external world were to come into the analytic situation?'

Analyst 'The dream is about the topic that we were discussing exactly. You bring about a contact that initiates from the hospital, and this is all right because it is not about you. Here nothing is any good unless it is about you, and you have no hope then. It shows that what you are fearing here is being awake while feeling no hope about contact with me here.' (Patient sleepy.) 'It is difficult for you to remain here and to be cut off from contact, in fact isolated.'

Patient 'Yes, when I hear you talk loving words, the idea of you and I being here together becomes remote.'

Analyst 'The precondition for the next stage is this difficult one in which you are here with me and yet isolated.' (Patient sleeps for several minutes.)

Patient 'It seems almost as if part of the difficulty about talking here is that unconsciously I am, so to speak, deliberately isolating myself. I have a need *not* to establish contact.'

Analyst 'Yes. You seem, however, to be going at an abstraction, trying to make the abstraction real.'

Patient 'Yes, that's what I'm trying to do, to convert the abstraction into a reality. It is tempting to evade issues by going to sleep, but it is not helpful to do so, and in a way I feel I've got you ranged against me here, for you have pointed out that sleeping can be valuable because of the dream that may go with it. I feel that sleeping produces a stalemate.'

Analyst 'The alternative is very difficult for you; it is to be awake here, but not in contact.'

Patient 'Yes, there seems to be only one solution, sleep, with the idea that I will wake and find everything changed and the problem solved.' (Sleepy. . . . Here he put his hand on his face and forehead, a rare occurrence, perhaps the first time it has happened.) *Pause*. 'It seems at times, but I've said it before, that every now and again I take stock and find I've been asleep and then I want to punish myself because I'm useless. It's wasting time.'

Analyst 'A moment ago you put your hand to your face. If I were a sensitive mother and you an infant, I would have known your face wanted contact and I would have brought your face against my breast, but you had to be the mother and the infant and your hand had to act the part of mother.' (Sleep overcame him at the beginning of this interpretation.)

Patient 'I'm still up against not being here. I don't feel it's any use.'

Analyst Here I repeated the interpretation.

Patient 'I grasped that, but I ought to have been speculating about what you would do; I would be horrified if you actually did anything. You seemed to imply that you would have to make a physical contact.'

Analyst 'Do you remember the headache that was outside your head, and my interpretation about having your head held, the day you had held a child's head.'[1]

Patient 'There is a paradox, which fits in here, which I have discussed with my colleagues, about patients attending our outpatients' department. I don't want to go on seeing people for whom I can't do much. But many enjoy coming to hospital, and even the long wait. Now I'm doing outpatients more, and each time I have to make a decision about future attendances. It has struck me that what they want is to have their hands held, that is to say, they are not content with verbal contact; they need some physical contact.'

Analyst 'And they miss it, don't they, if they are not physically examined?'

Patient 'They feel it's a waste of a visit if they are just spoken to. Even a minor examination makes all the difference.'

---

[1] See 'Withdrawal and Regression' in the Appendix to this volume.

Analyst 'I suggest that the subject is the loneliness which is more or less universal, and that that is the same subject as that of your being here, but isolated, not in contact with me.' (Sleepiness?)

Patient 'I'm trying to sum this up. This idea of physical contact. This sleepiness of mine today is new, that is to say, it is happening in a different setting. All this sleepiness today arises out of the conflict, wanting physical contact and being horrified if I got it.'

Analyst 'Do you remember, in the incident of the headache outside your head, you said that if I had actually held your head you would have felt it as a mechanical application of a technique? What was important was that the need was understood and felt by me.'

Patient 'At the level of feeling, I need physical contact, but feel horrified at the idea of getting it here. But I feel I ought to want it somewhere.'

Analyst 'The girl gave you physical contact which was important to you, but it was contact that belonged here but it was obtained outside. Now you have a conflict between needing and being horrified. As an infant your need was quite definite and simple. The question is, how much are you an infant here and now, and how much is it true to say that we are talking together about an infant?'

Patient 'It is an important stage of progress to recognize the need for physical contact. At first it was only an intellectual abstraction, the question whether as an idea it was attractive or not.'

Analyst 'Now, however, you are talking about real needs.'

Patient 'This may be rather obvious, but in some cases the contact I need can be verbal, that is if it comes at the right time. There are times recently when I've gone home and found my wife not concerned, offering no greeting. I have felt upset, but have not made a fuss because I know it's no use. But I have thought that if something had come from her at the right moment it need only have been a word.'

Analyst 'I would say that a correct interpretation that is well-timed is a physical contact of a kind.'

Patient 'Something occurred to me. I have noticed in the last few weeks quite a big change. Originally, a year ago, I enjoyed the cinema because for a few hours I could ignore my problem, identifying with the film characters, and therefore resenting the intervals with lights up. Now if I go to the pictures, which is rare, I feel worse when I go home, more out of contact and so bad-tempered. I don't any longer want to be lost in the film characters. Now it's all right if I go *with* someone, so that when we come out we have had the experience in common. I'm aware now that I used to go to the cinema to dig myself further back into remoteness. It is annoying that my wife will not discuss films. Either she has not been to the film yet, so she doesn't want to know the story, or else she has been, and that was some time ago and she has now got bored with it.'

(Because of the children the two can but seldom go together to the cinema.)

Tuesday, 28 June

Patient 'I have nothing to say, and this seems to have some positive quality.'

Analyst 'A thing in itself.'

Patient 'Yes. Ever since we talked about schizophrenia I have been more aware of altered feelings. I have been on the lookout. It has made me more critical about recognizing normality. Previously I was prepared to accept that the analysis might enable me to return to what I was like several years ago but this would be a return to unreality, and now I assume that I have always been abnormal. So there is nothing for me to compare the normal with. So carrying on all right is no longer adequate. Again this contributes to my feeling of hopelessness. If I have got to get somewhere I have no experience, so a prospect of arriving is less tangible. We can remove obstacles here, but what about positive steps? The first time I came to you I was not aware of any problem. My sole aim was to get somewhere different, to make progress possible. Mother offered me treatment for no very good reason. She said it could benefit me without my being aware of need. Perhaps mother knew something was wrong. At the moment I appear rather a fraud asking to be made different. This is something unparalleled in ordinary medicine.'

Analyst 'There basic health is taken for granted and the attempt is to alter illness.'

Patient 'Before I started I had an idea of positive health on the credit side, but since I have become a doctor I feel that has gone by the board, for health has no meaning. It would be an intellectual idea, having missed something and to feel convinced that it can be altered.'

Analyst 'The only thing that would be satisfactory would be if it happened.'

Patient 'My baby daughter had a first birthday and I forgot, although I talked about it the night before. The older daughter mentioned it as soon as she woke, and I was shaken by my own absence of excitement. How can I learn to get excited? A fundamental subjective process cannot be instilled, yet that is what I have come here for.' *Pause.* (Sleep?) 'At the moment I am up against a difficulty not knowing where to go or what is the next step. I could be silent for a long time, not as a joke but simply because I have nothing to say.'

Analyst 'You seem to be leaving out of account that this is experiencing something, being here but not having any contact with me.'

Patient 'I am aware of the general nature of the problem but I am not aware of the special aspects of the moment. It occurred to me that there is no good reason in treatment to refer to specific problems. Just now there is no point in saying what comes into my mind. I had forgotten that it was the expected idea (free association). It is unhelpful to remember things. I am trying all the time to avoid pointless use of words.'

Analyst 'In this case free association is not talking and being out of contact.'

Patient 'Ideas disappear as before, but now in order to think I have to be remote. It comes back to me that I cannot chatter, only by a very great effort, so what I say is not chatter but is forced words. There is no spontaneous lightness. I have the feeling of unreality because of the effort to be spontaneous. Effort is artificial in itself.'

Analyst 'Being remote is real, although it brings you out of touch.'

Patient 'Outside there is the same loneliness because of lack of contact. Other people are put off, so they don't make friends. My wife felt like that about me. She complains that I don't notice things. An example is that when someone talks my first reaction is to say nothing. There is nothing to say. But I want to be friends, so I talk in an effort to be friendly, but I am aware that it is hopeless all the time.' *Long Pause.* 'When I woke I felt I was smothered with hair.'

Analyst 'Possibly something to do with mother and yourself.'

Patient 'It feels like that, but what then? I feel that there is a connection between mothering and smothering.'

Analyst 'A mother may be able to be in touch with you when you are remote.'

Patient 'If that is so, it is rather difficult. Outside here there is no one to know what I need. In here, when I hint that I want you to say something, you never will. You seem pledged not to. It is a hopeless position to know that you have decided not to do the one thing needed.'

Analyst 'How am I to know what is needed? You are making a search for the experience of not being met because no one was there to be in touch with you.'

Patient 'How does this get anywhere?'

Analyst 'I think you are near feeling anger, which is all the time implied if you are reaching moments at which there was failure.' (Patient asleep.) 'You had a need then to be held with someone else in charge while you slept.'

Patient 'I am up against a difficulty that the mechanism here is essentially verbal. It is difficult to picture progress along a verbal level. It is too much like magic for me to expect to benefit from it. Yet in a way perhaps it is not so illogical.'

Analyst 'The couch is me more than if I were to actually hold you. The clumsiness of the whole matter would remind you only too well that you are not the infant you feel you are.'

Patient 'In mother's house or in my mother-in-law's house I not only have nothing to say but I go sleepy. In terms of what we said perhaps I am appealing for support, and I have a desire to sit or lie down. It seems that I cannot bother to be awake.' *Pause.* 'It occurs to me again, I am wondering whether the sleep represented a recognition of a failed desire to be fondled as a baby. I am dead to something. The difficulty is the fear of the anger. We have talked in the past about hidden anger. This reminds me of a situation of feeling annoyed with myself for being so cautious, not allowing anger to escape. I could stand a release of much more anger, and I am annoyed at holding up so big a barrier to progress, which depends on letting it go.'

Analyst 'There is a need for you to feel sufficiently integrated to stand the effect of being angry.'

Patient 'Now I feel I could stand more disruption.'

Analyst 'If I am right in all this, you are angry with me for not holding you, which is the original failure coming into the present.'

Patient 'I feel here too that when I have nothing to say there is some mechanism saying, "You are all right; is it worthwhile risking a disturbance? You might be able to manage." It is no good appealing to this voice. I am prepared for the risk, but the other part of me is too cautious.'

Wednesday, 29 June

Patient 'I had a dream last night. It has faded. It hinged round something near a true story of my wife and a man. It was nearly a nightmare. Perhaps I was fighting with him or struggling. The last two or three nights I feel I ought to have fought him more vigorously at the start, to have been less weak. The dream is a dramatization of what I wish had taken place.'

Analyst 'There seems to be something strengthening in you, enabling you to reach the struggle which has always been implied.'

Patient 'Yes, sometimes I have the feeling that my relationship to my wife might alter. I have felt that, if I approached her now and became more affectionate, she might possibly find me more acceptable. I have heard less about the man. Perhaps she is not seeing much of him. I have no more to go on than a subjective feeling.'

Analyst 'Often we see you get towards the idea of a struggle between two men and then a retreat from this position. Now you seem to have come up to it again.'

Patient 'I remember that we discussed a time or two ago about my wanting to be mothered or fondled and so on, and as I went away yesterday I thought perhaps I have wanted this from girls, and my wife has not any interest in this but would like to be fathered. On the bus I thought, I have a fear of being mothered. You remember the music teacher in the first analysis with you. To be mothered would be all right if it were by the right person. My mother-in-law is the wrong person. In part I despise myself about childish or effeminate attitudes. Unfortunately I chose my wife who just does not like mothering. If someone appeared only too anxious to supply affection and motherliness, then if I play with the idea of this I am filled with alarm.'

Analyst 'With me you get certain limited examples of mothering, but these lead you to see the absence of mothering from the right person at the right time.'

Patient 'I am not sure I understand this process. Whether in analysis one goes through what one has missed in token form like embryo in evolution? I can understand that. It seems more reasonable.'

Analyst 'There is a relationship between what you feel about women and what you feel about analysis. When I do well, you feel strengthened to meet the failures which have distorted you and angered you about this. Anger simply was not there because you were not organized into a strong enough position to be angry.'

Patient 'So I can only see two alternatives. One is to go through a mothering process, and the other is to be angry because of the absence of good mothering at the right moment.'

Analyst 'We shall see in the course of the treatment.' (Patient asleep.) 'It seems that, when you came towards the idea of a clash with father, you were thrown back on the question of whether it was worthwhile, and your relationship to your mother was not strong enough or well enough founded, so that you were thrown back on the weaknesses in this relationship.' (Patient sleepy.)

Patient 'I was not actually asleep. I had paused because you were going too fast. I was not keeping up, so I stopped, which was a reaction to your going too fast.'

Analyst 'If I went on ahead, that would be teaching and not psychoanalysis.'

Patient 'It is difficult for me to accept responsibility that I have to set the pace, but I can see why that must be.'

          Pause.

Analyst 'Just now when I went too fast I was exactly like your mother at her worst, or at any rate as you felt her to be at some critical early time. The present was the same as the past and implied in it all is anger with me.'

Patient 'There is a practical problem here with the small daughter who is fed on the bottle. We have tried to wean her on to a cup but she is not enthusiastic. I am torn between pushing her on and avoiding allowing her to become backward, relying on the bottle until she is too old and people would criticize and say it was absurd, but on the other hand I want to avoid the trauma of taking it away from her. There are two schools of thought: push and not deprive. Also in hospitals, when children come in with dummies, the first thing the nurses do is to deprive them of the dummy. Now it seems to me that this must be a bad policy just when the children are deprived of their home environment. It must make the separation harder, so with my own child I can see how my own background contributes to the dilemma.'

Analyst 'The children at hospital are usually older than a year, and at a year, which is the age of your little girl, it must be even more true that hurrying can do harm. But in regard to yourself the trouble was at a much earlier stage when you simply could not do with being pushed on, and with failures of adaptation.'

Patient 'It is better to meet the scorn of other people than to risk hurting a child.'

Analyst 'The scorn of other people just does not count when you are in charge of so small an infant.'

Patient 'The conclusion is that the idea of a struggle with the child is bad. Later the child knows what is happening and the struggle is less harmful, like when a child refuses to eat or to learn. I see now that there can be value in a struggle later when things have gone well at the beginning. There is the question of my wife's attitude about my sister's children who are naughty. She fears that the familiar pattern is reappearing. I do see now that she is actually alarmed at the struggle, which is not abnormal at their age as it means that they have not given in. All this seems remote from my problem but I suppose it has some bearing on it. The question is how to get back. To sum up, my own problem is how to find a struggle that never was. In the dream it was the struggle that was missing.'

Analyst 'You were not able to get the relief that the triangular situation brings when a child is in a clash with father; relief from the struggle with mother alone.'

Patient There was a renewal of the stopping here when he said, 'This is like going out. An annihilation of you is implied.' *Pause.* 'I realize here from time to time that there is danger in too much excitement because the idea of excitement involves rushing away. Anger is the same. If I was suddenly excited I would get up and tell you things and do things. Excitement is no good here.'

Analyst 'The risk is too great for you because of the clash.'

Patient 'A feature of excitement is irritation that it is not private. This applies to sexual matters. I have always had a difficulty that in sexual relationship with a girl there is no privacy, because there are two people. It is undesirable. On several occasions I have felt loneliness suddenly when in relationship with a girl, as if I had stopped seeing her. Also I upset my wife the first holiday we went on after marriage. We went with people and I did not want to be with her alone. I did not want to be excluded from the others, or else I feared what would happen if there were only two of us.'

Analyst 'A bit of each.'

Patient 'I also realize the difficulty with my wife about treatment here. I want to talk to her about here; I want somebody else in on it. I don't want one to the exclusion of the other. The trouble with mother is that it excludes father.'

Analyst 'On another occasion you said that what you needed was for the two parents to recognize you as an infant, so that there would be the three of you.'

Patient 'The idea of mother being perfect seems to exclude father. The word "mother" and "smother" seem to me to be related.'

Analyst 'You are trying to deal with mother's hate mixed up with her love.'

Patient 'Not that way. She eliminates the struggle with father because he joined in her plot being clever about it.'

Friday, 1 July

Patient 'The first thing that comes to me is something I noticed last week. Some doubt as to how to begin because you said I try too hard at the beginning, and so it struck me that to talk at the beginning is almost wrong. I ought to be wary about this.'

Analyst 'You feel it is unnatural to be the one starting.'

Patient 'The last two times I started with a tremendous rush, but on the whole I was thinking about this on the way here; that would be a natural form of behaviour.'

Analyst 'Being as careful as you are certainly prevents both silence and surprises.'

Patient 'Also I remembered that I had a clear dream last night, although I have forgotten it. It's curious; I remembered it one hour after waking;

I then lost it. There are two things in association with the dream. There is a semblance of truth and also a struggle in it, but this may be artificial.'

Analyst 'A bridge between your inner reality and external life, although you have forgotten this dream now. Do you think of it as having been pleasant or unpleasant?'

Patient 'Not as unpleasant as previous dreams.'

Analyst 'There seems to be a struggle.'

Patient 'Yes, I think it was with the wife's boy friend.' *Pause.* 'At the moment I am skirting round the various ideas to find somewhere to start. Ideas come and then get dismissed as incoherent, unimportant.'

Analyst 'What you are preventing is taking up unformed ideas and seeing where they get to. Perhaps they might not even get as far as being words but might be just sounds.'

Patient 'It is a jumble of words, not meaning anything. Odd bits and pieces – tokens.'

Analyst 'I am thinking of the period that we have spoken about before you could express ideas, when prattling or even just babbling was what you could manage. There is a question of what kind of audience you have and what you feel I am expecting.'

Patient 'There is also a fear of letting you have things that I have not had time to go through first. I am anxious lest you should be misled and chase the wrong ideas. Also there is a possibility of a deeper fear that I might get to an uncomfortable situation.' *Pause.* 'A lot of these ideas are related to things to do with work. There really is no real cause for anxiety. In the past in this sort of situation the interpretation was that I did not want to bore you with hospital matters. Now there is more the element of deliberately keeping you out of them. I don't want you reaching to all parts of my world. I have a feeling of danger that you might become too omnipotent. There must be some way to keep you out.'

Analyst 'You are telling me about positive elements in keeping me outside, which means having the right to your own inside. I think there may be something to do with mother here.' (Patient sleepy.)

Patient 'Today I seem sleepy and there is some excuse. Friday's a busy day and so on, but that isn't all.'

Analyst 'I am not sure that you know what I was saying.'

Patient 'Yes, I think I do know, but I was thinking of something while you were talking.'

Analyst 'I think I ought not to have wakened you.'

Patient 'I feel accused. I don't want to be caught.'

Analyst 'You were having a secret sleep and you feel that I discovered this secret.'

Patient 'There are various reasons. For one thing I insult you by sleeping; for another, I don't like the idea of you apologizing for sending me to sleep. There is a pattern of not wanting to find you too ready to withdraw and to apologize and so on. It puts me in the position of having to look after you.'

Analyst 'And also spoils the idea of a struggle.'

Patient 'If I apologize to my wife, she gets annoyed. Apologies can be overdone. An apology commands acknowledgement. It cannot be left; it expects some further action.' *Pause.* 'I suppose I distrust sleep. This is not the right place for it. It will be noticed and so I have to wake myself in order to forestall comment.'

Analyst 'If you sleep you leave me, like a few days ago when you said that you stopped because I was going too fast.'

Patient 'Yes, I could not keep up, so it was not worth trying. At the moment I am thinking in terms of progress in the analysis. Sleep is irritating in that, while I am asleep, there can be no communication here. Somewhere or other finding it difficult to talk here is related to difficulties outside which are rather new. I had a busy day today. I got behindhand with notes and things. It is a cause for worry. And it is new that these external worries are reflected in disjointedness here in the analysis.'

Analyst 'This is another example of there being less distinction between two aspects of your life.'

Patient 'Usually external problems stimulate me here. Now they only lead to confusion and sleepiness. It is outside things that are getting too confused.' *Pause.* 'I had an idea then associated with all this running away. Firstly, silence and sleep are the same as running away. Secondly, which is new, I feel today I got into a mess and I would like to run away from this situation. Once I talked to you about brushing past you, but I did not at the time recognize that I was fed up. Now I feel that there was confusion that cannot be coped with, and I wanted to go away and try again next time. It reminds me of a situation of a child dreaming. People say it's only a dream. The thing is to wake up. It's the same sort of quality. I would like to wake up, that is, get up, go away.'

Analyst 'The dream seems to take you towards the uncomfortable.'

Patient 'One idea is that you are critical of me for not playing my part. Also that I waste your time and I ought to justify coming here.'

Analyst 'How far has the hour been disrupted by my breaking into your sleep? It seems to me that what I did was rather like the original trauma that disrupted you.'

Patient 'The danger was that I was encouraged to be precocious. I could read very early indeed, and it strikes me now that this has a doubtful advantage.'

Analyst 'By early reading you lose being read to while going to sleep.'

Patient 'It occurs to me, one thing that has annoyed me about my wife for two years is that she is unwilling to talk last thing at night.'

Analyst 'Possibly she might talk and you go to sleep while she is talking.'

Patient 'But it is irritating to me that she has made a blunt declaration, "I am not going to talk." Communication is at an end. There is something also in it of an idea of myself needing her to be available until sleep. It is a hazy idea, but I find I am annoyed that she won't say goodnight. I would like conversation to be available until one of us goes off to sleep.'

Analyst 'There is a positive element, then, in my talking and your going to sleep. The lack of this positive element might have contributed to your finger-sucking.' *Pause.* (Here his hand was over his mouth and face.)

Patient 'Also if I make you too anxious about waking me I might produce a situation in which you are scared to do anything. It is an indefinite danger arising out of my sleeping that you might do nothing and I would never wake. This is all part of my anxiety about your being too apologetic and not being in command.'

Analyst 'There are two things I do. One is when I am good enough I displace your mother and others who failed. When I am bad I reactivate the bad past and it comes into the present.'

Patient 'Part of the anxiety is that if I put myself in your situation, and I thought of this while coming here in the train, I would not be able to manage these difficult matters. Recently you drew attention to the effects of your own actions. If I were doing the same thing what I did would be full of blunders. It seems you have got to be on top of everything.'

Analyst 'Certainly I make mistakes but there are times when these can be valuable if acknowledged.'

Tuesday, 5 July

(I was late on this day, which was already a postponed time. This had no perceptible effect on the material. There was an exceptional noise because of a cocktail party next door.)

Patient 'Oh! coming here today I was not thinking about how to start because there is no immediate or pressing problem except the vague problem of aim.'

Analyst 'These words, "vague problem of aim", seem to me to be quite fundamental to your illness.'

Patient 'I am not sure what I am aiming at.'

Analyst 'There are many ways in which this has appeared, one of which was that in the second analysis you were not able to come directly to me but I had more or less to go and look for you. Also you have said that in your first analysis you had no aim. At the beginning, like other infants, you had no aim, and this problem has remained with you.'

Patient 'I am not sure what you are meaning about "at the beginning".'

Analyst 'Put very crudely, when a baby has tasted milk he knows that his aim is to get at milk, but if no milk is presented the aim remains undirected. This idea can be spread over the whole of the details of infant care. It seems to me that your words, "vague problem of aim", state the whole thing, and there is no solution for you except that something comes from me.'

Patient 'This seems to be a general expression of a lot of problems in my life where I have no aim or objective. What sort of a job I am to take, for instance, and about the whole of my future. So far everything has depended on accidentals.'

Analyst 'Possibly that is the only thing that your mother failed you in, in meeting your original impulses and giving your aim a direction. In this way you have an exaggeration of a difficulty that is inherent in human development. It seems that mother was unable to be sensitive enough at the very beginning in the way that she could only be by an identification with her infant.'

Patient 'I don't quite see how.'

Analyst 'You will remember when you put your hand to your face and I said, "If I were a sensitive mother of an infant I would know that your face needed contact.'

Patient 'So the question now is, should I try to rectify the error or recognize that something is missing in my development?'

Analyst 'You have two alternatives: either finding me good enough or finding me failing you, in which case anger is implied, although you have not reached this stage.'

Patient 'I have to decide to find out whether it is possible to correct the omission.'

Analyst 'A thing that comes from this is that psychoanalysis takes you back not to something good that has been forgotten but to a failure or an absence of something.'

Patient 'It seems that I have to learn how to manage to find an aim. By contrast with my present aimlessness I feel I ought to have an aim now.'

Analyst 'What you are saying is that you feel hopeless and you are saying what you feel hopeless about. It is about this matter of aim.'

Patient 'Now is the time to alter. Perhaps I have to make a conscious decision.'

Analyst 'I think not.'

Patient 'So perhaps I have to go to you for something.'

Analyst 'Just here you have a dependence on me, and you are saying that at the moment you feel I am failing you. You are working away at the idea of the start of the hour, but it is the work done in the middle which elucidates this problem.'

Patient 'I would like to say that the start is not always awkward. In the last few weeks the difficulty in starting has been less or even absent.'

Analyst 'You remember you said that on two occasions you felt that you started with a torrent. The changes come through the work we do in the whole hour, and the change to be expected is that this problem of aim may disappear. What we do in the hour depends on the matter of subtleties in our relationship.'

Patient 'I recognize the need for subtlety. This presents a new difficulty or emphasis. There is not much point in my asking specific questions or bringing up concrete matters. An example occurred to me while I was waiting. I might discuss a specific topic, but what would be the point? The topic has not much to do with me, and it might cover up the difficulty about talking and be a bad way to start talking.'

Analyst 'A specific question limits itself.'

Patient 'I wanted to ask your opinion on an interesting topic, but it seems unlikely to get me anywhere.'

Analyst 'The question may contain something valuable, although I do see what you mean, that if I simply answer it I am being of no use.'

Patient 'But I think it is not so much that I want to know the answer as that the question might interest you yourself. So that might start you talking, just in the way that one deals with some chance meeting with a person, finding out their line, etcetera. It is an opening gambit to be abandoned later. The question was about a letter in the *British Medical Journal* this week. It had to do with the treatment of skin disorders by hypnosis. This seems a curious idea that a specific defect could be cleared up piecemeal. I have read something by Freud about hypnosis a long time ago which suggested that he started using it and abandoned it, but it seemed to me he never gave much of a reason. The idea of hypnosis suggests that I am trying to get something out of you, a short cut, or that you should take the initiative. So the question might have importance on its own.'

Analyst 'If I become the dominating figure, then that eliminates the problem of your having your personal aim met. This seems to represent again your extreme hopelessness that we might meet in a subtle way on equal terms.'

Patient 'About hypnosis, I always felt that it just could not happen to me. I cannot imagine how anyone could set about it. I would be so sceptical from the start. It is out of the question that I should get into a hypnotic state.'

Analyst 'It is interesting in view of the fact that sometimes you look as if you are asking for it when you go sleepy and want me to dominate, but this brings out what you have yourself expressed, which is that there is very great hostility wrapped up in this sleepiness. Nevertheless, the whole of this is a continued expression of your hopelessness about our meeting in a way in which there is a subtle interchange.'

Patient 'I must have been aware of the idea of a subtle interchange because I recognize that I have been looking for just something like that, without really knowing it. I could express my difficulty with women in this way, that I can only think of two ways of establishing a relationship. By one way it all comes from me; by the other way, which of course doesn't happen, it all comes from the girl, and I would not like it if it did. So I must have been aware that there could exist a satisfactory compromise which is described by these words, "subtle interplay".'

Analyst 'This which we now call subtle interplay has been happening all the time in the analysis. It is not something that might happen tomorrow but something that is happening now.'

Patient 'In a way, yes, but it so frequently gets broken off or does not develop. We break off and start again.'

Analyst 'At these points of breaking off I am doing exactly what was done badly originally, and you are affected in the present as at the beginning.'

Patient 'It occurs to me now that often I come here hopeless about starting and cannot see any way in which there could be a solution. Then half way through I notice suddenly that I have been doing what I thought to be impossible – talking and getting somewhere. It is as if I suddenly wake up and notice that I am doing something I thought out of the question.'

Analyst 'We are both engaged in this matter of subtle interplay. I think that the experience of subtle interplay is pleasurable to you because you are so vividly aware of hopelessness in this respect.'

Patient 'I would go so far as to say that it is exciting.'

Analyst 'The word "love" means a lot of different things, but it has to include this experience of subtle interplay, and we could say that you are experiencing love and loving in this situation.'

Pause.

Patient 'Again I notice something today that seems different. Could it be that there is more noise than usual?'

Analyst 'There is a great deal of noise today because of a cocktail party next door, and also the children that we are used to are in a more excited state and are playing more noisily than usual. I noticed that you did not make any remark about this at the beginning.'

Patient 'I noticed it but it did not seem worth mentioning.'

Analyst 'The fact that you did not comment on this at the beginning now comes in as a positive contribution to the hour, because that would have been simply getting away from the vague problem of aim. You would have started by reacting to an external event.'

Patient 'This expresses part of my difficulty with my wife. When I try to talk to her I do just this thing. I talk about concrete things that I know she is not interested in, and it gets nowhere. She must be aware that I am casting about for some way of breaking the silence and she rejects it all. She refuses to contribute. At times I feel like scolding her for not recognizing my need for chat. In fact I have scolded her.'

Analyst 'I am not in a position to judge what your wife would be like if you were normal, but here we have your wife on strike against being a therapist.'

Patient 'I have no means of judging what she would be like if I could take all these things for granted.' *Pause.* 'Here I am up against a difficulty in that she expects me to take a more decisive line. I feel there is no point. It has got to come naturally, and she won't understand that attitude. I have been speculating, if I were to go home unexpectedly and were to find her boy friend there. In the past I have just walked out. Ought I to take a stronger line, I wonder, and insist on his going? But I don't know if there is any point in being more decisive. I don't really know what I want to happen. I imagine a situation in which there is a test, but what is the test and what is the answer that I want? Do I want her to be sorry? Do I want to be tough with the man? Do I want to challenge her actually to defy me? I don't like the idea that I am not able to face up to the situation if it should arise.'

Analyst 'The thing that is absent in your relationship to your wife is subtle interplay, which we know in part depends on your inability to take this for granted. In a sense we have now to come round to an answer to the question, because it could quite reasonably be said that Freud abandoned hypnosis and developed psychoanalysis because he saw the value of subtle interplay between analyst and patient and realized that this very thing was eliminated in hypnosis.'

Wednesday, 6 July

Patient 'I was just thinking. It occurs to me to say that I had a dream last night. There is only a bit that I remember at the moment. I was having an exam (I am not sure of its nature) at the hospital. It was conducted by Professor "X" of my medical school. The practical was being done on patients that are in my care, so the examination was rather of the nature of a chat – a discussion without the examination of patients. It would have been silly to have examined them because I knew a lot about them anyway. In a way I have a sort of exam next week, the interview about the job that I am already doing as a locum; and also about a hospital. There is a connection with the fact that these interviews about jobs have nothing to do with medicine. It is a curious tradition that one is never asked questions about clinical medicine.'

Analyst 'I would take out of the dream the word "chat". You remember how it came in recently. There seems to be some sort of idea of a contact with the professor in a play area.'

Patient 'He is a genial man reputed for being friendly. I have just remembered that I saw him recently, when I dropped in at my hospital. As a matter of fact, I was disappointed because he did not recognize me, though I could hardly expect him to as I was only a student. But some of the other staff might have. Perhaps he is snobbish. He could represent a fatherly figure for me.'

Analyst 'He is a man that you would like to be able to have an easy relation to.'

Patient 'Yes, but he is inaccessible. At the moment I do not feel like challenging him.'

Analyst 'The fact that he is a genial figure makes the position tantalizing.'

Patient 'Yes, because others there do seem more willing to recognize students.'

Analyst 'If an exam were to be on your own patients you would come off rather well, would you not?'

Patient 'Professor X would be critical. He sets a high standard; you can't bluff him. Also it comes in that, although he has a genial personality, he demands a very high standard of work from his house physicians, so that they have no time off at all. At the time when I first worked I needed weekends, and the prospect of a job under Professor X would have been gruesome, with no time off at all. I feel alarmed at the idea. It's curious that he should demand such a standard from his house physicians and not tolerate the same thing for his own patients. A curious tradition, asking too much and taking advantage of the fact that such jobs are very much sought after. So there is a good deal of resentment about his genial character. I almost blame him for my not trying to get a job there because of his needing work without relief.'

Analyst 'So you would really have liked a job at your own hospital.'

Patient 'Yes, there are great advantages to be got from that. It's a matter of prestige, but in regard to experience the job is not good – fewer patients and less responsibility – but you can't overlook the prestige element. Also there builds into this a film that I saw last night, "The Women's World". The president of a large motor works invites three leading salesmen and their wives to stay with him. On the behaviour of these couples during the holiday he is to decide who to give an important job to.'

Analyst 'What a terrible situation!'

Patient 'It's like my own position – one interview and three other candidates.'

Analyst 'So the word "struggle" comes in as well.'

Patient 'I hadn't thought of that aspect. All the time in my hospital jobs I have not struggled for anything. I have hoped to be fitted in. It is an uncomfortable feeling. I don't seem to have the ability to fight my own way.'

Analyst 'The idea of struggle and of the rejection of the unsuccessful candidate certainly comes in at the present time through the film.'

Patient 'Yes. One of the characters in the film said, "What a pity we are forced to hate friends."'

Analyst 'So you are forced to hate the other three who are applying.'

Patient 'I was not aware of that, but I see it in the background. I have never been able to recognize this hatred. There has always been a lack of jealousy, and for some time I have known that it ought to be there. So I turn my hate against the system that compels one to compete. I remember in my first job I competed with three others, and I was pleased to get it. I never thought of the others as people. They were just competitors. I got an intellectual satisfaction.'

Analyst 'You were not in a position then to triumph over people.'

Patient 'I was only dimly aware of primitive rivalry. It seemed too childish to allow myself to gloat over the unsuccessful. As a small boy I might have gloated when favoured at home, but it was undignified, and this is not proper adult behaviour.'

Analyst 'Did you get there in childhood even?'

Patient 'The first idea that comes to me is that on occasion I got father's ear in competition with my sisters and gloated at having beaten them.'

Analyst 'Do you think that has had to do with your being a male when they were girls?'

Patient 'That may well have been. I feel that competition is robbed of significance because girls are different, so it is not on fair grounds. If it had been with a brother that I competed, that would have been a real victory.'

Analyst 'But you are implying an inherent victory. Simply that by being a male you have a superiority.'

Patient 'Yes, I suppose.' (Doubtful.) *Pause.* (Thinking.) 'I am stuck here. I think we are pressing too far.'

Analyst 'It may possibly be my fault.'

Patient 'I made too much of the absence of competition. Parts seem genuine enough. There is a general lack of concern.'

Analyst 'It seems that there is something here which may be true, but it is not the main thing at the moment.'

Patient 'I am not sure at all how much being a male really fits in except to emphasize loneliness. Also an inability to face up to competition is one thing I came here to see about.'

Pause.

Analyst Here I started an interpretation –

Patient 'Sorry, I lost which subject we were talking about. You mean, does coming here exclude others from coming? I am not convinced, as I think that is something that you have brought up. Or if it is there, I am not willing to recognize it. Perhaps there is something more in it, because my wife's criticism of my coming here and my own criticism of psychoanalysis is that it is a treatment only available to a very few. The treatment is not justified as it is only fortuitously available, and I have never really answered this question. I just ignore it. I need the treatment and that's that. At times the idea is uncomfortable.' *Pause.* 'Something I was thinking is perhaps an extension of the idea of wanting to be helped and being ashamed of it. I remember the criticism felt by the patients at the hospital of the role of the PSW, who did not seem to fulfil two important functions which are hers. She did not keep in touch with relatives, and she was not able to inform them when approached, and also she did very little to help patients into jobs, rehabilitation, and so on, after they left. This did not apply to me. The idea was, go out and find one if you want a job. I felt irritated. The idea of someone not doing what they were supposed to do.'

Analyst 'This is again to do with struggle.'

Patient 'It is the same with the work done by almoners in hospital. They are part of the family supplying parental responsibility, but I wonder if it is not looking after the patients too much. This is part of a criticism of the welfare state. I am annoyed that I myself expect and want a hospital organization to take over and look after patients so that they get social as well as medical care. In the same way, on leaving medical school the newly qualified doctor wants a job fixed up. This means weakness, immaturity. I do not feel clear about it.'

Analyst 'Included in it all is your inability to stand triumph, to accept your own aggressiveness.'

Patient 'About medical patients I find myself oscillating between complete care and complete abandonment. On the one hand I am pushed by the feeling that it is nice, comforting, to give social care. On the other hand I feel criticial. This is mollycoddling. The weakness in me is that I can't formulate my own opinion. A lot of my indecision is part of this not wanting to accept responsibility for myself and my own decisions because they are made by other people's decisions. I hide the difficulty about deciding things by saying it doesn't matter what I feel about it.' *Pause.* 'At the moment I feel I have wandered round. I have been too dilatory. I have not put pressure on one object. I feel confused. One thing is that I feel I have failed to impress you. Perhaps I was hiding that the criterion is whether I impress you or not.'

Analyst 'There seem to be two alternatives. Either there is something in the dream theme that I have missed and I have taken up the wrong points, or the other alternative is that I am right and that you are strongly resisting the idea that I put forward that the central theme is the hate of rivals. I have an idea that you feel I ought to be backing you up in the interview next week, as in fact I did do in your original interview. I am getting at this through the dream of Professor X.'

Patient 'The idea occurs to me that he might be one of the assessors, or someone like him, although this is very unlikely. Also I recognize that it is farcical complaining, because I am relying on the fact that I am already working in the job, so that they have some obligation towards me. I have wormed my way in. I feel guilty because I ought not to rely on prejudice in my favour.'

Analyst 'Because this again eliminates the struggle and the overthrow of rivals which is what you are trying to get to.'

Patient 'I can't afford to be honest and so I use unfair weapons, but it is not satisfying.'

Analyst 'It is difficult to know which would be satisfactory to you:
   1 To fight.
   2 That your work should be better than that of the others.
   3 To worm your way in, and
   4 That you might be the better man.
   'How would you feel if it were true that you were the best man in a general way of the candidates applying?'

Patient 'I don't know. Then there would be no competition.'

Analyst 'It is quite clear that the satisfying alternative is the first, but you are unable to dream the dream in which you fight to kill your rivals.'

Friday, 8 July

Patient 'The first thing that occurs to me is that I dreamed again the night before last of an exam. It was Professor X again, but the exam was more related to cases. Last night I dreamed of an exam again, but it was not Professor X. It seems that the subject of a test or viva must be more important for me in the unconscious than I am prepared to admit. Three nights in succession I have dreamed in this way. It is curious that I notice that I remember the dream on waking and then again an hour later recapitulate. After that I forget the dream completely till I arrive here, then I remember, but by that time the subject matter has become elusive. It is curious how dreams like this come back. Just as I become fully awake the dream is there, but I am still drowsy. Then it fades as I become alert.'

Analyst 'All the time there is the external fact of the interview next week.'

Patient 'Last time we spent a lot of time discussing this subject, but I am hazy about the form of the discussion.'

Analyst 'Perhaps you remember that an important part of the discussion was the relationship between you and those turned down.'

Patient 'Oh yes, I remember now. I notice today, it occasionally cropped up while I was doing outpatient work. In the rush I found myself tending to think of patients more as units than people – items of work to be got through. I found myself hoping or expecting to find nothing wrong, just to save myself from having to deal with them, and constantly had to pull myself up and to remember that these are people come for advice. I cannot expect them all to have nothing wrong. I repeatedly pulled myself up.'

Analyst 'The matter of people compared with units is like the people who are rivals but who do not turn up in the last two dreams.'

Patient 'The other side of the picture is of course that I only see people in the outpatients who have been twice or more before, so I am looking at the results of investigations, seeing whether there is a need for further treatment or whether to tell them they need not come again, or the people need regular check-ups. So I do not feel so bad about it, but I have to keep my eye open for the genuine patient. It is a curious situation that the conscience comes into it. There seem to be two kinds of consultant that I work for. One aims at seeing patients and discharging as soon as possible to the GP. The other tends never to discharge, so the outpatient department is filled with old patients. In that first case I have to put on a restraining hand, and in the second case it is the opposite. I find I tend to favour getting rid of patients, partly because I do not like long lists, and I justify myself by saying that I am saving the people unnecessary journeys. I find myself in the patient's position and reflect, "What would I like?" and so on. So it's like coming here. I really only just now realized that I am coming to your outpatient department and the object is to not have to go. It is a reflection on my need to make sure that you are aiming at getting rid of me.'

Analyst 'This business of your putting yourself in the patient's place and all that is one example of the subtle interchange.'

Patient 'That is what I try to do. Both extremes may be justified, but I try to strike a balance. I could have the entire population attending my outpatients. A guiding point is what is reasonable when one uses the patients' own feelings.'

Analyst 'This is a description of myself with you.'

Patient 'Yes, and with some patients one has to be on the lookout as they want to leave off, but one can see that they are not well. So here it is not just how I feel. I have to rely on you to know more than I do.'

Analyst 'The principle is that you come here in order not to have to.' *Pause.* 'I cannot yet see the relationship between this and the dreams.'

Patient 'One comment is whether one's attitude to people is suitable to the job. One's conscience comes into it.'

Analyst 'You say that the interviews for jobs do not take into account medical acumen. I wonder whether you feel that they also omit an assessment of your conscience in regard to patients.'

Patient 'They cannot assess this. There are only two ways of assessing this – the opinion of the consultant for whom one works and that of the patients. I feel in a way that I am still a fraud. I do not feel half as capable as others think I am. In medicine it is mostly bluff, and I have to ask myself, do I bluff more than the average?'

Analyst 'This is really an examination of myself. You are the one who has the chance to find out, as my patient, whether I bluff.'

Patient 'The patient can say how good my bluffing is. He may notice I am mystified and seem lost. It is bound to happen because I am not a good actor. I cannot disguise myself. If I cannot make head or tail of a story, I feel hot and bothered and show it. This is the same as wondering how you cope when you are lost here.'

Analyst 'Do patients prefer the actor or the doctor who shows when he is confused?'

Patient 'Well, the actor is rather popular, but patients get put off by bad acting.'

Analyst 'Joined up with this is your dislike of my being apologetic.'

Patient 'I don't like apologizing when I am not certain. Also dealing with other people, doctors and almoners, etc, I personally feel that I look vacant. The thing is, do they notice it? I am sure they don't notice it nearly as much as I feel they do. I just hope they accept it as a mannerism or a pose.'

Analyst 'I would like to remind you of the time when you stopped because I had gone on beyond you. (*See p. 164.*) I suppose this feeling that you look vacant is rather like this stopping or withdrawing or sleepiness that happens here.'

Patient 'Or I pretend to understand when I am at work but here mannerisms and stunts would be noticed as such. I find that satisfying and even useful. And when I am not here I forget that others are not so observant as you are, or that they do not know me and just would not notice. It is as if I imagine others act for you in your absence. Part of my sensitivity away from here is related to coming here where I am the topic.'

Analyst 'Yes, here you are the topic, but there they have their own thoughts as well, and their own topics.'

Patient 'This brings me back to the job and the examinations. I think I fear this interview. It means much more to me than the job. It is a judgement on me. Am I generally any good or not? So I am concerned about the others because some will fail if I get the job, so it is a judgment on me for not considering whether the others are more qualified than me. This is a subjective approach. As I have been locum in the job I am known, and if they do not employ me it is rather like a rejection, so that I am likely to keep the job. I feel in general that I would prefer not to apply for a job in the same group so as to avoid this problem. It is unfair to the employers if they have an obligation to be good to an employee. I am trading on that. If I turn out to be no good, I am taking a mean advantage applying for this job. I have accepted some responsibility for the choice of myself.'

Analyst 'There are three subjects: one is yourself, another is the job, and the third is the other candidates. What you are not mentioning is the fact that these people that you may be turning out could be friends. This came into the film.'

Patient 'I do feel I do not want to go on, not today at any rate. I would like to come back tomorrow. I feel uncomfortable; I have had enough; I would like to run away.'

Analyst 'The thing in front of you that is difficult for you is that you might be involved in triumph. This particular aspect of the interview is unacceptable to you, that there shall be a struggle and that you will fight and kill.'

Patient 'Yes.' (Sleeps.) 'When you were talking about triumph it occurred to me that part of the anxiety when things are too difficult, or when I have too much responsibility in a case, is that things have suddenly gone too far ahead, so I find myself alone on my own with no one to lean on out in mid air and so on. Running away means retreating. I want to go to mother's lap almost exactly as you described some time ago about a child walking to his mother and horrified to find himself on his own. Walking means separation. I can accept triumph if there is someone to share it with, even if I have to imagine someone, but that is hazardous. The imagination may fail, and I will be left holding the baby.'

Analyst 'To some extent this has to do with your being an only son. Do you remember my speaking of this before?'

Patient 'No.'

Analyst 'The fact that you had no brother may be an important factor. You said that in competition it took some of the gratification away if your rivals were sisters in relation to father.'

Patient 'I feel that triumph is hollow if there is no one to show it to.'

Analyst 'The difficulty here is between reality and fantasy. In a competitive game you can share your triumph with the other competitors if you win, but if it is a dream and your aim is to kill – (Patient deeply asleep.) – then you cannot share triumph with the rival.'

(The question seriously presented itself as to whether I had made a technical error taking the subject over to rivalry, that is, going on ahead too fast.)

Patient 'The last few minutes it has been very difficult to keep here at all. Perhaps I slept. I feel annoyed with myself for wasting time. There is absolutely no excuse.' (Sleeps again.)

Analyst 'There is the interview next week. The fact seems to be that this interview is in advance of you in your analysis. You are not really worried about the interview as such, but what it means to you, in terms of your relation to me, is something that you have not arrived at, and so you stopped. You cannot dream of killing the rival. Circumstances are behaving as I behaved the other day when I went on ahead.'

Patient 'If I were applying for a job in the usual manner, on equal terms, it might be easier.'

Analyst 'It might, but I am not sure whether you could manage such a thing easily at the present moment in your analysis.'

Patient 'It is hypothetical. It might be. I am not worried about either the interview or the job as such. It is a combination of uncertainty with the feeling that there ought not to be uncertainty.'

Analyst 'I think that you are not ready for open competition.'

Patient 'If it were an outside job I could afford to be indifferent. The trouble is that this is "in the family".'

Analyst 'Yes, just that.'

Wednesday, 13 July

On Tuesday, 12 July, the patient rang up at the time of his hour to say that the combination of the hot weather and his being very tired made him wish to miss a session.

Patient 'I felt exhausted last night. By the way, I didn't get the job. That and the heat made me unwilling to come. A local hospital has very little to say in the choice of its resident staff. Abbout the interview I felt unusually agitated, more than I have done on previous occasions. It is curious, because there was no reason. I felt that I was not the same person as in other interviews. For half an hour I was excessively bewildered and then felt relief. To get this job would not have been quite satisfactory for me. I had the feeling that it would be unfair taking an advantage. At least now with another job I shall be able to satisfy myself that I am on my own feet. Some of this may be myself reassuring myself. The advantage of this job was that I would be working in the same group and therefore must seem to be popular. It is not after all so impressive as one might think.'

Analyst 'You were saying these things before the interview last week.'

Patient 'This afternoon I feel more in favour of a break from treatment for a time. There are snags both ways. The advantage is that I would have more scope in selecting jobs. I feel that now coming to analysis depends on the job more than the other way round. The disadvantage would be that the process of analysis is incomplete, so that I ought to get it completed before having a gap. I feel like trying it out. It's difficult for me to judge.'

Analyst 'There are certain things that you have told me in previous sessions. You can see I am able to judge better than you. For instance, I can point out to you that in your description of the interview what has been left out is that you have been killed.'

Patient 'I noticed a curious thing. One of the other candidates came in to see me in the morning before the interview. I wondered why he did it. He said, did I think he might get the appointment and so on. It was silly to ask me. I wanted to say no, so as to limit the field. I felt hostility towards him. I think for the first time I felt hostility in such a situation and did not want to talk to him, and he did not want to talk to me.'

Analyst 'You seemed to be having the natural feelings belonging to this situation.'

Patient 'I was warned by the staff that their favouring me would not carry much weight. After I came out I felt more friendly to the others. When one had been selected there was a change of atmosphere among the three who were left. We had nothing to quarrel about any more.'

Analyst 'So you entered more than you usually have been able to do before into the rivalry situation.'

Patient 'That applies in general too; I am more able to feel rivalry when it is present. I am able to summon up more hostility about my wife's boy friend. Not that I have seen him recently. My wife avoids our coming into direct conflict. If we were to meet now I would be more positive in my hostility. Certainly not begging for mercy. In general I am tending to lay down the law more firmly. In my work this is partly due to an increase in experience, so that I am able to be more authoritative. Today, doing a ward round with the junior, I was able to make a definite diagnosis where he was not certain. And I did so without being apologetic. Some months ago the idea of being in authority was something I could only accept in theory. Now it feels more logical and it is less of an act; more natural. This was a clear-cut case; I could not help thinking why he did not notice what I noticed.'

Analyst 'So experience does not make you clever all the time; it makes the truth seem more obvious.'

Patient 'I wonder how I could not do it before.' *Pause.* 'At the moment I notice that you are not making any comment on whether I go on with analysis or not. Perhaps I do not want to feel I am coming here only because I want to, even if I have a good reason. It would be easier if I did not have to accept responsibility for this sort of decision. A criticism against coming here is that I would be able to say no; nevertheless I would like your view. How important is it for me to go on coming?'

Analyst 'I will say definitely that I prefer it if you can continue. Nevertheless there is the point that I am also pleased about the progress, which means that you might be able to put the job before the treatment.'

Patient 'Am I justified in thinking it could be done?'

Analyst 'I do just think it possible.'

Patient 'At the hospital where I was a patient, when I spoke about taking a job they said, "You can, but you need not." This implied a gamble. Now that I have made progress here, is it still a gamble?'

Analyst 'I think that it is all right for you to leave off, but there is more for you to get out of analysis around the subject of rivalry, which you are only just beginning to be able to accept with its full implications. So I will say again that it is better if you can come in September and get on with it.'

Patient 'I remembered this evening on the way here one of the chief jobs they offered me is in X, and I found myself not being very keen because it is further out. It is funny, I never thought about whether I could get here from it or not, only that it was too far from home.'

Analyst 'No doubt you have a good deal to discover in yourself as a result of the changes that have come about in the analysis recently.'

Patient 'In the old days, in the first treatment, you said that it was quite a good result for war time. Would you be making the same sort of comment now? Good but incomplete? A breakdown is likely to occur later on?'

Analyst 'No, I would not say that now.'

Patient 'Quite good enough is not good enough if I am due for a breakdown. How far is a breakdown inevitable? Probably it was when I left off the first treatment as I have never felt normal. I am concerned now that I do not really know what I want to do with my life.'

Analyst 'I am saying clearly that I do want you to come in September. If you do not come, I can see that there are advantages to be got out of the break.'

Patient 'I can keep comparing my views on psychoanalysis with my views of it ten years ago. I used to express strong views that psychoanalysis was unscientific, feeling that analysts were too dogmatic, almost sectarian. If one disagreed with an analyst, one became a heretic. So psychoanalysis seemed a bad thing. I held this view until I broke down. Now my experience is such that I do not know where I got those views from. It may have been mother's fault. This is quite a recent idea that I have had. Her rigid adherence to Freud and analysis I find is not shared by most analysts. Analysts as a whole I find do not say that Freud is right and everything else wrong. They think as they go along. My wife quotes my words belonging to the time when I was hostile, when I expressed fervent hostility to psychoanalysis, so my coming here now is regarded by her as a backsliding, doing something against my own principles. Also, ten years ago one thing that disturbed me was a book of Freud's in which he dabbled in anthropology. I can't remember –'

Analyst '*Totem and Taboo*?'

Patient 'Yes. He was arguing from theory, reconstructing the past through the present society. I have not read it for a long time, of course. I wonder if I would consider this a valid criticism now.'

Analyst 'It interests me that you refer to *Totem and Taboo* as unacceptable. Is not the theme of that book that the brothers come together to kill the father? The hostility between the brothers is suppressed for the purpose of the overthrow of the father.'

Patient (Laughs.) 'I never thought that I might have an emotional bias when I was critical then. At the time I was critical that Freud said that the oedipus complex was important in primitive society, which was, in fact, matriarchal. It seemed unlikely, considering the boys did not know their own fathers. Even daughters had no specific fathers. So it would be impossible to apply the same set of rules, but I must say I am very hazy about this and I have not thought of it for a long time. Perhaps I ought to get it out again.'

Analyst 'It is possible for anthropologists to criticize *Totem and Taboo*, but not, I think, along the lines that you were critical. I would say that the general view is that there was an awareness of parentage, only there were certain customs relating to the use of uncles and so on.'

Patient 'The idea of original sin plays an important part in it, I think, unless my memory is at fault. I had great hostility to the idea that since the dawn of time children have been concerned about the sexual relationships of their own parents. There is almost a religious bias running through the book colouring the whole attitude. As I was brought up an atheist (that was father's doing), the idea that I might have to accept religious ideas came to me as rather horrifying and made me antagonistic to psychoanalysis.'

Analyst 'I suggest that there is something you are leaving out of the subject presented in that book. The sin is associated with the killing of the father, but you are not saying anything about the central theme, which is that all those who were antagonistic to each other loved their mother, and it was love of the mother that made them want to kill the father in the primal scene.'

Patient 'I am hazy about sin and the way it came into this book.'

Analyst 'Original sin in this book seems to me to come in as the love of mother.'

Patient 'I have an inability to accept the idea of a universal hatred of the father. The idea is unpalatable, but I think there is more to be gained out of this to do with the present situation. In those days I was attracted by anything that was not dogmatic, but now I would say that I definitely favour flexibility. My criticism of medicine is the dogma in it. This must be so because we have been taught it.'

Analyst 'All this time you are paying a tribute to myself. You have often asked me to be more dogmatic, but as you have partly said, you value my flexibility and my willigness to try things out as I go along. This especially comes in in regard to the question, shall you leave off treatment or not?'

Patient 'The thing about dogma is that it cannot be wrong. The great master, Freud, the Pope, Stalin; the acceptance of dogma is something that takes the place of father. You assume that he cannot be wrong. A father-figure. It is a bad thing to let intellect rest on illogical emotions.' *Pause.* 'In a way, I seem to be ending on a theoretical note. Am I unconsciously but deliberately avoiding digging up something?'

Analyst 'There is an avoidance along the lines of using me in a general way as an analyst, or perhaps a mother-figure, and ignoring the fact that I am also a father-figure for you in your analysis. When I say I want you to come back I am a mother-figure, and this is valuable to you in so far as you are infantile. There is another way of looking at it, however, in which I, as father, say you must come back. Now you are in a position in which you can defy me. In a third way of looking at the matter, the analysis is mother that you want and I am father. Either I kill you or you kill me, because we are in rivalry. Often we discuss these matters, but here in the matter of whether you come back or not in September, there is a practical situation, and an emotional rather than an intellectul problem is before you.'

END OF TERM

(Almost nine months later, the patient sent the following letter.)

10 April

Dear Dr Winnicott,

I feel that I owe you an apology for not writing before. When I last got in touch with you I decided to stop at least until Easter while I was working at —— and then let you know.

On the whole it has proved very satisfactory and my plans, so far, are to continue as at present until my appointment expires next August.

I am not at all sure what I will be doing after that. It is not yet possible for me to plan that far ahead. I am tempted at times to abandon analysis as I now feel so well. On the other hand, I do realise that the process is incomplete and I may then decide either to resume with you, or should that no longer be possible, to start with someone else. It seems to me to be a great step forward that I can accept that idea fairly easily.

Should we not resume later on, I would like to use this opportunity to express my gratitude for all that you have done.

Yours sincerely,

APPENDIX

Withdrawal and Regression[1]

IN THE course of the last decade I have had forced on me the experience of several adult patients who made a regression in the transference in the course of analysis.

I wish to communicate an incident in the analysis of a patient who did not actually become clinically regressed but whose regressions were localized in momentary withdrawal states which occurred in the anaytic sessions. My management of these withdrawal states was greatly influenced by my experience with regressed patients.

(By withdrawal in this paper I mean momentary detachment from a waking relationship with external reality, this detachment being sometimes of the nature of brief sleep. By regression I mean regression to dependence and not specifically regression in terms of erotogenic zones.)

I am choosing to give a series of six significant episodes chosen out of all the material belonging to the analysis of a schizoid-depressive patient. The patient is a married man with a family. At the onset of the present illness he had a breakdown, in which he felt unreal and lost what little capacity he had had for spontaneity. He was unable to work until some months after the analysis started, and at first he came to me as a patient from a mental hospital. (This patient had had a short period of analysis with me during the war, as a result of which he had made a clinical recovery from an acute disturbance of adolescence, but without gaining insight.)

The main thing that keeps this patient consciously seeking analysis is his inability to be impulsive and to make original remarks, although he can join very intelligently in serious conversation originated by other people. He is almost friendless because his friendships are spoiled by his lack of ability to originate anything, which makes him a boring companion. (He reported having laughed once at the cinema, and this small evidence of improvement made him feel hopeful about the outcome of the analysis.)

Over a long period his free associations were in the form of a rhetorical report of a conversation that was going on all the time inside, his free associations being carefully arranged and presented in a way that he felt would make the material interesting to the analyst.

Like many other patients in analysis, this patient at times sinks deep into the

---

[1] Read at the XVIIème Conférence des Psychanalystes de Langues Romanes, Paris, November 1954, and to the British Psycho-Analytical Society, 29th June, 1955; and published in Dr Winnicott's *Collected Papers* (1958), which has been reissued under the title *Through Paediatrics to Psycho-Analysis* (Winnicott 1975). See the Introduction to this volume, p. 1; also p. 20, note 2.

analytic situation; on important but rare occasions he becomes withdrawn; during these moments of withdrawal unexpected things happen which he is sometimes able to report. I shall pick out these rare happenings for the purpose of this paper from the vast mass of ordinary psychoanalytic material which I must ask my reader to take for granted.

Episodes 1 and 2

The first of these happenings (the fantasy of which he was only just able to capture and to report) was that, in a momentary withdrawn state on the couch, he had *curled up and rolled over the back of the couch*. This was the first direct evidence in the analysis of a spontaneous self. The next withdrawn moment occurred a few weeks later. He had just made an attempt to use me as a substitute for his father (who had died when the patient was 18) and had asked me my advice about a detail in his work. I had first of all discussed this detail with him, pointing out, however, that he needed me as an analyst and not as a father-substitute. He had said it would be a waste of time to go on talking in his ordinary way, and then said that he had become withdrawn and felt this as a flight from something. He could not remember any dream belonging to this moment of sleep. I pointed out to him that his withdrawal was at that time a flight from the painful experience of being exactly between waking and sleeping, or between talking to me rationally and being withdrawn. It was at this point that he just managed to tell me that he had again had the idea of being *curled up*, although in actual fact he was lying on his back as usual, with his hands together across his chest.

It is here that I made the first of the interpretations which I know I would not have made twenty years ago. This interpretation turned out to be highly significant. When he spoke of being curled up, he made movements with his hands to show that his curled-up position was somewhere in front of his face and that he was moving around in the curled-up position. I immediately said to him: 'In speaking of yourself as curled up and moving round, you are at the same time implying something which naturally you are not describing since you are not aware of it; you imply the *existence of a medium*.' After a while I asked him if he understood what I meant and I found that he had immediately understood; he said, 'Like the oil in which wheels move.' Having now received the idea of the medium holding him, he went on to describe in words what he had shown with his hands, which was that he had been twirling round forwards, and he contrasted this with the twirling round backwards over the couch which he had reported a few weeks previously.

From this interpretation of the medium I was able to go on to develop the theme of the analytic situation and together we worked out a rather clear statement of the specialized conditions provided by the analyst, and of the limits of the analyst's capacity for adaptation to the patient's needs. Following this the patient had a very important dream, and the analysis of this showed that he had been able to discard a shield which was now no longer necessary since I had proved myself capable of supplying a suitable medium at the moment of his withdrawal. It appears that *through my immediately putting a medium around his withdrawn self I had converted his withdrawal into a regression*, and so had enabled him to use this experience constructively. I would have missed this opportunity in the early days of my analytic career. The patient described this analytic session as 'momentous'.

There was a very big result from this detail of analysis: a clearer understanding of the part I could play as analyst; a recognition of the dependence which must at times be very great even although painful to bear; and also a coming to grips with his reality situation both at work and at home in a completely new way. Incidentally he was able to tell me that his wife had become pregnant and this made it very easy for him to link his curled-up state in the medium with the idea of a foetus in the womb. He had in fact identified with his own child and at the same time had made an acknowledgement of his own original dependence on his mother.

The next time he met his mother after this session he was able for the first time to ask her how much the analysis was costing her, and to allow himself to feel concerned about this. In the next sessions he was able to get at his criticisms of me and to express his suspicion that I was a swindler.

Episode 3

The next detail came some months later, after a very rich period of analysis. It came at a time when the material was of an anal quality and the homosexual aspect of the transference situation, an aspect of analysis which especially frightened him, had been reintroduced. He reported that in childhood he had had a constant fear of being chased by a man. I made certain interpretations and he reported that while I had been talking he had been *far away, at a factory*. In ordinary language his 'thought had wandered'. This wandering off was very real to him, and he had felt as if he was actually working at the factory to which he had gone when he ended the earlier phase of his analysis with me (which had had to be terminated because of the war). Immediately I made the interpretation that he had gone away *from my lap*. The word lap was appropriate because in his withdrawn state and in terms of emotional development he had been at a stage of infancy, so that the couch had automatically become the analyst's lap. It will readily be seen that there is a relationship between my supplying the lap for him to come back to, and my supplying the medium on which depended his capacity to move round in a curled-up position in space.

Episode 4

The fourth episode that I wish to pick out is not so clear. It came in a session in which he said that he was unable to make love. The general material enabled me to interpret the dissociation in his relation to the world; on the one hand spontaneity from the *true* self which has no hope of finding an object except in imagination; and, on the other hand, response to stimulus from a self that is somewhat *false* or unreal. In the interpretation I pointed out that he was hoping to be able to join up this split in himself in his relation to me. At this point he sank into a withdrawn state for a brief period, and then was able to tell me what had happened when he was withdrawn; *it had become dark, clouds had gathered and it had started to rain; the rain had beaten down on his naked body*. On this occasion I was able to put into this cruel, ruthless environment himself, a newborn baby, and to point out to him what kind of environment he might expect should he become integrated and independent. Here was the 'medium' interpretation in reversed form.

Episode 5

The fifth detail comes from the material presented after a break of nine weeks which included my summer holiday.

The patient came back after the long break saying that he was not sure why he had come back; and that he found it difficult to start again. The main thing he reported was a continued difficulty in making a spontaneous remark of any kind either at home or among friends. He could only join in a conversation, and this was easiest when there were two others present who were taking the responsibility by talking to each other. If he made a remark he felt he was usurping the function of one of the parents (that is to say in the primal scene) whereas what he needed was to be recognized by the parents as an infant. He told me enough about himself to keep me in touch with current affairs.

The fifth episode was reached through consideration of an ordinary dream.

The night after this first session he had a dream which he reported the following day. It was unusually vivid. He went on a weekend trip abroad, *going on the Saturday and returning on the Monday.* The main thing about the trip was that he would meet a patient who had gone abroad from a hospital for treatment. (This turned out to be a patient who has had a limb amputated. There were other important details that do not specifically concern the subject of this communication.)

My first interpretation was the comment that in the dream *he goes and comes back.* It is this comment that I wish to report, since it joins up with my comments on the first two episodes in which I had provided a medium and a lap, and with that on the fourth episode in which I put an individual in the bad environment that had been hallucinated. I followed with a fuller interpretation, namely that the dream expresses the two aspects of his relationship to analysis; in one he goes away and comes back, and in the other he goes abroad, the patient from hospital standing for this part of himself; he goes and keeps in touch with the patient, which means that he is trying to break down the dissociation between these two aspects of himself. My patient followed this up by saying that in the dream he was particularly keen to make contact with the patient, implying that he was becoming aware of dissociation or splitting in himself, and wishing to become integrated.

This episode could be in the form of a dream dreamed away from analysis because it contained both elements together, the withdrawn self and the environmental provision. The medium aspect of the analyst had become introjected.

I further interpreted: the dream showed how the patient dealt with the holiday; he had been able to enjoy the experience of escaping from the treatment while at the same time he knew that although he had gone away he would come back. In this way the particularly long break which might have been serious in this type of patient was not a great disturbance. The patient made a particular point that this matter of going off and away was closely associated in his mind with the idea of making an original remark or doing anything spontaneous. He then told me that he had had, on the very day of the dream, a return of a special fear of his, that he would find that he had suddenly kissed a person; it would be anyone who happened to be next him; this might turn out to be a man. He would not make such a fool of himself if he found he had unexpectedly kissed a woman.

He now began to sink more deeply into the analytic situation. He felt he was a little child at home, and if he spoke it would be wrong; because he would then be in the parents' place. There was a feeling of hopelessness about having a spontaneous gesture met (and this fits in with what is known of the home situation). Much deeper material now emerged and he felt that there were people going in and out of the doors; my interpretation that this was associated with breathing was supported by further associations on his part. Ideas are like breath; also they are like children, and if I do nothing to them he feels they are abandoned. His great fear is of the abandoned child or the abandoned idea or remark, or the wasted gesture of a child.

Episode 6

A week later the patient (unexpectedly from his point of view), came up against the fact that he had never accepted his father's death. This followed a dream in which his father had been present and had been able to discuss current sexual problems with him in a sensible and free way. Two days later he came and reported that he had been seriously disturbed because he had had a *headache*, quite different from any that he had ever had before. It dated more or less from the time of the previous session two days earlier. This headache was temporal and sometimes frontal and *it was as if it were situated just outside the head*. It was constant and made him feel ill and if he could have got sympathy from his wife he would not have come to analysis but would have gone to bed. He was bothered because as a doctor he could see that this was certainly a functional disorder and yet it could not be explained in terms of physiology. (It was therefore like a madness.)

In the course of the hour I was able to see what interpretation was applicable and I said: 'The pain being just *outside* the head represents your *need to have your head held* as you would naturally have it held if you were in a state of deep emotional distress as a child.' At first this did not mean very much to him but gradually it became clear that the person who was more likely to have held his head at the right moment and in the right way when he was a child was not his mother but his father. In other words, after his father's death there was no one to hold his head should he break down into experiencing grief.

I linked up my interpretation with the key interpretation of the medium, and gradually he felt that my idea about the hands was right. He reported a momentary withdrawal with a feeling that I had a machine which I could activate and which would supply the trappings of sympathetic management. This meant to him that it was important that I did not hold his head actually and in fact, as this would have been a mechanical application of technical principles. *The important thing was that I understood immediately what he needed.*

At the end of the hour he surprised himself by remembering that he had spent the afternoon holding a child's head. The child had been having a minor operation under local anaesthetic and this had taken more than an hour. He had done all he could to help the child but without much success. What he had felt the child must need was that his head should be held.

He now felt in rather a deep way that my interpretation had been the thing for which he had come to analysis on that day, and he was therefore almost grateful to his wife that she had offered no sympathy whatever and had not held his head as she might have done.

SUMMARY

The idea behind this communication is that if we know about regression in the analytic hour, we can meet it immediately and in this way enable certain patients who are not too ill to make the necessary regressions in short phases, perhaps even almost momentarily. I would say that *in the withdrawn state a patient is holding the self* and that if immediately the withdrawn state appears *the analyst can hold the patient*, then what would otherwise have been a withdrawal state becomes a regression. The advantage of a *regression* is that it carries with it the opportunity for correction of inadequate adaptation-to-need in the past history of the patient, that is to say, in the patient's infancy management. By contrast the *withdrawn* state is not profitable and when the patient recovers from a withdrawn state he or she is not changed.

Whenever we understand a patient in a deep way and show that we do so by a correct and well-timed interpretation we are in fact holding the patient, and taking part in a relationship in which the patient is in some degree regressed and dependent.

It is commonly thought that there is some danger in the regression of a patient during psycho-analysis. The danger does not lie in the regression but in the analyst's unreadiness to meet the regression and the dependence which belongs to it. When an analyst has had the experience that makes him confident in his management of regression, then it is probably true to say that the more quickly the analyst accepts the regression and meets it fully the less likely is it that the patient will need to enter into an illness with regressive qualities.

REFERENCES

Freud, S. (1895). *Studies on Hysteria* in Volume 2 of *The Standard Edition of the Complete Psychological Works of Sigmund Freud* (London: The Hogarth Press; New York: Norton).

Giovacchini, P. L. (ed.) (1972). *Tactics and Techniques in Psychoanalytic Therapy* (New York: Science House; London: The Hogarth Press).

Nietzsche, F. (1886). *The Gay Science*. Translated, with commentary, by Walter Kaufman (New York: Vintage Books, 1974).

Winnicott, D. W. (1931). *Clinical Notes on Disorders of Childhood* (London: Heinemann).

— (1935). 'The Manic Defence' in Winnicott 1975.

— (1936). 'Appetite and Emotional Disorder' in *ibid.* (1975).

— (1945). 'Primitive Emotional Development' in *ibid.* (1975).

— (1948a). 'Paediatrics and Psychiatry' in *ibid.* (1975).

— (1948b). 'Reparation in Respect of Mother's Organized Defence against Depression' in *ibid.* (1975).

— (1949a). 'Birth Memories, Birth Trauma, and Anxiety' in *ibid.* (1975).

— (1949b). 'Mind and its Relation to the Psyche-Soma' in *ibid.* (1975).

— (1951). 'Transitional Objects and Transitional Phenomena' in *ibid.* (1975).

— (1952). 'Anxiety Associated with Insecurity' in *ibid.* (1975).

— (1954a). 'Withdrawal and Regression' in *ibid.* (1975), and reprinted as the Appendix to this volume.

— (1954b). 'The Depressive Position in Normal Emotional Development' in *ibid.* (1975).

— (1954c). 'Metapsychological and Clinical Aspects of Regression within the Psycho-Analytical Set-Up' in *ibid.* (1975).

— (1955). 'Clinical Varieties of Transference' in *ibid.* (1975).

— (1956). 'The Anti-Social Tendency' in *ibid.* (1975).

— (1958). 'The Capacity to be Alone' in Winnicott 1965.

— (1960a). 'Ego Distortion in Terms of True and False Self' in *ibid.* (1965).

— (1960b). 'The Theory of the Parent–Infant Relationship' in *ibid.* (1965).

— (1963a). 'The Development of the Capacity for Concern' in *ibid.* (1965).

— (1963b). 'Psychiatric Disorder in Terms of Infantile Maturational Processes' in *ibid.* (1965).

— (1963c). 'Psychotherapy of Character Disorders' in *ibid.* (1965).

— (1965). *The Maturational Processes and the Facilitating Environment* (London: The Hogarth Press; New York: Int. Univ. Press).

— (1970). 'The Mother–Infant Experience of Mutuality' in *Parenthood*, edited by E. J. Anthony and T. Benedek (Boston: Little, Brown & Co.).

— (1971). *Playing and Reality* (London: Tavistock Publications; New York: Basic Books).

— (1972). 'Mother's Madness appearing in the Clinical Material as an Ego-alien Factor' in Giovacchini 1972.

— (1973). 'Delinquency as a Sign of Hope' in *Adolescent Psychiatry*, II, edited by S. C. Feinstein and P. L. Giovacchini (New York: Basic Books).

— (1975). *Through Paediatrics to Psycho-Analysis* – a reissue of Winnicott's *Collected Papers* (London: Tavistock Publications, 1958), with an introduction by M. Masud R. Khan (London: The Hogarth Press; New York: Basic Books).

INDEX

Compiled by Madeleine Davis